T0360784

SWISS MONETARY HISTORY SINCE THE EARLY 19TH CENTURY

This book describes the remarkable path which led to the Swiss franc becoming the strong international currency that it is today. Ernst Baltensperger and Peter Kugler use Swiss monetary history to provide valuable insights into a number of issues concerning the organization and development of monetary institutions and currency that shaped the structure of financial markets and affected the economic course of a country in important ways. They investigate a variety of topics, including the functioning of a world without a central bank, the role of competition and monopoly in money and banking, the functioning of monetary unions, monetary policy of small open economies under fixed and flexible exchange rates, the stability of money demand and supply under different monetary regimes, and the monetary and macroeconomic effects of Swiss banking and finance. *Swiss Monetary History since the Early 19th Century* illustrates the value of monetary history for understanding financial markets and macroeconomics today.

Ernst Baltensperger is Professor Emeritus of macroeconomics at the University of Berne and former director of the Study Center Gerzensee of the Swiss National Bank. He studied economics at the University of Zurich and received his PhD in economics from Johns Hopkins University. He has been an advisor to the Swiss National Bank and the Swiss government and served as an editor of several academic journals.

Peter Kugler is Professor Emeritus of monetary economics at the University of Basel. He has held previous positions as professor at the University of Basel (statistics), the University of Berne (econometrics), and the University of Vienna (economics). He served as a member of the scientific advisory board of the Deutsche Bundesbank and has been an external advisor to the Swiss National Bank and the Swiss government.

STUDIES IN MACROECONOMIC HISTORY

SERIES EDITOR: Michael D. Bordo, Rutgers University

EDITORS:

Owen F. Humpage, *Federal Reserve Bank of Cleveland*
Christopher M. Meissner, *University of California, Davis*
Kris James Mitchener, *Santa Clara University*
David C. Wheelock, *Federal Reserve Bank of St. Louis*

The titles in this series investigate themes of interest to economists and economic historians in the rapidly developing field of macroeconomic history. The four areas covered include the application of monetary and finance theory, international economics, and quantitative methods to historical problems; the historical application of growth and development theory and theories of business fluctuations; the history of domestic and international monetary, financial, and other macroeconomic institutions; and the history of international monetary and financial systems. The series amalgamates the former Cambridge University Press series *Studies in Monetary and Financial History* and *Studies in Quantitative Economic History.*

Other books in the series:

Peter L. Rousseau and Paul Wachtel, Editors, *Financial Systems and Economic Growth* (2017)

Øyvind Eitrheim, Jan Tore Klovland, and Lars Fredrik Øksendal, *A Monetary History of Norway, 1816–2016* (2016)

Jan Fredrik Qvigstad, *On Central Banking* (2016)

Michael D. Bordo, Øyvind Eitrheim, Marc Flandreau, and Jan F. Qvigstad, Editors, *Central Banks at a Crossroads: What Can We Learn from History?* (2016)

Michael D. Bordo and Mark A. Wynne, Editors, *The Federal Reserve's Role in the Global Economy: A Historical Perspective* (2016)

Owen F. Humpage, Editor, *Current Federal Reserve Policy Under the Lens of Economic History: Essays to Commemorate the Federal Reserve System's Centennial* (2015)

(continued after Index)

Swiss Monetary History since the Early 19th Century

ERNST BALTENSPERGER

University of Berne, Switzerland

PETER KUGLER

University of Basel, Switzerland

CAMBRIDGE
UNIVERSITY PRESS

University Printing House, Cambridge CB2 8BS, United Kingdom

One Liberty Plaza, 20th Floor, New York, NY 10006, USA

477 Williamstown Road, Port Melbourne, VIC 3207, Australia

314-321, 3rd Floor, Plot 3, Splendor Forum, Jasola District Centre, New Delhi - 110025, India

103 Penang Road, #05-06/07, Visioncrest Commercial, Singapore 238467

Cambridge University Press is part of the University of Cambridge.

It furthers the University's mission by disseminating knowledge in the pursuit of education, learning and research at the highest international levels of excellence.

www.cambridge.org
Information on this title: www.cambridge.org/9781107199309
DOI: 10.1017/9781108185523

First published 2017

A catalogue record for this publication is available from the British Library

Library of Congress Cataloging in Publication data
Names: Baltensperger, Ernst, author. | Kugler, Peter, author.
Title: Swiss monetary history since the early 19th century / Ernst Baltensperger, University of Berne, Switzerland, Peter Kugler, University of Basel, Switzerland.
Description: Cambridge, United Kingdom ; New York, NY : Cambridge University Press, 2017. | Series: Studies in macroeconomic history | Includes bibliographical references and index.
Identifiers: LCCN 2017007124 | ISBN 9781107199309 (hardback : alk. paper)
Subjects: LCSH: Money–Switzerland–History. | Monetary policy–Switzerland–History. | Finance–Switzerland–History.
Classification: LCC HG1152 .B253 2017 | DDC 332.4/9494–dc23 LC record available at https://lccn.loc.gov/2017007124

ISBN 978-1-107-19930-9 Hardback

Contents

Figures

Tables

Foreword

I hope readers will derive as much pleasure from this book as I have.

The publication explores the monetary history of Switzerland, beginning in the early nineteenth century, when multiple local and foreign currencies were in use in my country. The introduction of the Swiss franc in 1850 is the first watershed event the book discusses, followed as it was by a period in which several commercial banks vied with each other to issue bank-notes. This phase came to an end with the creation of the Swiss National Bank (SNB) in 1907. The book also surveys the history of Switzerland's exchange rate regimes, which range from a currency union in the late nineteenth and early twentieth centuries to the autonomous monetary policy geared toward price stability we have in place today. It rightly draws attention to the remarkable variety of monetary regimes Switzerland has operated throughout its history.

The analysis is both thought-provoking and admirably clear. In monetary history, as in every other field of history – and indeed in life more generally – some things are easy to explain, others more difficult. Equally, simple explanations can often be excessively simplistic, and complex explanations unnecessarily convoluted. One of the merits of this book is that it resists the temptation to cast a veil over those things that are less easily explained, and does not hesitate to unmask certain overly simplistic explanations. The authors achieve this by fleshing out the chronological account with in-depth analysis of underlying economic topics.

I have found this book both enjoyable and engaging. Such works are eminently useful, not only for professional and lay historians, but also for monetary policy analysts and commentators. When the SNB's Governing Board makes decisions, it does so within the framework of a monetary policy strategy, which is itself anchored in a legal and constitutional mandate; these structures are both products of history. In seeking to understand the evolution of monetary policy frameworks, readers will gain greater knowledge of the wider context in which we operate and deeper insight into the decisions we take. This book is an excellent guide to Swiss monetary policy, past and present.

Thomas J. Jordan,
Chairman of the Governing Board,
Swiss National Bank

Acknowledgments

This book is an outgrowth of a book on the history of the Swiss franc that the first named author published in German in 2012. While that book was aimed at a general, nonspecialized Swiss- and German-language audience, the present one addresses a more specialized, international readership and includes many materials not covered in the former book. Thus, this is in large parts a new and different book.

The production and publication of this book has been substantially supported by the Swiss National Bank through all its phases. We gratefully acknowledge this support, without which the book would probably not have come into existence. While completing this work, we have greatly benefited from discussions with many colleagues and friends, among them Peter Bernholz, Patrick Halbeisen, Nils Herger, Thomas Jordan, Carlos Lenz, Thomas Moser, Dirk Niepelt, Georg Rich, Kurt Schiltknecht, and Mathias Zurlinden. We are especially grateful for numerous helpful comments and suggestions by Stefan Gerlach, Marcel Savioz, and Tobias Straumann, and to two anonymous referees; all read the entire manuscript in its pre-final stage.

Introduction

This book presents a monetary history of Switzerland in the nineteenth and twentieth centuries. At present, the Swiss franc is soaring and full of vitality. Yet in 1850, when it first came into being, nobody would have predicted that it would become one of the most successful and strongest currencies in the world over the course of the years to follow. In fact, during the first half-century of its existence, the Swiss franc remained a satellite currency of the French franc, tending not infrequently toward weakness in the market for foreign exchange. At the beginning of the twentieth century, however, it embarked on a remarkable path, which led it to become the strong international currency that we know today. These facts alone make it an interesting object of study.

Beyond this, Swiss monetary history provides valuable insights into a number of issues that remain of great interest today. The organization of monetary institutions and their development over time shape the structure of financial markets and affect the economic course of a country in important ways. Their study thus remains highly relevant for understanding where we stand today. Regarding Switzerland, the following topics come especially to mind:

Money without a central bank: Switzerland did not have a central bank until the early twentieth century. Not until 1907 – just 110 years ago – did the Swiss National Bank (SNB) commence operations. Until then, the history of money in Switzerland was a history of specie and – following the emergence and dissemination of banknotes as a means of payment, particularly in the second half of the nineteenth century – a history of private and public note-issuing banks. During this period, the banking industry had a central place in the history of money in Switzerland. With the exception of the United States, all other major industrial countries had centralized banknote issue before.

Competition and monopoly in money and currency: Swiss monetary experience provides interesting insights into the roles played by competition and monopoly in the provision of money and monetary services. Prior to 1850, Switzerland offered a rare example of real currency competition, with free choice of currency denomination in banknote issue, comparable to the blueprint proposed by Hayek (1978). In 1850, by introducing the new Swiss franc as its national currency, Switzerland decided in favor of a centralized government monopoly with regard to the definition of the monetary unit and the right of coinage. With regard to banknote issue, Switzerland did retain competition until 1907; nevertheless, in 1881, the previously unregulated competition in banknote issue became heavily regulated under a new federal banknote act. Thus, Swiss monetary history provides a sequence of interesting examples of different regimes concerning competition and monopoly in money provision.

The functioning of a monetary union under a nineteenth-century metallic standard: From 1865 until the end of 1926 (officially), Switzerland was a member of a currency union, the so-called Latin Monetary Union, based on a treaty between France (as the leading country of the union), Belgium, Italy, and Switzerland (in 1868 Greece also joined). Swiss monetary history, along with that of the other union partners, thus offers an example of the workings of a currency union under nineteenth-century conditions. The Latin Monetary Union has often invited comparisons to today's European Monetary Union. It is important to note, however, that the Latin Monetary Union represented a much lesser degree of financial and currency integration. In particular, the definition and legal base of member country currencies remained national, without any transfer of monetary sovereignty to the union level.

Monetary policy of a small open economy under fixed and flexible exchange rates. Over the course of its history, Switzerland has assembled ample experience with regimes of both fixed and flexible rates of exchange. In the nineteenth century, and in the twentieth century until the breakdown of the Bretton Woods system at the beginning of the 1970s, fixed rate arrangements were the rule. In various instances, though, these fixed rate regimes were suspended over more or less extended periods of time (the Franco-Prussian War, World War I, the postwar period until 1925), or confidence in them was severely shaken (the Great Depression of the 1930s). The latter experience in particular has led Switzerland to feel "a certain scepticism about a fixed rate system and a willingness to live in a world of floating currencies" (Bordo and James 2007, pp. 90–1). It was learned that fixed rates were advantageous, as long as mutual agreement among the system's participants about the objectives, procedures, and possibilities of monetary policy allowed it to function reasonably well. These conditions absent, however, a fixed rate system could become disruptive and the source of severe tension. This experience paved the way for Switzerland – in contrast to many other small and medium-sized countries – to adopt a regime of flexible exchange rates in in January 1973, after the demise of Bretton Woods. A floating exchange rate has become the rule ever since.

The extraordinary strength and stability of the Swiss Franc over the unstable twentieth century: In the nineteenth century, and up to World War I, the Swiss franc was a relatively "normal" currency, frequently assessed even as relatively weak. In the twentieth century, on the other hand, the Swiss franc has embarked on a course of extraordinary strength and stability. In 1914, one US dollar was equivalent to 5.18 francs; at the time of writing the dollar exchanges for roughly the equivalent of 1 Swiss franc. The British pound sterling was worth about 25 francs in 1914; currently its value is about 1.3 francs. The relative decline of the former partner currencies in the Latin Monetary Union, the French franc and the Italian lira, was much more pronounced. Their value in terms of Swiss francs at the time of their integration into the euro in 1999 could be measured only in thousandths. This nominal strength of the franc derives from two different sources: first, a "PPP (purchasing power parity) component" stemming from relatively low trend inflation created by the pronounced stability orientation of Swiss monetary policy, and second, a "real component" resulting from relative productivity differences and other real factors. In this book, analysis of the performance of the Swiss franc in the exchange market over the past one and a half centuries provides interesting insights regarding these issues.

The "Swiss interest rate island:" Swiss interest rates are low in international comparison. In the period of exchange rate flexibility since 1973, this can be attributed in part to a relatively low inflation rate and exchange rate appreciation. However, analysis shows that these factors cannot fully explain the Swiss interest rate puzzle. Neither can Swiss banking secrecy and tax benefits: The low interest rates are also documented for Swiss franc assets created outside Switzerland, and most fixed interest rate securities deposited in Switzerland by foreign investors are denominated in foreign currencies. The Swiss interest rate bonus developed over the entire twentieth century. The exceptional political, economic, and monetary stability of Switzerland led investors to pay a premium for holding Swiss franc fixed income assets. In this book, empirical analysis of Swiss interest rates in an international perspective provides interesting information on this stability bonus under different currency and exchange rate regimes, both in the nineteenth and the twentieth centuries.

Swiss money demand and supply under different monetary regimes. The changes from a metallic monetary standards, to the Bretton Woods system, and finally to a pure de facto paper standard with flexible exchange rates obviously led in turn to strong changes in the processes governing money supply. Moreover, we should expect a change in monetary dynamics under these different regimes. For instance, domestic prices and nominal income, as well as the money supply, have to adjust under a metallic standard, whereas changes in nominal income, interest rates, and the exchange rate work as shock absorbers under flexible exchange rates. In contrast, there is no strong *a priori* reason for there to be a fundamental change in money demand across different monetary regimes. In this book, empirical analysis of Swiss money demand and money supply for the entire period 1851 to 2010 sheds light on these questions.

The monetary and macroeconomic effects of Swiss banking: In the nineteenth century, without a central bank, the history of money in Switzerland was a history of specie and of private and public note-issuing banks competing with each other. In contrast, in the twentieth century, with the country now having a central bank, the banking system no longer played the same central role for the analysis of money and monetary processes. Under central banking, a currency is supplied and shaped by the central bank, not by commercial banks. Of course, banks are part of the environment which influences the central bank and the results of its actions, along with many other actors and influences. In this sense, their role needs to be taken into account in order to understand monetary policy and its effects. It is erroneous, however, to see the banking sector and its structure – including banking secrecy – as the primary force shaping macroeconomic variables such as the price level, exchange rates, or the level of interest rates and their fluctuations. Nevertheless, this does not mean that a well working and efficient financial sector is not important for economic development. In this book, analysis of the linkages between the financial sector, Swiss GDP, and trade and current account balances for the period from 1890 to 2010 provides information on this relationship.

The book is divided into three parts. Following an introduction, Part I provides a brief overview of the Swiss political system and of the general economic development of Switzerland since the formation of the federal state in 1848. This may provide helpful background information for international readers not familiar with the details of Swiss politics and the Swiss economy.

The subsequent two parts contain the main body of the book. Part II presents a chronological review of Swiss monetary history in the nineteenth and twentieth centuries.[1] It is written in a style which makes it accessible to a general reader who is interested in economic developments and history but has no specialized technical training. It begins with a review of the processes leading to the creation of a Swiss national currency in 1850 and, more than fifty years later, the establishment of a Swiss central bank, covering, among other aspects, Swiss participation in the Latin Monetary Union and the changing roles of competition and monopoly in banknote issue. In the twentieth century, after the establishment of a Swiss central bank, the SNB became the main actor in Swiss monetary policy. In a sequence of chapters, the book covers the SNB's policies under the international gold standard during the years up to World War I; Swiss monetary and currency policies in World War I and the postwar period up to the outbreak of the global economic crisis at the end of the 1920s; Switzerland's situation during the Great Depression and the intensive debate about devaluation of the Swiss franc; the SNB's policies during World War II and the subsequent reform of the international monetary system at Bretton Woods; the postwar period under the Bretton Woods fixed exchange rate regime; and finally the radical reorientation of monetary policy under the system of flexible exchange rates following the collapse of the Bretton Woods regime at the beginning of the 1970s.

Part III presents a number of thematically organized chapters analyzing key questions and issues of general interest, covering the entire period under consideration, or major parts of it (limitations being partly due to data availability). This part of the book, in contrast to the preceding one, includes some technical analysis and requires a certain amount of formal knowledge. It includes chapters dealing with the Swiss experience with currency and note-issue competition in the nineteenth century; stability and structural breaks in money demand and money supply over the entire period from 1851 to 2010; Swiss interest rates over the period from 1837 to 1970 (the "Swiss interest rate island"); the Swiss franc's exchange rate from 1850 to 2010; and, finally, the monetary and macroeconomic effects of Swiss banking in the period from 1890 to 2010.

---

[1] This part of the book is based on the German-language text in Baltensperger (2012).

PART I

POLITICAL AND ECONOMIC
DEVELOPMENT OF SWITZERLAND

1

The Swiss Political System and General Economic Development since the Formation of the Federal State (1848)

This chapter provides a brief overview of the political and economic development of Switzerland since 1848. The political system and its evolution are outlined in the first subsection. Then we consider economic growth and inflation performance in the following two subsections. In the latter part we compare developments in Switzerland with those in the UK and the United States. These two countries are selected for two reasons. First, they are considered to be benchmark economies: the UK was the economically leading country during the nineteenth century and lost this position to the United States in the twentieth century. Second, they both still have the same currency today as in the nineteenth century; thus a comparison of long-run price level and inflation developments is meaningful. This is not the case for Germany, the dominant economy of continental Europe, which has used six currencies over the past 150 years (thaler/gulden, mark, reichsmark, ostmark, D-mark, euro), with the mark and the reichsmark finishing their lives through implicit default (the mark with German hyperinflation of 1922/3, the Reichsmark with inflation and restricted convertibility into the D-mark in the currency reform after World War II) and an explicit default on the bonds of the Third Reich after its collapse in 1945.

THE SWISS POLITICAL SYSTEM 1848–2010

Swiss democracy as we know it today essentially dates back to 1848. Prior to 1848, the Swiss cantons understood themselves as independent, sovereign city and regional states linked to each other in a loose, treaty-based confederation. The central objective of this confederation was originally to guarantee collective security through mutual military assistance. A brief attempt to transform this system into a united Helvetic Republic during the period of French occupation, initiated after the French invasion of Switzerland in 1798, proved unsuccessful and short-lived, not least because it was forced on the country by foreign domination. In 1803, this effort was abandoned again. In the 1830s, liberal movements led to political change and constitutional reforms in many cantons, especially the industrialized, liberal, and predominantly Protestant cantons that included most of the major cities. Increasingly, cultural and religious tensions between these and the more rural, conservative, and Catholic cantons centered in the heart of old Switzerland built up. In 1845, the latter signed a separate treaty (the *Sonderbund*) to protect their common interests. An escalation of the situation resulted, leading to a short civil war in 1847 (the *Sonderbundskrieg*), which ended after only twenty-six days with a small number of casualties and a clear victory for the liberal side. This paved the way for the formation of the modern Swiss confederation in 1848.

The federal constitution adopted in 1848 transformed Switzerland into a federal state made up of twenty-five (today twenty-six) cantons. A number of hitherto cantonal rights were transferred to the national level. In principle, foreign relations, national defense, customs and tariffs, the issue of currency, and legislation concerning measures, weights, transportation, and communication were assigned to the confederation, with other affairs remaining domains of the cantons and their communes. A national government was established, with a federal two-chamber parliament, the Federal Assembly, as the legislative power; an executive authority, the Federal Council, as the executive power; and the Federal Supreme Court as the judicial power. Certain minimum standards for democratic institutions at the cantonal level were also enacted. The federal constitution experienced "total" revisions in 1874 and then again in 2000, and specific points have been amended, according to procedures to be explained below, on many occasions since 1848. Nevertheless, the basic structure of the Swiss political system has remained unchanged in most regards since 1848.[1]

The Federal Assembly consists of the National Council, initially including one member per 20,000 inhabitants (111 in 1848), elected every four years by the people directly using proportional rules (the total number of seats was later fixed at 200), and the forty-six-member Council of States, with two members per canton (one for six so-called half-cantons), elected by popular vote according to cantonal rules. The Federal Council includes

---

[1] For a detailed account of the Swiss political system and its institutions, see Linder (1994, 2012).

seven members chosen by the Federal Assembly. The seven Federal Councilors make up a team sharing equal rights. Each Federal Councilor heads a department of the federal administration, with all major decisions being taken at regular meetings either by consensus or by majority voting. Every year, one member of the Federal Council in turn is elected as Federal President. In this function, however, he acts only as *"primus inter pares,"* with very limited special powers, mostly of a representational nature. The members of the Federal Supreme Court are elected by the Federal Assembly.

A pronounced federalist structure, which leaves much decision power with the cantons and their communes; the separation of power between the legislative, executive, and judicial authorities; and direct democracy are pillars of the Swiss form of democracy. Switzerland's political system is unique in the strong role that it assigns to direct democracy and its institutions. While it leaves the election of the federal government to parliament (in contrast to many other democracies), it provides citizens, at the national level, with two important instruments of direct democratic influence: the referendum and the initiative. Both of these instruments have evolved in important ways over time. At the cantonal level, similar instruments have been developed.

The *referendum* is a constitutional right of the citizens to force the federal authorities to submit new legislation, or important treaties, to a popular vote. In certain cases – when a change of the constitution is involved or when important international treaties are proposed – a referendum is mandatory. Approval in the popular vote then requires a double majority of the people and the cantons. In other cases – involving simple parliamentary acts and proposals for regulation – a referendum is optional. In these cases a popular vote can be forced by the signatures of 50,000 citizens, to be collected within ninety days of parliamentary decisions. In this case, a majority of the people (but not of the cantons) is required for approval in the popular vote. This second type of referendum was introduced in 1874, while the mandatory referendum goes back to 1848.

The *popular initiative* is a formal proposition by a citizen or a group of citizens asking for a constitutional amendment or a change of an existing constitutional provision. If the initiative is signed by at least 100,000 citizens within eighteen months, it must be submitted to a vote of the people and the cantons. Prior to the vote, the Federal Council and the Federal Assembly will discuss the initiative and give (non-binding) advice on whether to accept or to reject the proposal. Alternative formulations may also be proposed by them. As with the mandatory referendum, acceptance in the popular vote requires both a majority of the voters and of the cantons. The constitutional initiative goes back to 1848 in the case of total revision of the constitution; for partial revisions or amendments, it was introduced in 1891.

After 1848, Swiss politics at the federal level was first dominated by the winners of the *Sonderbundskrieg*, the Liberals and the "Radicals" – until 1891, the Federal Council included only representatives of this side of the political spectrum. However, over time Switzerland found ways to overcome this limitation and develop a pronounced culture of power-sharing between all relevant groups of society: between Catholics and Protestants, between liberals and conservatives, between bourgeois and social democrats, between organized labor and employers, between the German-speaking majority and the French, Italian, and Romantsch-speaking minorities. "This has led to social integration, peaceful conflict-resolution by negotiation, and national consensus amongst a once fragmented and heterogeneous population" (Linder, 1994, p. xvi). Switzerland thus became a model of a democracy of consensus, and of political stability. Along with a strongly federalist structure, the institutions of direct democracy, by making political positions more easily contestable and encouraging incentives to compromise, have played a significant role in this process.

The direct-democratic instruments of the referendum and the initiative were an important element in the development of Swiss-style liberal democratic corporatism, as discussed by Katzenstein (1985, 2003). Political decisions were threatened by referenda, and this led to the inclusion in political decisions of organizations with the power to start a referendum. This characteristic of Swiss politics at first worked in favor of the most important business association, founded in 1869, the *Schweizerische Handels- und Industrieverein*. The labor organizations and trade unions initially had much less political influence,[2] until the integration of the Social Democrats in the political decision-making process in the 1930s.

Apart from the institutional framework, "Swiss-style" democratic corporatism was fostered by the fact that Switzerland was a small state with a highly open economy. Despite its smallness and a lack of natural resources such as metals, coal, oil, and the like, Switzerland went through an early

---

[2] The *Arbeitersekretariat* was founded in 1887 and was supported by the federation in similar ways as the *Schweizerische Handels- und Industrieverein*. However, other labor organizations were founded earlier: The industrial unions, such as the *Grütliverein* for craftsmen and the *Schweizerische Typographenbund* for typographers, were founded in 1843 and 1858, respectively, and the Swiss Federation of Trade Unions (Schweizerische Gewerkschaftsbund) was created in 1880 (Degen, 2014).

process of industrialization. This was only possible by relying on international trade and taking a relatively positive attitude toward free trade. The dependence on foreign economic and political developments created a perception of vulnerability in economic success – typical of small states, according to Katzenstein (1985) – which favored the emergence of a democratic corporatism relying on negotiated change rather than market forces alone. Moreover, this characteristic may also help to explain the country's long-lasting preference for the gold standard and fixed exchange rates, which were definitely abandoned only in the early 1970s, when controlling inflation was no longer possible under a fixed exchange-rate regime (Straumann, 2010, pp. 276–307).

ECONOMIC GROWTH: PER CAPITA GDP, COMMAND GDP, AND GNP

The usual indicators for the international comparison of economic performance are per capita gross domestic product (GDP) estimates as provided by Angus Maddison and his followers. This data set was recently updated and revised and includes data from 1 AD to 2010 (Bolt and van Zanden, 2013). GDP is expressed in 1990 "international dollars," which should lead to comparable values for different regions and countries across the world. This data series is plotted in Figure 1.1 for Switzerland, the UK, and the United States for the period from 1851 to 2010.

From Figure 1.1 we see that all three countries had very similar per capita GDPs, with a slight advantage for the UK around 1850. During the second half of the nineteenth century, Great Britain lost its leading position, and Switzerland is indicated to be the country with the strongest growth record up to World War II. Subsequently, the United States led for fifteen years, but then lost this position to Switzerland until 1975. After the transition to flexible exchange rates in the 1970s we note weaker Swiss economic growth, nearly allowing the UK to close the gap on Switzerland.

This pattern may appear surprising with respect to Switzerland as, in the past, it was mostly seen as a late developer among today's highly developed countries. Indeed, the revision of the Maddison data from the 2007 release (data up to 2003) led Swiss real per capita GDP in 1850/1 to be revised upward by one third. This dramatic change in reported data is mainly caused by the fact that until recently, Swiss economic history was an under-researched topic. To a large extent, this gap was closed by the "Wirtschaftsgeschichte der Schweiz im 20. Jahrhundert" project

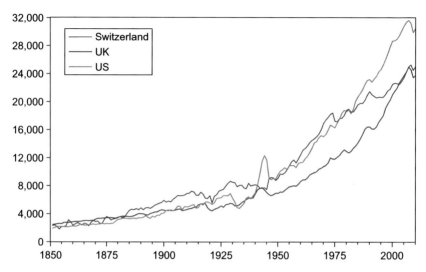

Figure 1.1: Per capita GDP in 1990 dollars, 1851–2010
Data source: Bolt and van Zanden (2013)

(Halbeisen, Müller, and Veyrassat, 2012), which provided revised GDP figures for Switzerland from 1851 to 1947 (Müller and Woitek, 2012).

A second aspect which stands out and deserves discussion is the seemingly weak growth in Switzerland from 1980 onwards. There exist, however, two special factors causing a sizable negative GDP bias in real income estimation for Switzerland. First, the huge current account surpluses experienced by Switzerland since 1980 and the resulting very high net foreign asset position (growing to ca. 125 percent and 142 percent of GDP in 1999 and 2010, respectively) led to a high level of net capital income from abroad, as reflected by a gross national product (GNP) level exceeding GDP by about 6 percent on average since 1990 (Figure 1.2).[3] In 2005, GNP was about 13 percent above GDP, whereas capital losses on foreign securities and a strong appreciation of the Swiss franc reduced this value again to a mean of 6 percent in 2010. Second, the improvement of the Swiss terms of trade related to the trend in real appreciation of the Swiss franc is not reflected in Swiss real GDP measures (Kohli, 2004). The reason is simply that exports and imports are deflated separately for the calculation of real GDP. In order to make this effect visible, a command base GDP

---

[3] Reliable Swiss GNP and net foreign asset data have unfortunately only been available since 1990 and 1999, respectively.

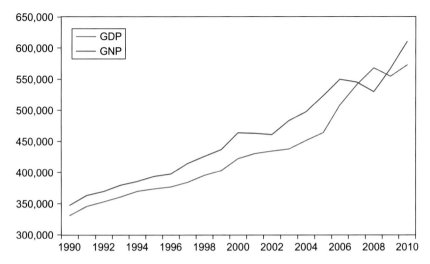

Figure 1.2: Swiss GDP and GNP, 1990–2010, millions SFr
Data source: SNB Monthly Statistical Bulletin, Table P4, www.snb.ch/de/iabout/stat/statrep/ statpubdis/id/statpub_statmon_arch_xls_de

is usually calculated (Kehoe and Ruhl, 2007). In this framework, the nominal surplus in the trade of goods and services is deflated by the import deflator. This measure then reflects the increased real import possibilities arising from a trade balance surplus.

Figure 1.3 shows the development of these two alternative real income measures for Switzerland and Figure 1.4 displays the terms of trade series (export price index/import price index) since 1980.[4] The difference in the two measures is sizable: The average growth rate of command base GDP is 2.0 percent, whereas "usual" GDP mean growth is only 1.6 percent from 1981 to 2010. Over a period of thirty years, this seemingly small difference in growth rates amounts to an accumulated difference in levels of approximately 13 percent. Note that for the UK and the United States, the differences between GDP and GNP and between GDP and command base GDP are very small and negligible. The large difference between GDP and command base GDP for Switzerland is really exceptional for a highly developed country (Kehoe and Ruhl, 2007).

---

[4] The end year of the sample was chosen as a result of the availability of the Maddison data up to 2010.

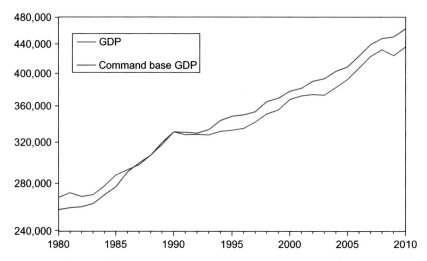

Figure 1.3: Swiss real GDP and command base GDP, 1980–2010, millions 1990SFr
Data source: Own calculations using data from Swiss economic and social history database
(Table Q16b), www.fsw.uzh.ch/hstat/nls_rev/overview.php

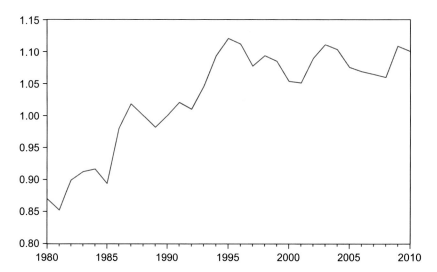

Figure 1.4: Swiss terms of trade, 1980–2010, 1990 = 1
Data source: Own calculations using data from Swiss economic and social history database
(Table Q16b), www.fsw.uzh.ch/hstat/nls_rev/overview.php

In conclusion, we see that Switzerland has performed well in economic development and growth, compared to the benchmarks set by the UK and the United States, since the formation of the federal state in 1848. It must be stressed that the seemingly weak growth suggested by GDP figures since 1980 is corrected if the real appreciation of the Swiss franc and the correspondingly improved terms of trade, as well as the income from the very large stock of net foreign assets, are taken into account. The really interesting question thus is what caused this trend in real appreciation and the sustained current account surpluses behind the strong net foreign asset position.

CONSUMER PRICES AND INFLATION

Figure 1.5 shows a plot of the consumer price index (CPI) series for Switzerland, the UK, and the United States since 1850. Note that a logarithmic scale is used as there is a very strong divergence of CPI developments since 1970. We observe a remarkable long run co-movement of CPI levels up to 1950, even though gold convertibility was suspended in all countries during World War I and reintroduced again at different times

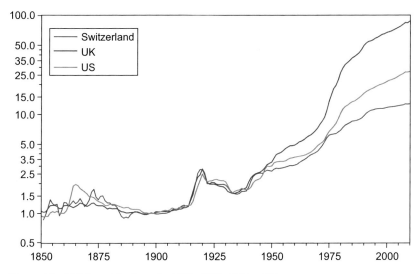

Figure 1.5: CPI, logarithmic scale, 1850–2010, 1899 = 100
Data source: Own calculations using data from Swiss economic and social history database (Table H39), www.fsw.uzh.ch/hstat/nls_rev/overview.php. UK and US, Officer and Williamson (2013)

in the 1920s, and the gold standard was suspended at different dates again in the 1930s. Medium-run divergence can be explained by local events; in particular, we see the separate development of US consumer prices during and after the Civil War with suspended convertibility of the dollar ("greenback inflation" of the 1860s). This common international trend of the log price level disappears at the beginning of the 1950s, and since the transition to flexible exchange rates in 1973 we note an accelerating divergence of the price levels in the three countries. The average inflation rates from 1950 to 2010 were 2.6 percent in Switzerland, 5.7 percent in the UK, and 3.7 percent in the United States, respectively. Over sixty years, this resulted in tremendous differences in price level developments between the three countries. From the end of the nineteenth century to 2010, consumer prices rose by factors of 13 in Switzerland), 27 in the United States, and 88 in the UK. An obvious question is what factors account for the comparatively exceptional inflation performance of the Swiss franc. Much of the rest of this book deals with precisely this question.

PART II

A CHRONOLOGICAL REVIEW OF SWISS MONETARY HISTORY IN THE NINETEENTH AND TWENTIETH CENTURIES

In Part II of this book, we present a chronological account of Swiss monetary history over the past two centuries. Its purpose is to provide the reader with the main facts and allow him or her to understand the processes governing this history and the factors shaping them.

We begin with the period leading up to the creation of a national Swiss currency in the context of the political unification of the country, culminating in the monetary reform of 1850. We continue with a review of the consequences of this reform, including the Swiss participation in Europe's most important currency union of the nineteenth century, the Latin Monetary Union, and with a discussion of the slow and at times painful process toward full centralization of banknote issue and the establishment of a national central bank, the Swiss National Bank, in the years 1905–7. We then review Swiss participation in the policies governing the international gold standard before the outbreak of World War I, the monetary policy of the Swiss National Bank during World War I and in the afterwar period, Swiss monetary policy during the Great Depression and in World War II, and Swiss monetary policy in the fixed exchange rate period of Bretton Woods. Finally, monetary policy in the era of flexible exchange rates following the demise of the Bretton Woods system at the beginning of the 1970s, with the ensuing radical reorientation of monetary policy, is reviewed and discussed from a Swiss perspective, leading up to the present.

In the subsequent Part III, we will follow a complementary approach and present a thematically organized analysis of a number of key issues and questions of general interest from a more fundamental point of view, covering the entire period under consideration or major parts of it.

2

Creation of a National Currency (1848–1881)

The Swiss currency and the Swiss financial system as we know them today have essentially developed over the past two hundred years, parallel to the creation of modern Switzerland in the nineteenth and twentieth centuries. Decisive moments shaping the course of future events were, of course, the creation of the Swiss federal state with the federal constitution of 1848, and the subsequent monetary reform of 1850. Nevertheless, it is informative to also look first at the period leading up to these events.

MONEY AND FINANCE IN SWITZERLAND BEFORE 1850: CHAOS OF COINS AND CURRENCIES

Up to the monetary reform of 1850, Switzerland did not have a common, national currency – except for a brief interlude during the so-called Helvetic Republic imposed on Switzerland during the period of French occupation around the end of the eighteenth and beginning of the nine-teenth centuries (1798–1803). Monetary exchange and payments were characterized by a bewildering multitude of currencies and coins of domestic as well as foreign origin – guilders, francs, ducats, pounds, shillings, thalers, crowns, kreuzer, heller, batzen, pfennig, and many more. Conditions like this have marked money and finance not only in Switzerland but also in other parts of Europe for long periods of time.

In the area covering present Switzerland, the privilege to mint coins and issue money increasingly shifted from feudal and church sovereigns to independent cities and regionally defined republics (cantons) between the end of the fourteenth century and the sixteenth century. As Switzerland has no silver and gold deposits to speak of, it was necessary to import the raw materials for minting coin. This, along with the growth of trade with surrounding regions (including the export of mercenary services as an important source of revenue), encouraged increasing use of foreign coins and currencies. Next to the confusing multitude of coins and currencies, the dangers of counterfeit, debasement, and deterioration (usage, money clipping) were constants in the history of coin. Between the beginning of the fifteenth and the end of the eighteenth centuries, for instance, the metal content of a Lucerne gulden declined from 5.32 to 0.82 grams of gold, or from 40.11 to 9.61 grams of silver.[1]

The franc made a first, though unsuccessful, appearance as Switzerland's national currency in 1798: It was imposed on the Swiss cantons under the sign of foreign occupation, after France's invasion of the country. Under French supervision, the country experienced its first attempt at monetary unification. With the Helvetic Republic, the central government received exclusive power to coin money. The monetary unit was the Swiss franc, divided into 10 batzen or 100 rappen (centimes). The Helvetic Republic, however, found little acceptance and was a political failure; with Napoleon's Mediation Act of 1803, this short-lived episode quickly came to its end. The power to issue money was returned to the cantons. Some cantons retained the franc as their monetary unit; others went back to other currency denominations.

Money circulation in Switzerland at this time existed mostly of large-denomination foreign silver or gold coins with "full" metal content (corresponding to their nominal legal value, so-called *Kurantgeld*) on the one hand, and a multitude of small-denomination, "undervalued" cantonal coins (with a metal content below their nominal value, so-called *Scheidemünzen*) on the other.[2] Domestic coin was characterized to a high degree by money debasement and qualitative uncertainty. The cantons published lists of "official" exchange rates between their money and alternative monies; however, these were not always consistent. Furthermore, these official "tariffs" were binding for official transactions (of public institutions) only. Under such conditions, domestic currencies tended to be avoided, especially for large payments and long-term contracts. It goes without saying that these conditions were not particularly favorable for trade and financial exchange.

In 1819, nineteen of the twenty-four cantons existing at that time agreed to introduce the "old Swiss franc," defined as the equivalent to 6.665 grams

---

[1] Körner (1991). A detailed review of coin money in Switzerland between 1500 and 1800 is offered by Furrer (1995).
[2] Halbeisen and Müller (1998), p. 65. On monetary conditions in Switzerland in this period, see Blaum (1908), Schlesinger (1936), and Weisskopf (1948).

of silver, as a common currency unit. This step had only limited significance, however, as no coin was minted in this common currency. The old
Swiss franc was never more than a pure accounting unit. Its uses remained
limited to exchange between cantons and as a standard of reference for
valuing other monies. The recipients of old Swiss francs remained subject
to the risk of their being paid out in coins of different origins and
qualities.[3] According to Halbeisen and Müller (1998, pp. 67–8), complaints
about "money confusion" declined somewhat after the 1830s, with a
certain stabilization of small-coin circulation and an increasing dominance
of the South German gulden in the eastern half of Switzerland. Nevertheless, the multitude of currency standards and coins in circulation and the
inconsistencies in cantonal tariffs remained major inconveniences.

Banking developed relatively late in Switzerland. Although private banks
in several cities, especially Geneva, did already play a significant role in
international wealth management and capital export in the eighteenth
century and earlier, there were no old trade and commercial banks of
importance comparable to those in some other European countries.
Ritzmann (1973) argues that the economic structure of Switzerland up to
the early nineteenth century generated little demand for private credit.
Funding was easily satisfied by self-finance, direct investment, and simple
money-change institutions. Furthermore, cities and communities were
typically creditors, rather than debtors, with large public assets in some
cases (accumulated not least through the "export" of soldiers' services).
The first banks were created to manage these funds – they were typically
invested abroad – rather than to extend domestic credit.[4] Thus Ritzmann
speaks of Swiss banks in this era as "organizers of capital exports."[5] In the
nineteenth century, a wave of foundation of small, regional savings banks
followed – as was the case in many other European countries – serving the
same purpose for low-income households and the general population,
which at this time started to accumulate modest wealth.

Banknotes did not play a major role as a means of payment in Switzerland before 1850. The first Swiss banknotes were issued in 1825 by the
Deposito-Cassa der Stadt Bern, an institution founded that year by the city

---

[3] Pestalozzi (1839) discussed the difficulties created for the economy by this complicated
 and confusing currency system. His contribution may serve as an example of the
 controversial debate accompanying the attempt to overcome this unsatisfactory state.
[4] Banks founded for this purpose include the *Bank Malacrida*, founded in 1702 in Berne;
 Bank Leu & Co., founded in 1755 in Zürich; and similar institutions in other cities such as
 Geneva and Basel.
[5] On all this, see Ritzmann (1973), p. 22.

of Berne – at this time still under a conservative, "patrician" regime – with management of the city's financial wealth as its main task. The banknote business of the Deposito-Cassa remained small, though – not only in absolute terms, but also compared to that of other Swiss note-issuing banks to be founded later on. One reason was that its banknotes (at least initially) were denominated in the old Swiss franc, which, due to its uncertain value (in relation to other currencies), was not very popular. Another major reason was that the notes it issued had a limited period of validity and possessed a rather high nominal value (with 500 old Swiss francs equaling 3.3 kilograms of silver). Especially in rural areas, they were used for large payments and trans-regional transactions only.

The 1830s and 1840s saw the foundation of a number of additional note-issuing banks. The background to these dynamics was a shift of political power from conservative to liberal regimes in many cantons. Inspired by the Parisian revolution of 1830, cantonal constitutions were reformed and the rule of the old patrician powers came to its end. Economically, this led to a period of optimism and development and, as a result, to a growing demand for credit and instruments of payment. New discount and note-issuing banks, modeled after foreign examples, were set up to satisfy this need.[6] In 1834, the *Cantonal Bank of Berne* was founded as a public note-issuing bank by the canton of Berne – now under a new, liberal regime. Its notes were denominated in French francs and included small denominations (of one écu, the French silver five-franc piece). It was only slightly more successful than the Deposito-Cassa, however. In the following years, a number of important commercial and note-issuing banks were founded as private shareholder companies in other major cities: In 1837 the *Bank in Zürich* and the *Bank in St. Gallen*; in 1844 the *Bank in Basel*; and in 1846 the *Banque du Commerce de Genève*. Additionally, two smaller note-issuing banks started business during the 1840s: In 1845 the *Banque Cantonale Vaudoise*; and in 1848 the *Banque de Genève*. The currency denomination of the notes of the Bank in Zürich was the Brabant thaler, that of the Bank in St. Gallen the gulden, and that of the banks in Basel and Geneva the French franc. Although demand for these banks' notes exceeded that for the notes of the two banks in Berne by a considerable margin, the note-issuing business of Swiss banks in general remained weak and not very successful throughout the first half of the nineteenth century.[7]

---

[6] Ritzmann (1973), pp. 37–8.   [7] See Table 8.1 in Chapter 8.

Compared to coin, the banknote remained unsubstantial as a means of payment throughout this period.

This was not specific to Switzerland but reflected the situation in all of continental Europe at this time. Up to the middle of the nineteenth century, means of payment on the continent – in contrast to Great Britain – consisted almost entirely of coin, especially silver coin, which existed in great variety. A major reason for this was the strong fragmentation of political and monetary power, which was not favorable to the spread and the large-scale adoption of banknotes. In France, furthermore, and in all the areas under its cultural influence, paper money had been totally discredited since the catastrophic experiment in the early eighteenth century by John Law (who had introduced a highly inflationary paper-money regime resulting in the so-called "Mississippi Bubble" and, when the bubble burst in 1720, one of the biggest financial crises known in history) and the equally disastrous episode involving the issue of paper-money "assignats" during the French revolution. In contrast, Great Britain was far ahead in the development of payments habits in this period. According to Cameron (1967), shares in money circulation for England and Wales in 1800 were 40 percent coin, 50 percent banknotes, and (already) 10 percent bank deposits. In 1844, the corresponding numbers were 25 percent for coin, 20 percent for banknotes, and 55 percent for deposits.

Of great interest is the fact that the nonexistence of a national currency left Swiss banks in this period totally free to determine the currency basis for the banknotes they issued.[8] Swiss history for this period thus provides a rare example of real currency competition of the type proposed by Hayek (1978).[9] Weber (1988) analyzes this example and declares it a success, as it was characterized by stable purchasing power of the paper money issued and a lack of bank failures and financial crises – and this in a period which was full of political unrest and turbulence. The Swiss note-issuing banks, he shows, selected the most stable of the existing currencies in use at the time as a base for their notes, that is, made them convertible into one of these at fixed terms. The most stable currencies at this time were foreign currencies. Weber argues that it was competition that forced banks to behave this way, that is, to link their notes to currencies with a large circulation

---

[8]   Even after the introduction of the new Swiss franc in 1850, banks in most cantons remained free to issue notes in foreign currencies, although they soon stopped making use of this option. Only the federal Banknote Act of 1881 formally prescribed the Swiss franc as the common denominator.

[9]   Many other examples of banknote competition refer to competition between banks issuing notes denominated in a common national currency.

and stable purchasing power, thus preventing them from over-issue of their notes. While this is convincing, this positive assessment is put into perspective by the fact that banks' note-issue business remained small. Even given their stable purchasing power, the use of banknotes as a means of payment remained unimportant, as customers did not see much advantage to notes vis-à-vis coins, especially for smaller transactions and in rural areas. The high costs of note issue and circulation, especially the high metal reserves needed to create confidence, also helped limit the development of this business.[10] We will return to a more general assessment of Switzerland's nineteenth-century experience with currency and note-issue competition in Chapter 8 of this book.

THE MONETARY REFORM OF 1850: BIRTH OF
THE SWISS FRANC

The social and economic developments of the 1830s and 1840s caused increasing political tensions between the industrialized, liberal, and predominantly Protestant cantons (including most of the bigger cities) and the rural, conservative, and mostly Catholic cantons (centered in the heart of old Switzerland). The result was a civil war, fortunately brief and relatively unbloody, which was won decisively by the liberal forces. Assisted by political moderation and a spirit of reconciliation on the part of the victorious side, this allowed the adoption of a liberal federal constitution and the creation of the modern Swiss confederation. Thus Switzerland was transformed from a loose confederation of independent, sovereign cantons into a liberal, federal republic.

These were times of radical change not just politically, but also economically. Cantonal tariffs were abolished. Weights and measures were unified. Postal services were nationalized. And, last but not least, the authority to mint coin was transferred from the cantons to the confederation and a common national currency was introduced. Thus, the (new) Swiss franc came into existence, replacing the multitude of cantonal and foreign coins and currencies previously in use. Note, however, that the authority to charter and regulate banks and their activities, including the issue of paper money in the form of banknotes, still stayed with the cantons. Only the revised federal constitution of 1874 and the federal Banknote Act of

---

[10] See Table 8.2 in Chapter 8.

1881 based on this constitutional revision would change that.[11] Most cantons were very liberal in licensing banks and regulating the issue of banknotes. The number of note-issuing banks increased steadily after 1850. In 1881, thirty-six such banks existed, with twenty cantons owning at least one.

The monetary reform set up by the constitution of 1848 found its concrete form in the federal Coinage Act (*Bundesgesetz über das Eidgen-össische Münzwesen*) of May 7, 1850. This act introduced the franc as Switzerland's monetary unit and defined it in complete analogy to the French monetary standard.[12] In other words, the Swiss franc was to be the precise equivalent of the French franc. It was set up as a silver currency, with a silver content of 4.5 grams, equal to that of the French franc. It was subdivided into 100 centimes or rappen. Its shape and size were equal to that of the French franc. Silver coins of five, two, one, and 0.5 francs were minted, as well as "small" coins with denominations of twenty, ten, five, two, and one centimes made up of alloys of "non-precious" metals, such as copper and nickel.[13] The old coins previously in use were withdrawn from circulation between August 1851 and August 1852.[14]

It is of interest to note that the objectives of this monetary reform at the time were not highly ambitious.[15] The central concern was that of simplification and unification of monetary affairs – overcoming the monetary confusion of the past. There was no question of creating a totally independent, internationally unique currency system. On the contrary, the guiding idea was adherence to one of the common and established (foreign) currency standards of the time. Two candidates were under serious consideration: the French franc, widely used in the western part of Switzerland (including Berne and Basel), and the South German gulden, which

---

[11] Before 1881, regulation of banks and banknote issue varied considerably between cantons and was very limited in scope (for more, see the subsection of this chapter entitled *Banknotes and Bank Regulation: From Free Banking to the Banknote Act of 1881*, and Chapter 8). Its aim was essentially customer protection and ensuring the stability of banks. See Toniolo and White (2015) on the historical evolution of financial stability objectives in several countries in Europe and America.

[12] With one (seemingly) minor exception: the French monetary standard was formally a bimetallic (gold-silver) standard, while the Swiss franc was defined as a pure silver currency. More on this below.

[13] Gold coins were only minted after 1883.

[14] More than 300 different types of domestic coin were turned in, in addition to a similar number of foreign coins.

[15] According to Halbeisen and Müller (1998, p. 65), the monetary reform was neither seriously contested nor nearly as emotional an issue as, e.g., the tariff reform.

had become increasingly important in the eastern part of the country (including Zurich and St. Gallen). There was heated debate between the supporters of these two currency standards, finally won by the adherents of the French system.[16] The main arguments for the French franc were its much greater international weight and its reliance on the decimal system. An additional handicap of the South German system was its uncertain future in view of political developments aimed at German political unification.

The new Swiss coins were initially minted abroad.[17] Without direct access to precious metals, and in view of the costs of minting – a process which presumably exhibits some economies of scale – the import of coins from foreign mints, especially from France (Paris and Strasbourg), appeared to be the economically superior solution. In principle, everyone was free to have silver minted into coin at foreign mints. In future times, however, the dependence on foreign suppliers created by the lack of a domestic mint would increasingly be viewed as a problem.

Furthermore, the new Swiss silver coins were minted in very limited quantities only. The idea was that the demand for such coins would be satisfied by equivalent foreign coins to a large extent – up to 80 percent, according to Weisskopf (1948, p. 83). In 1852, all silver coins corresponding to the French (and thus the Swiss) currency standard – from France, Belgium, Sardinia, Parma, the old Cisalpine Republic, and the former Kingdom of Italy (Napoleonic time) – were formally declared equivalent to the corresponding Swiss coins. In this way, a strong dependence on foreign countries, especially France, for the provision of silver coin emerged.

As it turned out, the new currency had an unfortunate start. According to the Coinage Act of 1850, the Swiss franc was meant to be a pure silver currency, modeled after the French franc. However, in formal terms, the French currency standard used as a guide was a bimetallic (silver-gold) standard: French law of 1803 allowed not only a silver coinage (the standard form used at the time), but also a (rarely used) gold coinage of the French franc. As it happened, worldwide demand for silver strongly grew in the period after 1850, with several countries introducing silver currencies (e.g., India and other British colonies). At the same time, the

---

[16] See, e.g., the spirited exchange between Pestalozzi (1849), a major critic of the French system, and Speiser (1849), an outspoken adherent of the French system (who was to become the federal government's main expert on currency matters).

[17] The Swiss (federal) mint started operations only in 1855.

supply of gold increased sharply, due to massive gold findings in California and Australia. As a consequence, the valuation of silver increased relative to that of gold on the international market. Gresham's Law came into operation. In France, gold coinage replaced silver coinage, silver left the franc area for other uses, and gold took the place of silver as the dominant monetary metal. In Switzerland, the new silver coins were quickly pushed out of circulation by French gold coins. By 1855, they had almost completely disappeared. French gold coins were exchanged at par (which means that the Swiss silver coins must have earned a premium). Few new silver coins were produced, as their production became too expensive.

Swiss authorities effectively tolerated these developments. French gold coins were accepted at par not only by banks and other institutions, but also by the federal treasury. De facto, the silver standard foreseen by Swiss law was replaced by a gold standard according to French coinage specifications within a few years of the new currency's existence. Under the new international conditions, maintaining the silver standard defined by the act of 1850 would have meant giving up the fixed peg to the French franc. Instead, the preference for maintaining a firm link to the French system proved much stronger. The decision, without much discussion, was to maintain this fixed link. In 1860, these developments were legalized through a revision of the coinage act. French gold coins, and equivalent gold coins of other states, were declared legal tender. The original silver standard was replaced by a bimetallic (gold-silver) standard, with gold and silver parities exactly corresponding to those of the French franc: 1 franc = 4.5 grams of silver = 0.2903226 grams of gold (implying a relation of 15.5 grams of silver = 1 gram of gold).

THE LATIN MONETARY UNION

In 1865, a monetary union was formed between France (as its leading country), Belgium, Italy, and Switzerland (three years later, Greece also joined) – the so-called "Latin Monetary Union." Switzerland was itself partly responsible for the developments leading to this international arrangement. In 1860, in response to the scarcity of silver, Switzerland lowered the fineness (i.e., the actual silver content) of its silver coins with a nominal value of less than five francs to 80 percent. The purpose of this was to make it unprofitable to melt down these coins. However, this led to difficulties with countries relying on the French monetary system, especially France, Belgium, and Italy, where the fineness of equivalent coins was

90 percent (Belgium; France until 1864) or 83.5 percent (Italy; France after 1864), respectively. Swiss coins were exported and started to drive French, Italian, and Belgian coins out of circulation, since the "cheap" Swiss coins could be exchanged in these countries into equivalent coins with a higher intrinsic value. As a consequence, neighboring countries became unwilling to accept Swiss coins at par, and France stopped accepting them at all in April 1864. French silver coins in turn began to drive the (still more valuable, in comparison) Belgian coins out of circulation. In response to these disturbances, an international conference with France, Italy, Belgium, and Switzerland as participants convened in Paris in 1865 (the first of several such conferences over the decades to come).[18]

From this conference, an international treaty emerged which established a monetary union between the countries involved, based on the French bimetallic standard and its parities. Silver coinage (for coins with a nominal value of less than five francs) was harmonized at a fineness of 83.5 percent. Gold coins and (the full-valued) silver five-franc pieces were declared legal tender in all participant countries. Silver coins with a nominal value of less than five francs had to be accepted by participant-country government cashiers for payments of up to 100 francs.[19] As already mentioned, Switzerland minted its own silver coins in limited amounts only, and no Swiss gold coins were produced until the 1880s. While the Latin Monetary Union did regulate coinage, it did not regulate the issue of paper money in the form of banknotes. This was left to the participating countries.

The Latin Monetary Union gained some influence beyond the realm of its formal treaty states. A number of other countries linked their currencies in informal ways to the Union and its bimetallic standard, without becoming formal contract states – among them the Vatican, Romania, Bulgaria, Spain, Serbia, Venezuela, and Argentina – creating a currency block extending over a vast economic space. In spite of this, however, the future was to belong to the gold standard, with Great Britain leading the way.[20]

The Swiss federal government, according to Weisskopf (1948, p. 95), initially had high expectations concerning the benefits of this international agreement and viewed it as a first step toward the creation of a fully universal monetary system, improving trade, international relations, and

---

[18] On these developments, see, e.g., Eichengreen (1996), p. 16; Einaudi (2001), p. 33.
[19] Ritzmann (1973), p. 91.
[20] See, e.g., Redish (1994); Eichengreen and Flandreau (1996, 1997); Flandreau (2000).

economic development for all participants alike.[21] The reality was more modest, however. The new monetary union functioned rather imperfectly from its very beginning. For one, its conception as a bimetallic currency standard implied the risk of instability due to fluctuations in market gold-silver valuation, well known from monetary history and theory. Beyond that, the lack of harmonization of the regulation of paper-money issue – which stayed at the national level – proved troublesome almost from the outset in view of the growing importance of banknotes as a means of payment in these times. An overissue of paper money in Italy, and the subsequent suspension of banknote redemption there in May 1866, created a premium for silver coin in Italy and caused Italian coins to flood other member countries, including Switzerland.

Most importantly, the increasing preference for national objectives in all areas of public policy, characteristic of this period of the rising nation state, made it difficult to enforce adherence to union rules by all participants. Arguments between union member states about the right to coin silver were frequent, leading to treaty renegotiations (and, in 1884, even a temporary cancellation of the treaty by Switzerland). In spite of all this, the Union was to exist, at least formally, until the end of 1926 – although, in practical terms, it did not play much of a role after the outbreak of World War I.

It is important to note, however, that compared to today's European Economic and Monetary Union, the Latin Monetary Union represented a much lesser degree of financial and currency integration. The definition and legal base of member-country currencies remained national. No transfer of monetary sovereignty to the Union level took place, and there was no common monetary authority. In essence, the Latin Monetary Union was an international agreement to use a common (metallic) monetary standard – the French one – more comparable to the fixed exchange rate arrangement of Bretton Woods after World War II than to the Economic and Monetary Union of our day. An exit and return to an independent monetary course, in principle, was possible at any time. Of course, a fully autonomous monetary policy as we know it today was not feasible under the metallic monetary standards of the nineteenth century, in any case.

A major shock to the fragile structure of this international arrangement was not long in coming. The outbreak of the Franco-Prussian War in July 1870 forced France to prohibit gold exports and suspend the convertibility

---

[21] Halbeisen and Müller (1998), p. 75. Similar hopes were shared by other participating countries.

of banknotes.[22] Thus the rules of the still young monetary union were already broken – if only temporarily, and for comprehensible reasons. For Switzerland, with its strong monetary dependence on France, this had disastrous consequences and led to a severe liquidity crisis and financial distress – the *Geldcrisis* of 1870. The policy of importing coin from abroad and abstaining from sufficient domestic production, which had seemed economical and advantageous under normal conditions, completely cut off the country from its supply source of money and turned out to be a great disadvantage under conditions of war. As the public's liquidity preference (demand for coin) increased three- to fourfold due to the insecurity of the times, a dramatic scarcity of cash arose and the risk of a complete break-down of the monetary system seemed real. Swiss note-issuing and credit banks were no longer able to honor their payments obligations, to discount bills, and to extend credit. Some cantons were forced to introduce a general payments moratorium (the canton of Berne was one example).[23]

In order to alleviate the situation, at the end of July and in August, respectively, the federal government declared the English sovereign (a one-pound gold coin with wide availability) and the American dollar to be legal tender. By changing their holdings of bills drawn on these currencies into coin, Swiss banks thus were able to increase the volume of payments instruments and to ease the liquidity squeeze. This reduced the existing tensions to a considerable degree. The quick end to the war – as early as the end of January 1871, France capitulated and peace negotiations took place – allowed complete normalization of the situation. Thus the monetary crisis of 1870 was but a brief encounter with financial distress and chaos. Nevertheless, it had a deep effect on public opinion and served as a reminder of the dangers of excessive monetary dependence on foreign powers. It also gave strong impulses to the emerging debate concerning the desirability of a centralized Swiss note-issuing bank.[24]

After 1870, the Latin Monetary Union, and the international monetary order overall, underwent serious change. A number of countries shifted from a silver or silver-gold standard to a pure gold currency – most importantly the newly founded German Reich, followed by Sweden, Denmark, Norway,[25] and the Netherlands, but also the United States,

---

[22] Italy, Russia, and the Austrian-Hungarian Empire also suspended convertibility.

[23] For a vivid contemporaneous description of this crisis and what it meant for business and trade, see Keller (1871).

[24] More on this in the next chapter.

[25] In view of their interdependence, the three Scandinavian countries established their own monetary union in 1873 – the Scandinavian Monetary Union.

which had been on a bimetallic standard before the Civil War led to a period of inconvertible paper money ("greenbacks"). This increased the monetary demand for gold, while monetary silver reserves were released. Additionally, the supply of silver rose due to important new silver discoveries in Nevada and other places. As a consequence, the price of gold increased relative to that of silver and, measured against the official parities of the Latin Monetary Union, gold became the scarce ("dear") metal again and silver the abundant ("cheap") one. In the Union countries, it became profitable to exchange gold for silver and have it coined. Thus silver returned to its role as the monetary metal of the Latin Monetary Union and the Union returned to an effective silver standard, with the silver five-franc piece as its most characteristic coin.

In the years to come, the Union had continual problems with an oversupply of paper money in some countries and excessive coinage of silver. It responded by introducing minting quotas, and in 1878 even by suspending free coinage. Arguments between member countries about the rights to mint small (undervalued) silver coins were frequent, and several renegotiations of the treaty took place. In 1893, Italian small silver coins – which had flooded the union area once more since the 1880s – were nationalized, that is, their acceptance was restricted to Italy only, effectively ending the existence of a unified monetary area. In the context of the ongoing renegotiations, Switzerland made several moves toward switching to a pure gold standard; however, these proved to be unsuccessful.[26]

BANKNOTES AND BANK REGULATION: FROM FREE BANKING TO THE BANKNOTE ACT OF 1881

The banknote as a means of payment suffered from a lack of acceptance in Switzerland for a long time. Banknotes were not legal tender. They were largely seen as an imperfect, and not especially favored, substitute for "real" money (coin). Between 1850 and 1870, growth of banknote circulation remained very modest. The subsequent five-year period, however, witnessed a dramatic change: Note circulation jumped by a factor of four, rising from 19 million francs in 1870 to 77 million francs in 1875. Afterward, growth returned to normal levels. Overall, banknote circulation increased from 7.6 million Swiss francs in 1850 to 235 million francs in 1906 (see Figure 2.1).

---

[26] Halbeisen and Müller (1998), pp. 76–7.

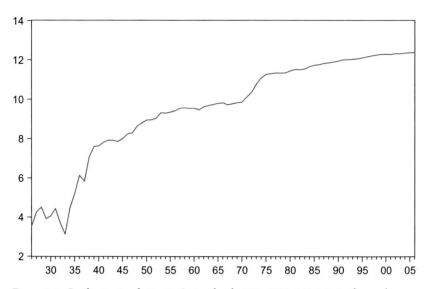

Figure 2.1: *Banknote circulation in Switzerland, 1825–1906, 1,000 Swiss francs, logs*
Source: Weber (1992), p. 194, based on Jöhr (1915)

According to Ritzmann, it was the return to a de facto silver currency after 1870 that greatly helped to make banknotes – up to this point still in modest use in Switzerland – more popular as a means of payment. The public was not enthusiastic about the return of the "heavy" silver coins for bigger payments and increasingly began to accept paper money.[27] In addition, a strong expansion of business activity in this period contributed to an increasing demand for money overall, including notes. Rapid economic growth in new, politically unified Germany (the postwar boom of the so-called *Gründerjahre*) strongly boosted the Swiss economy, too.

As we have seen, the first Swiss note-issuing banks were founded between the 1820s and the 1840s. By 1850, eight such banks existed. As there was not yet a common national currency, these banks were free to denominate their banknotes in the currencies of their choice. Formally, this remained true even after 1850. Until 1881, when a federal act regulating banknote issue was passed, banks were subject to no restrictions in this regard. However, banks were quick to adopt the new Swiss franc as their

[27] Ritzmann (1973), p. 91.

common currency denominator. A few banks, for example, the Bank in Zürich and the Bank in St. Gallen, issued notes in both Swiss francs and in foreign currency for some time. The demand for foreign currency notes was small, however, and their issue was soon stopped.

In general, banking from 1850 to 1881 was characterized by very little government intervention and a high degree of competition, including note-issue competition. There were no federal restrictions at all, and the cantons were liberal in licensing new banks and regulating their activities. A large number of new public and private banks were established, some – but not all – entering the note-issue business.[28] The increasing number of public (cantonal) banks did not lower note-issue competition, as these banks were not given a banknote monopoly or other privileges by their cantons.[29] Private banks usually had to meet certain minimal standards regarding liquidity and capital reserves according to their statutes, which had to be approved by the canton, and in some cantons an upper limit on their banknote issue was set. The purpose of these measures was to promote customer confidence, however, and not to prevent competition.

The period of free banking up to 1881 was reviewed by Weber (1992), who presents a positive view of note-issue competition during this period. He argues that competition forced banks to behave in a responsible way, avoiding over-issue of notes and contributing to stable financial conditions. Other authors, among them Jöhr (1915) and Ritzmann (1973), have presented a more pessimistic view, stressing the inefficiencies of the payments system under this regime. These inefficiencies are reflected in the fact that, up to 1870, banknotes did play a rather minor role as a means of payment in Switzerland. We will return to this debate and present our assessment of the Swiss experience of note-issue competition in Chapter 8 of this book.

---

[28] For instance, the *Schweizerische Kreditanstalt* (today's *Credit Suisse*), founded in 1856 in Zurich, and the *Bank in Winterthur* (the predecessor bank of today's *UBS*), founded in 1862 in Winterthur, both opted from their beginnings not to engage in the note-issue business. The dynamics of the Industrial Revolution – with its rapid growth of railway construction and the foundation of important industrial firms, in which Switzerland was very much active – led to the creation of these and other large commercial banks between 1850 and 1880.

[29] An exception was the canton of Zurich. The cantonal banking act of 1869 favored the newly established *Zürcher Kantonalbank* at the expense of the older (and private) *Bank in Zürich*. There even was an (unsuccessful) legislative attempt to grant it a cantonal note-issue monopoly.

In the course of the 1860s and 1870s, dominant political opinions in Switzerland shifted. The so-called "Democratic Movement" gained ground, favoring a more restrained form of liberalism, direct democratic institutions (such as the popular initiative), and a more pronounced role for government. Besides leading to the foundation of new public (cantonal) banks in numerous cantons, this paved the way toward a revision of the federal constitution in 1874 and – influenced by growing concerns about perceived inefficiencies of the existing payments system – the passing of a federal banking legislation in 1881.

The revised constitution gave the Confederation the authority to enact law regulating the issue of paper money at the national level – but without giving it the right to establish a federal monopoly on note issue. Banknote issue was, in principle, still left under cantonal rule. Nevertheless, the constitutional revision prepared the ground for legislation which effectively ended the era of free, unregulated banking in Switzerland. A first attempt at such legislation in 1876 was unsuccessful, after a negative popular (referendum) vote. In 1881, however, a bill regulating the issue and redemption of banknotes *(Bundesgesetz über die Ausgabe und Einlösung von Banknoten*, short: *Banknotengesetz* or "Banknote Act") was successful. The formation of a "Concordat" as a defensive move by the note-issuing banks after the vote of 1876 – two thirds of these banks participated and agreed to mutually accept their notes at par, to provide each other with balance sheet information, and to maintain a clearing center at the Bank in Zurich – could not stop this process. After the Banknote Act of 1881, the issue of banknotes was still left to competition between a large number of issuing banks (thirty-six of them at the time); however, these banks were now constrained by numerous restrictions they had not known before, aimed at making the banknote a much more homogeneous product than it had previously been and increasing the efficiency and safety of the payments system. That this would eventually lead to a full centralization of banknote issue and the establishment of a Swiss central bank cannot come as a surprise.[30]

The central regulations introduced by the new Banknote Act were the following:

- *Liquidity reserves*: Note-issuing banks were required to maintain metal (gold, silver) reserves equaling at least 40 percent of their note issue. Banks without public (cantonal) guarantees were required to

---

[30] More on this in the following chapter.

hold high-grade domestic or foreign public (or, under restrictive conditions, private) bonds against the remaining 60 percent of their note issue.[31]

- *Equity capital*: Note-issuing banks had to maintain equity capital equal to 50 percent of their note issue or more.
- *Banknote redemption*: Banks were required to mutually accept their notes at par, as long as the issuing partner bank itself honored its redemption obligations.
- *Taxation*: Taxation of note issue by cantons was limited to 0.6 percent (plus a federal and cantonal fee of 0.2 percent).
- *Banknote standardization*: Banknotes were standardized with regard to form and denomination, with notes between 50 and 1,000 Swiss francs (previously, some banks had issued notes of smaller denominations).
- *Bank supervision*: Federal supervision of note-issuing banks was established, introducing regular (weekly, monthly) reporting duties.

---

[31] This requirement, of course, gave a certain advantage to cantonal banks.

3

The Long Road to a Swiss Central Bank
(1881–1914)

Initial, vague ideas on the establishment of a central note-issuing bank for the whole of Switzerland were already in circulation before 1850.[1] However, it was only after the creation of the federal state and the currency reform of 1850 that implementation of such ideas became feasible. And even then it was more than half a century before the Swiss National Bank (SNB) finally saw the light of day.

From 1850 onwards, a number of different projects and proposals were discussed.[2] The debate became particularly lively as a result of the crisis of 1870 that was triggered by the inconvertibility of the French franc, in turn caused by the Franco-Prussian war.[3] Encouraged by frequent complaints concerning the inefficiency of the existing payment and banknote system, the question of the desirability, or even necessity, of a central bank was raised repeatedly, with advocates and adversaries of a federal banknote monopoly arguing their respective cases. On the opponents' side, most important were, first, a deeply rooted fear of an excessive concentration of power with the central government, and, second, the fiscal interests of the cantons. The advocates, for their part, stressed the inefficiency of the existing system and the need to protect banknote holders from possible over-issue and deterioration in the quality of banknotes.

---

[1] Ritzmann (1973), p. 93.

[2] See, e.g., Burckhardt-Bischoff (1865) or Rüttimann (1865) for early contributions to this discussion.

[3] In the aftermath of this crisis a committee of experts was appointed by the federal government, and the Swiss Chamber of Commerce and Industry (*Schweizerischer Handels- und Industrieverein*) commissioned appraisals of the current system.

THE CONSTITUTIONAL REVISIONS OF 1874 AND 1891

The federal constitution of 1848 left the authority to regulate banks and the issue of banknotes to the cantons. As we saw in Chapter 2, in 1874 the federal constitution was revised in the wake of the rise of the "Democratic Movement." By establishing a federal authority to regulate banknote issue, this revision brought a compromise between the two camps described above in terms of monetary and banking matters. On the pivotal issue of a banknote monopoly, however, the opponents of full centralization once again won the day. The new article on currency and banknote emission, article 39, read as follows:

The Confederation has the authority to enact general regulations on the issue and redemption of banknotes by means of legislation. However, it may not establish any monopoly for the issue of banknotes; neither may it pronounce any legal obligation for the acceptance of the same.

The Banknote Act of 1881 was based on this article. It brought considerable improvements to the efficiency of the payment system and security of banknote holders, but continued to allow competition between independent issuing banks.[4] In a sense, it also took into account the need to limit banknote circulation by restricting the maximum issue to a fixed multiple of paid-in capital.

However, the idea of full centralization of the note-issuing business was still on the table and more proposals were to come. One tenacious advocate of a central bank for the whole of Switzerland, to be established on a private basis but with government oversight, was Conrad Cramer-Frey, an important businessman and politician.[5] In 1881 the issuing banks, in a second "Concordat," agreed to extend and improve their banknote clearing. The number of private issuing banks declined, and over time the cantonal banks became more and more dominant in the business of banknote emission. Thus public sector influence gained ground.

In 1880, a popular initiative for yet another revision of the constitution was rejected. In 1891, however, 60 percent of the voters approved a revision of constitutional article 39. The revised article now stated:

The authority to issue banknotes and other similar monetary symbols rests exclusively with the Confederation.

---

[4] See Chapter 2 for the details of the 1881 Banknote Act.
[5] See, e.g., Cramer-Frey (1880).

Thus, the new constitutional article brought a decisive change in the crucial matter of banknote monopoly. Competition in banknote issue was no longer foreseen.

However, from the acceptance of the revised constitutional article, a decade and a half was to elapse before the precise form of the new central bank was determined and the SNB was able to start operations. During this phase, existing note-issue banks still continued business. The political debate concerning the new central bank focused on the choice of legal form (private vs. purely state-owned solutions), the location of the headquarters (Berne or Zurich) and the fiscal interests of the cantons. An initial implementation law in 1896 foresaw a purely state-owned bank but was rejected by the people in a referendum vote. A second proposal in 1899 failed due to disagreement on the headquarters issue. A third and final draft compromised on the headquarters question by proposing official seats in both Zurich and Berne, and was successful. It came into effect on 6 October 1905 as the Federal Act on the Swiss National Bank (short: National Bank Act). The support of the cantons was obtained through a profit-sharing arrangement.[6] The SNB effectively started business in June 1907.

Compared to most other central banks, the SNB was a latecomer to the scene. Among the important central banks of the industrialized world, only the US Federal Reserve – which was established with the Federal Reserve Act of December 1913 – came even later. A few central banks, notably the Swedish Riksbank (founded in 1668) and the Bank of England (dating back to 1694), have a very long history. The original function of these banks was managing government debt accumulated through wars and expensive extravagancies of aristocratic rulers. Most European central banks, however, were established in the nineteenth century: the Banque de France in 1800, the Austrian National Bank in 1816, the German Reichsbank in 1876, and the Banca d'Italia in 1893, to name but a few of the most important ones. The function of nineteenth-century central banks was different, though, from that of their early predecessors, namely preventing and easing financial panics and the consequences of abrupt capital flows, and increasing the efficiency of the payments system. In some cases, these central banks were created in response to particular financial crises. The German Reichsbank was founded in the aftermath of the crash of 1873, and the US Federal Reserve System as a result of discussion about the

---

[6] On the political debate relating to the establishment of the SNB, see Zimmermann (1987).

causes and resolution of the panic of 1907.[7] In Switzerland, as we have seen above, the crisis of 1870 played such a role in the genesis of the SNB.[8]

WHY OPINION TURNED IN FAVOR OF A CENTRALIZED BANKNOTE MONOPOLY

An obvious question to ask at this point is why public opinion in Switzerland shifted in the way just described. Why did centralization increasingly gain favor? It seems natural to relate this change in attitude to the general debate about the role of a state banknote monopoly that had taken place in Britain during the first half of the nineteenth century between the adherents of the banking school, the currency school, and the free banking school. In that debate the view had prevailed that free competition in the issue of banknotes as a means of payment – unlike the production of most other goods – was problematic and not to be recommended. Ritzmann (1973, p. 96) has argued that this theoretical discussion is unlikely to have had too much of an impact on the Swiss debate, since it took place at an academic level which was inaccessible to most Swiss at the time. He is probably right in the sense that the Swiss debate was based more on practical matters. It goes without saying, though, that these were indirectly linked to the issues discussed in the earlier British debate. In particular, the idea that free banknote issue inevitably leads to overexpansion of banknote circulation and subsequent outflows of monetary metal (gold and silver) was a frequent theme of the Swiss debate of the 1880s and 1890s. However, other factors played a role, too.

One important and frequently mentioned criticism of the existing system which had a strong impact on the discussion (see, e.g., Kalkmann, 1900, p. 29) referred to the inadequate elasticity of money circulation over the course of the year and the fluctuations in money market conditions resulting from it. Pronounced seasonal fluctuations in interest rates and market liquidity were considered disruptive by many business participants. The conditions for discount credit from Swiss note-issuing banks were designed to keep banknote circulation as stable as possible. This was because taxation of note issue was geared to banks' total allocation (or quota) of note issue (simply known as "banknote issue"), irrespective of actual banknote circulation. In other words, banknotes withdrawn from

---

[7] Bordo and James (2007), p. 30.
[8] For a general discussion of central banking and its historical evolution see Capie, Goodhart, and Schnadt (1994).

circulation were still taxed. Banks were therefore strongly motivated to make full use of their issue quotas and had an incentive to neutralize seasonal cycles in money demand – which, due to the agricultural cycle, was typically higher in the second half of the year than in the first – by adjusting their discount rates. Consequently, interest rates were subject to considerable seasonal fluctuations, and these fluctuations were regularly accompanied by a surplus of liquidity in the first half of the year and a liquidity shortage in the second.

Even though criticism of the monetary conditions prevailing at the time is easy to understand, it is important to note that the inadequate elasticity of money was mainly due to the rules of note-issue taxation just described. It did not represent an inherent feature of the system of note-issue competition and could easily have been changed without destroying this system. Moreover, inelasticity of liquidity provision was, to a certain extent, a general characteristic of the metallic currency systems prevalent at the time.

From 1885 onwards, and particularly in the 1890s, a chronic outflow of currency metal ("silver drainage") became an important additional factor. The Swiss franc developed a tendency toward chronic weakness, and in the metallic currency system of the time this induced an outflow of silver from Switzerland. Swiss issuing banks suffered serious depletion of their silver reserves.[9] Swiss interest rates in this period were systematically higher than French interest rates – that is, the Swiss franc was characterized by an interest rate "malus," rather than the interest rate "bonus" to which we have become accustomed over the past 100 years (Figure 3.1). Note, however, that this Swiss interest rate malus was less pronounced or even inexistent before 1880. In Chapter 10 we will provide an econometric analysis of the level of Swiss interest rates in an international perspective.

The redemption of banknotes was very uneven across the country and heavily concentrated on issuing banks close to the border. Before long, these banks ran out of silver reserves. They did not have the option of suspending banknote redemption or of devaluing the currency – this would have been a matter for the Confederation. They reacted by repurchasing silver, at a market price higher than the parity rate they received

---

[9]   It should be noted that what is involved here is currency weakness and drainage of currency (metal) reserves in general, and not the well-known problem of bimetallism, where gold is exchanged for silver after a change in the relative market price of both metals. At this time, gold was practically unavailable in the market due to the "gold premium policy" in France. Part of the statutory banknote coverage of Swiss banks was held in gold.

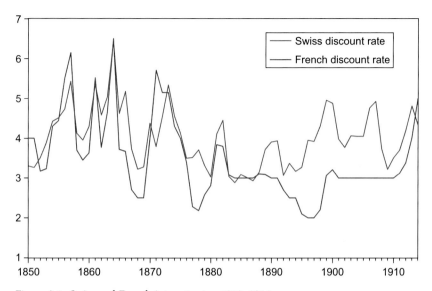

Figure 3.1: Swiss and French interest rates, 1850–1914
Source: Homer and Sylla (2005), Tables 23, 27, 29, 33, 34, 61, 63, 65, 69, 71

when redeeming their notes, and re-importing it as quickly as possible. Consequently, their note-issue business became less attractive. Naturally, this reaction of the banks also meant that the external drain on metal reserves continued. In the 1890s, silver drainage became chronic. Banks close to the border approached the Bank Concordat for help and demanded that "drainage costs" be shared. There were also efforts to coordinate discount policies. Interest in banknote business declined in general, and resistance to a central bank diminished.

"It was not silver drainage that tipped the scales, but, on the contrary, the paradoxical fact that the note issuing banks prevented this drainage, destroyed Switzerland's international currency adjustment and – to top it all – nearly destroyed themselves in the process," to quote Ritzmann's summary of this episode.[10] Ritzmann sees this as evidence that private issuing banks did not function properly within the competitive note-issue system. He argues that the idea of a central note-issuing bank gained popularity in Switzerland after private issuing banks had clearly demonstrated their inadequacy in the area of currency policy. Ritzmann therefore

---

[10] Ritzmann (1973), p. 96.

attributes responsibility for the swing in opinion and the change in the system to the poor functioning of the existing institutional arrangement as a result of competition between issuing banks.

Note-issue competition is also the most important point for Neldner (1996, 2003). He argues that, for fundamental reasons, such competition tends to result in over-issue and adverse effects caused by it; sees the Swiss experience from 1881 to 1905 as evidence in favor of the nineteenth-century currency school point of view; and interprets the shift in opinion in favor of the central bank approach as a reaction to the resulting distortions. In the past, Kalkmann (1900), Landmann (1905), and Jöhr (1915) have argued in a similar vein.

However, this is an incomplete story. The developments described certainly represent an important part of the picture. But they do not by themselves make note-issue competition the culprit. The developments described implied that the banks' note-issue business was no longer as profitable as it had previously been. Consequently, the issuing banks should have scaled back their volume of operation. Had they done so, no over-issue would have occurred and the problem would have vanished. The real question, therefore, is: Why did they fail to react in this way? Was it the collectivization of the issuing business via the Bank Concordat? Was it the regulation of this business through the Banknote Act? Or is it really, as suggested by the authors cited above, note-issue competition *as such* that exhibits an intrinsic tendency to over-issue? In our opinion, the proper way to look at these questions is as follows.[11]

Note-issue competition as such does not necessarily lead to over-issue, monetary overexpansion, and instability. As the Swiss experience between 1825 and 1881 shows, it can be perfectly compatible with stable monetary conditions and purchasing power. However, this is true only as long as the banknotes of competing suppliers remain differentiated and distinct products. Then competition displays its disciplinary effects and forces banks to remain sound, for fear of losing market share or even being driven out of business. But while this is a favorable situation, the resulting system also exhibits significant weaknesses. It is complicated for the users of banknotes and implies potentially heavy information and monitoring costs. These weaknesses have the effect of making the banknote unattractive as a means of payment. In turn, they create strong incentives for enforcing common quality standards – be it through regulation or through cartel-like arrangements – aimed at making

---

[11] A more detailed version of our view is presented in Chapter 8.

the banknote more homogeneous as a product and rendering the system more efficient. This is precisely what happened in Switzerland with the Banknote Act of 1881. But such standardization makes competition unable to perform its disciplinary role. It introduces an externality into the system and creates an incentive for banks to overexpand, since the results of individual overexpansion are borne no longer by the individual bank but instead by the industry and the market as a whole. It is not surprising, therefore, that overexpansion occurred after 1881 and the Swiss franc developed a tendency toward chronic weakness in the 1880s and 1890s.

Seen from this perspective, it was the quest for efficiency and stability that caused dissatisfaction with the competitive system and was, in the final analysis, responsible for the change toward centralization of the note-issue business. The system resulting from competition was functional and stable, but not efficient. Efficiency considerations led to regulatory interventions, which in turn destroyed the disciplinary effects of competition, and eventually led to its demise and centralization.

INSTITUTIONAL STRUCTURE, MANDATE, AND INSTRUMENTS OF THE SWISS NATIONAL BANK

The newly founded Swiss central bank opened its doors for business in 1907. It was created as a joint-stock company, not an uncommon legal form for a central bank in Europe at this time. Two fifths of the shares were assigned to the cantons, one fifth to the former note-issuing banks, and the remaining two fifths to private investors. However, a very particular form of joint-stock company was chosen, governed by special provisions of federal law and under pronounced public influence. The rights and privileges of shareholders were strongly limited in favor of the public sector by the National Bank Act. As already mentioned, the politically difficult choice of headquarters was decided by creating two official seats, one in Zurich and one in Berne, with a distinction being made between the legal and administrative seat (Berne) and the seat of the Governing Board (Zurich). Additional branch offices were opened in Basel, Geneva, and St. Gallen (and later also in several other places).

The highest managing and executive body of the SNB was the Governing Board (*Direktorium*), including three members appointed by the Federal Council (rather than the shareholders). In contrast to many other central banks, there was no dominant Governor with the power to determine the concept and course of central bank policy on his own. The Chairman of the Governing Board was but *primus inter pares*; in most respects the three members of the Board had equal standing, and decisions were taken by majority vote. Each member of the Governing Board managed one of the SNB's three major departments. Supervisory bodies were a forty-member Bank Council – with twenty-five members named by the Federal Council, including the president and vice president, and the other fifteen by the shareholders – and a seven-member Bank Committee selected from among them (including the Bank Council's president and vice president), responsible for closer oversight.

These supervisory bodies were subject to significant political influence. This was deemed useful for ensuring the SNB's independence from the banking and finance industry. Government pressure in favor of easy public credit was not seen as much of a danger in those days. Potential abuse of the central bank was related much more to commercial banks' efforts to induce the central bank to accept bills of exchange of low quality and speculative nature. Consequently, independence from banks was more important.[12] On various occasions, the Bank Council and the Bank Committee took active part in monetary policy discussions. In accordance with the National Bank Act (article 52), the Bank Committee was assigned an advisory role with regard to the setting of the official discount rate and the SNB's rate for loans. The independence of central bank policy from politics and the clear separation of the authorities of Governing Board and Bank Council regarding monetary policy decisions, well established today, only developed over the twentieth century. Apart from this, however, the organizational structure defined at the SNB's inception is, broadly speaking, still valid today.

The Federal Council chose three experienced bankers as the first members of the SNB's Governing Board. Heinrich Kundert, formerly director of the Cantonal Bank of Zurich, the biggest of the old issuing banks, was appointed as the first chairman of the Governing Board. Rodolphe de Haller, previously partner in a Geneva bank, was the Board's first vice president, and August Burckhardt from the Cantonal Bank of Basel was named as the third member. The first president of the SNB's Bank Council was Johann Hirter, a representative of the canton of Berne and president of the National Council, formerly a strong advocate of a state central bank. Paul Usteri, a liberal politician from Zurich, was selected as the Council's first vice president.

The main tasks of the SNB, according to the National Bank Act (article 2), were to regulate the circulation of money and to promote the efficiency of

---

[12] Bordo and James (2007), p. 35.

the country's payments system. To this end, the National Bank Act entitled the SNB to issue banknotes. The SNB's note-issue privilege was at first granted for a limited period of twenty years only; afterward, it was to be renewed every ten years. The SNB's banknotes were to be issued in relatively large denominations of 50, 100, 500, and 1,000 francs, meaning that they were not really designed for normal, everyday transactions. The notes were not (yet) legal tender. Only the gold and silver coins of the Latin Monetary Union had this status; banknotes were just a substitute for this "real" money. The SNB was obliged to exchange its notes at par for legal metallic money and to hold metal reserves of at least 40 percent against its note issue.

The history of the formation of the SNB makes clear that the new central bank was expected to ensure an elastic provision of money "according to the needs of commerce" and to further the system of payments and payments clearing. An active monetary policy role in the modern sense, on the other hand, was not – and could not be – a part of its mandate, as its freedom to create liquidity and money was strongly constrained by the convertibility requirements of the metallic currency system of the time. The SNB had to be capable to exchange its notes for metal, either silver or gold, at any time. The SNB was careful from the beginning to hold its metal reserves at or above the required 40 percent. In fact, for reasons of confidence-building and for fear of sudden large drains, actual metal coverage (held for the larger part in gold) was often far above the statutory requirement, fluctuating around 70 percent in the period from 1907 to 1914. Nevertheless, through some variation in its metal reserve ratio, the SNB could contribute to the desired elasticity in money provision to a certain degree. The 1905 National Bank Act gave the SNB no explicit objectives for exchange rate policy. The convertibility obligation for its notes implied, however, a stabilization of the Swiss franc around the official parities. Had the SNB issued notes in excess, the exchange rate of the Swiss franc would have tended toward weakness, notes would have been exchanged against metal, and an outflow of metal reserves would have occurred.

The National Bank Act specified the types of activities the SNB was allowed to engage in, setting it apart from commercial banks and their business. For the Bank's issue business, the former issuing banks which the SNB succeeded served as a model. Three main instruments of liquidity provision were foreseen by the Act: discount and Lombard credit,[13]

---

[13] Discount credit is (short-term) lending to banks against the collateral of short-term bills, with a discount representing the interest on the loan. Lombard credit is (short- to medium-term) lending against the collateral of securities (or a similar claim).

transactions in foreign currency and precious metals, and the purchase and sale of domestic securities. The relative importance of these instruments did change considerably over time, however. Up to the 1920s, central bank credit, especially in the form of discount credit, served as the major instrument for liquidity creation. Later on, gold and foreign exchange transactions increasingly played an important role. Purchases and sales of securities and Lombard credit, on the other hand, remained of minor importance.

The act restricted discount of bills to those with a maturity of at most ninety days. Beyond the legal requirements, the SNB felt committed to the principle known as the real bills doctrine – a common view shared by all central banks at the time – according to which only so-called commercial bills should be discounted, not "speculative" or "noncommercial" bills (also known as "finance bills," *Finanzwechsel*).[14] Commercial bills, issued to finance "real" transactions with a specified date of completion, such as crops to be harvested or the shipping of goods from foreign places, would be self-liquidating; lending on the collateral of such bills thus was seen as unproblematic. Financing speculative activities by discounting noncommercial bills, in contrast, was viewed as dangerous and undesirable.

Board chairman Kundert summarized this position as follows:

The totality of purely commercial bills in a country represents the maximum of circulating money that it can require, and the note issue needs to be set according to this norm. If the National Bank is to establish a healthy circulation, it must exclude from its discount all so-called finance bills, as well as bills that can be prolonged at maturity.[15]

Though adhering to this position on fundamental grounds, in practice the SNB was soon forced to depart from this principle. The limited supply of commercial bills induced it to relax its discounting rules, especially after the outbreak of World War I and the increase in liquidity preference caused by it. In the 1920s, pressure from the commercial banks rendered adherence to the doctrine virtually impossible.

Purchases and sales of foreign currency served the stabilization of exchange rates around parity. The SNB intervened when currency market turbulence arose and the so-called gold-points were reached, that is, the

---

[14] This represented a departure from the practice of the former note issuing banks.
[15] Kundert (1907), p. 18; cited in Bordo and James (2007), p. 37.

exchange rates for which the import or export of currency metal became profitable under the metallic currency system of the time.[16] The SNB built up a portfolio of foreign currency bills and gold depots and deposits at important foreign finance centers, especially Paris.

Open market operations, that is, purchases and sales of securities by the central bank, have long played a minor role in Switzerland. Although the 1905 National Bank Act did not exclude the acquisition of government securities by the SNB, it allowed this only for temporary investment of liquid reserves. This restriction was not changed until 1953, and even then with a limitation to papers with a maturity of at most two years. Only the revisions of the most recent times gave the SNB more flexibility in this respect.

A brief comparison of the SNB and the US Federal Reserve, founded a few years after the SNB, seems to be warranted. Switzerland and the United States shared many monetary features before the foundation of their central banks. There was a common currency issued by the federation from the beginning, and the regulation of banks and note issue rested initially with cantons and member states, respectively. Moreover, in both countries the federation started to regulate and harmonize bank note issue in the second half of the nineteenth century (in the United States, the introduction of national banks and the greenback came in the 1860s). However, the Federal Reserve System was initially much less centralistic and more "regional," as the twelve district Federal Reserve Banks enjoyed a considerable degree of freedom in their discount policies until the open market committee was founded in response to the Great Depression in the 1930s.

FIRST STEPS OF THE NEW CENTRAL BANK: THE SNB UNDER THE INTERNATIONAL GOLD STANDARD

The first seven years of the SNB's existence turned out to be the final years of the classical age of the international gold standard – an era which would come to its end with the outbreak of World War I. Characteristic features of this period were strong worldwide confidence in the stability and convertibility of the British pound and a high

---

[16] Transactions and transportation costs created a wedge between the gold- (or silver-) points and the parity rate.

priority assigned by all national governments to maintaining gold convertibility of their currencies, as compared to domestic national policy objectives.[17]

The young Swiss central bank was quickly confronted with a first major challenge. Its first year of business, 1907, was one of great international currency turbulence and financial panic. In autumn 1907, the Bank of England had to raise its discount rate to 7 percent as a consequence of this crisis, and the German Reichsbank raised its rate as high as 7.5 percent. The SNB was fairly successful in meeting this first test; Switzerland came through the period without great financial and real economic disturbances. The SNB had to raise its discount rate, too, but only to a relatively moderate level of 5.5 percent. The interest rate differential between Switzerland and France fell significantly after 1907.

The old private and cantonal note-issue banks withdrew from the note-issue business until 1910 (they were legally allowed to continue its operation during a period of transition). Real economic conditions in Switzerland were robust and the price level stable. The SNB began to develop patterns and principles of policy guiding its actions in pursuit of its mandate. It goes without saying that these were strongly influenced by the international monetary environment the SNB faced.

Article 18 of the National Bank Act required the Bank to issue notes "according to the needs of commerce." Article 20 asked for a minimum 40 percent coverage of note issue in gold or silver, and article 22 obliged the SNB to exchange its notes on demand into gold or silver coin according to the conditions of the Latin Monetary Union ("convertibility"). The metal coverage and convertibility provisions of the National Bank Act reflected the conventional view of the time that banknotes were not money, properly speaking, but only a substitute for "real," metal money. This was mirrored by the fact that banknotes were not legal tender. Since most foreign currencies were also defined in terms of gold and/or silver and were freely convertible, this implied fixed exchange rates between them: 25.222 Swiss francs per pound sterling; 5.182 Swiss francs per US dollar; 123.46 Swiss francs per 100 marks; and 100 Swiss francs per 100 French francs, to name but the most important

---

[17] For a detailed discussion of the SNB's monetary policy in the period from 1907 to 1929 see Ruoss (1992); see also Guex (1993). Extensive presentations of details from this period are also provided in Bordo and James (2007) and Straumann (2010).

currency pairs. Exchange rate fluctuations were possible within the limits set by the gold- or silver-points only.[18]

Beyond that, the SNB was subject to no quantitative constraints in its note-issue policy. The Bank Council was apparently worried at first that this might allow over-issue of money, but the Governing Board dispelled these worries by pointing to the implicit constraints offered by articles 18 and 20 and by reasserting its determination "to limit note issue to required and adequate levels" (Ruoss, 1992, p. 16). The National Bank Act indeed gave the SNB considerable short-run discretion in this regard – a discretion nevertheless warranted in view of the task of ensuring "elasticity" in the supply of money assigned to the Bank. However, the SNB could not engage in an active monetary policy as we know it today, aimed at domestic objectives such as the national price level, national employment, or national income. The central long-run constraint faced by the SNB – or any other central bank – was, of course, implied by the metallic currency system prevalent at the time, and its convertibility provisions. Should a central bank create too much of its money, its currency tended to lose value vis-à-vis other gold-standard currencies. The price of gold implied by this movement tended to exceed its statutory level. As a consequence, banknotes were presented for redemption in gold and the central bank began to lose metal reserves. As this development threatened the central bank's long-run capability to meet its legal obligations, it had to reverse course and once again provide money at a more moderate pace. By raising the discount rate, it could create tighter monetary conditions and protect its metal reserves. Maintaining generous metal (gold, silver) reserves and thereby ensuring maintenance of the convertibility requirement thus became the central objective of the SNB's policy from the beginning. Within these constraints, the SNB tried to keep the discount rate and interest rates as low as possible, in support of commerce and economic development.

There was a certain asymmetry in the Swiss rules, however. In contrast to most other central banks of the time, the SNB was not legally obliged to acquire gold and silver at the parity rates; it only had to sell these metals in exchange for its notes at these rates. The SNB thus would have had some

---

[18] As mentioned above, the gold- and silver-points are the exchange rates at which the export or import of currency metal became profitable in the metallic currency systems prevalent at the time. They deviate from the parity rates due to transactions and transportation costs.

scope to tolerate a certain Swiss franc appreciation (gold price decline).[19] The principle of free coinage would have set limits to this, however.[20] But the SNB considered it an obvious task to maintain the Swiss franc at parity and to prevent deviations from the parity rate in both directions from the beginning.

Up to the outbreak of World War I, the dominant policy instrument of the SNB – and all other central banks of the time – was discount policy. The central elements of discount policy were the setting of the central bank's discount rate and the definition of the securities ("paper") admissible for central bank discount. As explained above, admissibility was defined by the SNB according to "real bills" considerations, at least as a matter of principle. The motivations for adjustments in the discount rate were studied by Ruoss, using minutes of the Governing Board and annual reports of the Bank.[21] The discount rate was reviewed by the Governing Board at weekly meetings. Between June 1907 and June 1914, twenty-two changes in the discount rate were made, always in steps of half a percentage point, with the traditional seasonal pattern reflecting fluctuations in the demand for money (with a falling rate until midyear and an increasing rate in the second half of the year, peaking in autumn around Martinmas). The discount rate varied between a minimum of 3 percent (reached twice, in February 1909 and in February 1910) and a maximum of 5.5 percent (reached in November of the crisis year 1907). For a comparison: The Bank of England changed its discount rate thirty-eight times during the same period of time.[22]

The decisive factor in the determination of the discount rate was the development of the SNB's metal reserve ratio: A declining coverage ratio implied a tendency toward discount rate increases and an increasing ratio a tendency toward rate reductions (see Figure 3.2). There was no automatic response in this, however. In addition to the metal coverage ratio, exchange rate movements and international interest rate differentials played a role, too (with rate increases when the Swiss franc tended toward weakness).

---

[19] See, e.g., Ruoss (1992), pp. 17–18.

[20] In principle, everyone was free to take gold to the mint and have it coined at a fee (of 15 francs per kilo), within the limitations set by the mint's capacity.

[21] See Ruoss (1992), pp. 46–55.

[22] France, on the other hand, hardly changed the discount rate before 1914, instead using variations in the size of its domestic portfolio in order to stabilize the interest rate in the French money market. Apparently, the gold standard was less uniform in this respect than is usually thought: see Morys (2013) and Bazot, Bordo, and Monnet (2014).

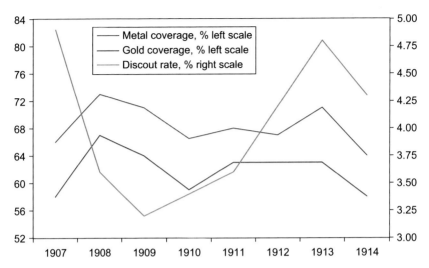

Figure 3.2: Metal coverage of note issue (yearly averages, in %) and SNB discount rate (in %), 1907–1914
Data source: Ruoss (1992), p. 50

Occasionally, business cycle developments were also considered. The SNB left no doubt, however, that maintaining convertibility was its central objective and that generous holdings of metal reserves served as its main instrument in pursuing this goal. Its determination in this gave it a certain freedom for short-run flexibility in the pursuit of its tasks. Actual metal reserves at all times far exceeded the legally required (40 percent) level. They were subject to considerable fluctuations, however (see Figure 3.2).

In summary, the first seven years of SNB policy can be assessed as rather successful. The SNB was able without delay to establish itself as a reliable partner of the international monetary system and to develop rules and principles guiding its participation in the mechanisms of the international gold standard. The commercial banks adjusted quickly and without difficulty to the presence of the new actor. Problems with the adequacy of liquidity provision, which had been frequent in the preceding decades, vanished. The disciplined policy of the young central bank thus brought favorable results.

4

World War I and the Postwar
Period (1914–1929)

The outbreak of World War I at the end of July 1914 brought dramatic changes to the international environment faced by Switzerland, and the world overall, creating novel and difficult challenges for Swiss monetary policy and the SNB. The international gold standard, which had ruled the world for decades, quickly broke down. Many countries – among them France, Germany, Russia, and also Switzerland – suspended gold convertibility in order to protect their monetary metal reserves. The United States prohibited the export of gold. Great Britain formally maintained the gold standard but severely restricted banknote redemption and international trade in gold.

With the suspension of gold convertibility, a central regulatory element of the gold standard was lost, and with it the disciplining force that it had imposed on its members in the past. The currencies which had been firmly linked to each other through the fixed parities for gold lost their common anchor. Exchange rates of major countries involved in the war were far less than perfectly flexible, though, as exchange control measures and bilateral exchange rate agreements were frequent. Beyond that, it is clear that the suspension or limitation of gold convertibility at the time was not viewed as a permanent break with the gold standard tradition, but rather as a temporary measure adopted to protect monetary metal reserves in times of crisis and war.[1] After the war, most observers and policymakers believed, the world would return to the gold standard again. Contrary to expectations, however, it would take more than a decade for gold convertibility

---

[1] The gold standard can be understood as a "rule with escape clauses," which can be suspended temporarily under specified conditions without jeopardizing the system in a fundamental way (see, e.g., Bordo and Kydland 1995).

and fixed exchange rates to be established anew, and the system would never be the same again.

Switzerland was, luckily, able to maintain neutrality throughout the war. Nevertheless, economically it shared many experiences with the belligerent countries. In Switzerland, as elsewhere, the war led to a dramatic increase in consumer prices and to very precarious economic conditions in general, causing severe social tension and unrest. For the first time in its existence, the Swiss National Bank was exposed to strongly critical public debate.[2]

LIQUIDITY CRISIS AND SUSPENSION OF CONVERTIBILITY, BANKNOTES AS LEGAL TENDER

As in other countries, the outbreak of the war caused a panic-driven rise in the demand for cash. At first, the SNB remained confident that its high metal coverage of note circulation (exceeding 70 percent at the outset) would allow it to meet this increased demand without too much of a problem. Nevertheless, it was concerned about the decline in its precious metal reserves and – through moral suasion, but without explicit prohibition – attempted to slow down the export of silver and gold.

Large-scale withdrawals from savings accounts quickly led to strong increases in banks' demand for central bank credit and in banknote circulation. Over the week from July 23 (Austrian ultimatum to Serbia) to July 31 (three days after the Austrian declaration of war against Serbia), SNB discount and Lombard credit rose from 108 to 247 million francs, and note circulation increased from 268 to 409 million francs. Metal coverage of the SNB's note circulation declined sharply within a very short period of time.

On July 30, the SNB responded to these developments by raising the discount rate and the Lombard rate by one percentage point each and by asking the Federal Council to suspend the gold and silver convertibility of its notes, that is, its obligation to redeem notes at par in either gold or silver. At the same time, it applied for authorization to issue (smaller denomination) 20-franc notes and to have its banknotes declared legal tender, making

---

[2] For discussions of Swiss monetary and economic policies during World War I and the postwar period see, e.g., Ruoss (1992), Guex (1993), Straumann (2010), and Halbeisen and Straumann (2012).

them a means of payment which had to be accepted by everyone in the cancellation of debt and financial obligations, absent any convertibility into metallic money.

Focusing on the maintenance of its metal coverage requirement, the SNB went on to raise its discount rate further; the peak value was reached at 6 percent in August 1914. Additionally, the SNB attempted to restrain the growing *demand* for money – which it viewed as an irrational public response to the crisis – by trying to limit access to the discount window and asking banks to pursue a restrictive stance in meeting requests for cash withdrawals. Not unexpectedly, these ill-designed measures proved ineffective, and the strong increase in liquidity demand forced the SNB to expand its discount credit and its banknote supply further, the latter now especially in new, smaller denominations of 5, 10, and 20 francs. Banks' quotas for discount credit were raised by 40 percent and requirements for discountable paper lowered. Over the month of September, finally, a certain normalization occurred, which allowed the SNB to lower the discount rate back down to 5 percent.

A byproduct of the war and this liquidity crisis was the foundation of the *Darlehenskasse der Schweizerischen Eidgenossenschaft*, a lending institution of the Confederation supposed to issue *Darlehenskassenscheine*, a debt instrument meant to serve as a banknote substitute and thereby reduce the scarcity of payment instruments and liquidity. The National Bank took a skeptical view of this project, not least since the *Darlehenskassenscheine*, in contrast to the banknotes issued by the SNB itself, were not supposed to be covered by metallic reserves. The *Darlehenskasse* started business on September 21, 1914. As it turned out, the liquidity crisis, and hence the need for a substitute instrument of liquidity, was essentially over by this date. The *Darlehenskasse* never gained much importance; ten years later it was liquidated again.

Due to the liquidity crisis of 1914, the Swiss National Bank was exposed to intense public criticism for the first time in its history. It was accused of insufficiently and tardily providing liquidity, especially banknotes of small denominations. Indeed, the SNB did view the increased demand for such notes, which then were hoarded on a large scale by the public, as an irrational reaction by market participants, and hence tried to constrain the increase in note circulation. The SNB's main concern remained maintaining a high metal coverage of note circulation. In this sense, its actions may have effectively been counterproductive; in particular, its call for banks to restrict cash withdrawals may have increased perceived liquidity scarcity and created additional uncertainty.

THE SNB AND PUBLIC FINANCES DURING THE WAR

The outbreak of the war caused federal expenditures to rise quickly, especially due to the costs of army mobilization, as well as declining tariff revenues (the Confederation's most important source of revenue at the time). The financial situation of the cantons and communities, and that of the federal monopoly enterprises (such as the federal railways), also got worse. The Confederation introduced new forms of taxation (war tax, war profit tax), but also resorted to substantial debt financing. Nine series of long-term "mobilization bonds" were issued over the wartime period. The strong use of the capital market quickly led to a significant rise in capital market rates beyond 5 percent after the outbreak of the war, causing public and political concerns and calls for measures to keep interest rates low. The SNB was not willing to directly respond to such demands by lowering its official interest rates, but instead suggested that the Confederation should resort to the use of central bank credit. The federal government was initially hesitant to follow this advice. Nevertheless, the SNB discount of *Bundesreskriptionen,* short-term obligatory notes issued by the federal government or its monopoly enterprises with a maturity of up to three months, soon became an important source of finance for the Confederation and its monopoly enterprises. By the end of the war, paper of this kind was outstanding to the amount of about 500 million Swiss francs, about 60 percent of it placed on the books of the SNB (see Table 4.1).[3] This contributed to a strong increase in banknote circulation.

Mostly, these bills were issued by the government and its enterprises "to finance the procurement of goods"; consequently, they were treated by the SNB like commercial bills, acceptable for discount according to its principles (although, in contrast to usual practice, they were regularly renewed). The rescriptions issued by the federal railways, however, which primarily served to cover the railway system's annual deficits, were viewed as finance bills and accepted by the SNB only with much reluctance. The SNB's acquisition of rescriptions can be seen as a kind of open market operation and an extension of the SNB's set of available policy instruments. The management of its portfolio of rescriptions gave the SNB an extra instrument for governing money market conditions. In particular, the sale

---

[3] This remains the only instance of serious fiscal pressure on monetary policy in SNB history, a fact greatly conducive to the development of the country's monetary stability tradition.

Table 4.1: *Rescriptions issued by the federal government and the federal railways,*
1914–1929

	Total circulation	SNB holdings	Open market
End of year	in millions, CHF	in millions, CHF	in millions, CHF
1914	59	58	1
1915	111	75	36
1916	256	123	134
1917	382	233	149
1918	492	312	180
1919	538	301	237
1920	559	280	279
1921	499	287	212
1922	359	325	34
1923	280	155	125
1924	98	78	20
1925	109	68	41
1926	94	83	11
1927	72	72	0
1928	54	54	0
1929	39	39	0

Source: Schweizerische Nationalbank (1932), p. 469

of rescriptions back to the market (*Rückdiskontierung, Rückplatzierung*)
became the major instrument for absorbing liquidity from the market
during the war. The discount rate was no longer used to any great degree
and was left unchanged at 4.5 percent until close to the end of the war (see
Figure 4.1).

Over most of the war period, however, liquidity creation by the SNB
increased extensively. Short-term (private) interest rates declined, reaching a level of about 2 percent by mid-1916. Long-term rates, on the other
hand, continuously rose and reached a level of roughly 5.5 percent by the
end of the war. Given the government's reliance on the capital market
and the continuous build-up of inflation pressure, this is no surprise.
Rather, it may seem surprising that the pronounced rise in inflation did
not push up long-term rates even more. It was not until the last year of
the war that the SNB began to show some concern about the excess of
liquidity it had allowed to build up and to start restraining money growth
again, finally raising the discount rate shortly before the war came to its

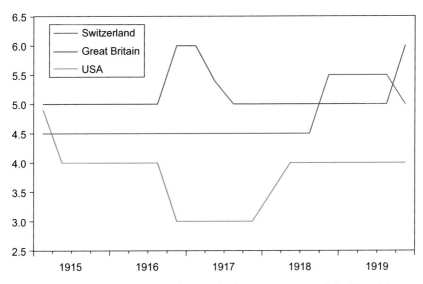

Figure 4.1: Official discount rates of Switzerland, Great Britain, and the United States, 1915–1919 (in %, monthly averages)
Data source: Ruoss (1992), p. 115

end. Throughout the war, however, the SNB's Board was not really conscious of the dangers to price stability emanating from its course, according to Ruoss (1992, pp. 97–8).

WARTIME INFLATION

Over the four years of war, consumer prices in Switzerland rose by more than 100 percent, not much less than consumer prices in Great Britain (see Figure 4.2). Nominal wages increased too, but by considerably less, so real consumer incomes declined substantially. These developments caused massive social unrest and tension, culminating in a nationwide strike (*Generalstreik*) in November 1918. They also led to intense public criticism of the National Bank and its policies.

As a result of the SNB's policy decisions – easing banks' access to the discount window, large-scale acquisition of *Bundesreskriptionen* – and also reinforced by a sizeable inflow of gold in 1916, partly due to SNB purchases of gold from Germany (which was in need of foreign exchange), the volume of central bank money increased strongly. In 1914 it rose by almost 50 percent, in 1915 by 3 percent, in 1916 by 19 percent, in

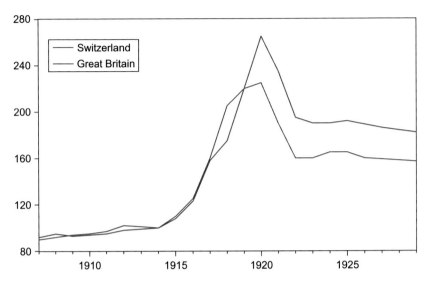

Figure 4.2: Prices in Switzerland and Great Britain, 1907–1929
Data source: Ruoss (1992), p. 26

1917 by 26 percent, and in 1918 by 33 percent. Banknote issue rose from an average of 335 million Swiss francs in 1914 to 733 million in 1918. This immense growth in liquidity was without doubt largely accountable for the high – and, for Switzerland, unprecedented – inflation experienced over the period of war. The annual inflation rate rose up to 25 percent by the end of the war; consumer prices more than doubled over this period of time. Increased scarcity of certain categories of goods and higher prices for imports undoubtedly played a role, too. But consumer prices could never have risen as much as they did without the money growth allowed by the SNB.

The problem of inflation – which affected other countries, such as Great Britain and the United States, in similar ways during the war – was a frequent topic of discussion at SNB Governing Board meetings in these years, particularly in relation to the issue of adequate cost-of-living compensation. Fundamentally, however, the SNB did not see itself as accountable for the rise of inflation. Its view was that price increases were principally caused by the development of import prices and that there was little the SNB itself could do about this. In particular, it saw no potential problems with regard to its discount of *Bundesreksriptionen*, viewing these like commercial bills resulting from credit extended for "real" commercial purposes. The resulting increase in banknote circulation, the SNB argued, could not possibly be "excessive" and a cause of inflation, since it reflected a justified need for means of payments based on "real" economic activities which had to be satisfied by the central bank.[4]

Nevertheless, the SNB's responsibility for the course of inflation became the subject of controversial and heated public debate. Edmund Kellenberger, the economics editor of the Bernese newspaper *Bund* and a lecturer (later professor) at the University of Berne, published a series of critical newspaper articles in 1918, blaming the SNB for excessive monetary expansion and holding it responsible for the resulting rise in inflation. The Free Economic League (*Freiwirtschaftsbund*), a political association built on the ideas of Silvio Gesell and leaning toward projects of a managed index currency with a price stability goal developed by Irving Fisher and others, incessantly made similar charges.

The SNB could not be convinced, however. It stuck to its argument, shared by other central banks at the time,[5] that it had neither the power nor the mandate to control prices and the price level in general, and thus could not be made accountable for movements in these. It failed to understand that this view, which may have had its defense under the metallic standards ruling the world before the war, was inappropriate in a world of suspended convertibility. Nevertheless, the SNB was not at ease with the situation and finally took measures intended to slow down banknote expansion, raising the Lombard rate (by half a percentage point) to 5.5 percent in July 1918 and the discount rate (by a full percentage point) to the same level in October 1918. Public pressure may have played a certain role in these decisions.[6] Probably much more important as a motivation for the SNB, however, was its concern about the decline in the metal coverage of banknote circulation.[7]

What explains the monetary policy behavior of the SNB during the period of war? A central part of the answer is provided by the – seemingly paradoxical – fact that the SNB (and most other central banks of the time) remained strongly attached to the gold standard and its rules, even though

[4] See, e.g., Ruoss (1992), p. 102, based on the minutes of the Governing Board meeting of August 1916. The argumentation of the SNB, of course, reflected the ideas of the real bills doctrine.

[5] For instance, the US Federal Reserve; see, e.g., Meltzer (2004), p. 184 or Bordo and James (2007), p. 46.

[6] Peaking eventually in the already mentioned *Generalstreik* of November 1918.

[7] Straumann (2010), pp. 39–40, also emphasizes this view.

this standard was suspended and not in place at the time.[8] Additionally, the governors of the SNB (and most of their colleagues abroad) still believed firmly in the old central bank tradition of the real bills doctrine – a view which was relatively harmless under the metallic monetary systems of the past, but became dangerous under the present conditions of suspended convertibility. A further important aspect was that the SNB, again like the central banks of many other countries, felt obliged to keep interest rates low in order to ease the financial strain on the state and allow government to finance its deficits at bearable costs. The liquidity flood associated with this low interest rate policy contributed to inflation pressure. At the same time, it helped limit governments' interest and debt burdens. For this reason, wartime inflation is a historically frequent event.

Why did long-term nominal interest rates not increase much more, given the strong rise in inflation? Interest rates on long-term bonds rose by about 1 percentage point to roughly 5 percent until mid-1916 and to about 5.5 percent until the end of the war. The most obvious answer to this question is that, as already mentioned above, the suspension of convertibility was not viewed as a long-term departure from the gold standard and its rules, but only as a temporary deviation in times of emergency. For after the war, a return to the metallic currency and to the old gold parity was commonly expected. For this reason, long-term price-level and inflation expectations remained firmly anchored.[9]

RECESSION, POSTWAR DEFLATION, AND RETURN TO
THE PREWAR GOLD PARITY: MONETARY POLICY
WITHOUT FIXED EXCHANGE RATES

Swiss currency policy after the war was dominated by the expectation of a return to the international gold standard. Switzerland, like Great Britain, aimed at reestablishing the prewar gold parity. It would take almost seven years for this goal to finally be reached, in 1925. The transition period in between was marked by deflation, recession, and unemployment. Switzerland shared this recession-plagued postwar experience with other countries, including Great Britain and the United States. Both of these pursued deliberate policies of deflation – policies of monetary restriction aimed at pushing the price level back toward what it had been before the war.

---

[8] See again Straumann (2010), p. 39.
[9] A slow and imperfect adjustment of nominal interest rates to inflation was characteristic of the gold standard period.

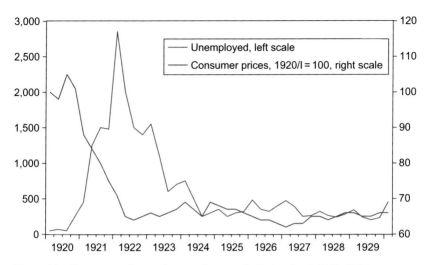

Figure 4.3: Consumer prices and unemployment in Switzerland, 1920–1929
Data source: Ruoss (1992), p. 141

Between September 1920 and May 1922, consumer prices in Switzerland fell by about 40 percent. The number of those unemployed rose from 3,500 in the first half of 1920 to roughly 100,000 in February 1922. These numbers – reflecting the registered number of workers seeking employment – are likely to substantially underestimate real unemployment, as the incentive to register was low, given the lack of obligatory unemployment insurance. In 1923, conditions slowly improved again, but remained weak for some time. The development of Swiss consumer prices and unemployment is shown in Figure 4.3.

In international comparison, though, the degree of monetary tightness in Switzerland remained moderate. Discount policy was relaxed again relatively early, in summer 1919, and the decline in Swiss central bank money turned out to be comparatively modest. Nevertheless, the SNB's policy is likely to have substantially contributed to the postwar recession of 1920-2. To some extent, the strong public criticism of the SNB's (inflationary) wartime policies may have been responsible for the SNB's turn to monetary restriction after the war. According to Ruoss, however, the SNB's main motivation was not so much the fight against inflation, but rather its goal to cut down its large holdings of *Bundesreskriptionen*, and the public sector financing implied by it, once the war was over.[10]

---

[10] Ruoss (1992), pp. 127–128.

The SNB was worried in particular about the federal railways rescriptions, which it viewed as finance bills.

Developments in the markets for foreign exchange also contributed heavily to the recessive tendencies of the Swiss economy. The currencies of the European neighbor countries depreciated strongly over the postwar period – in contrast to the US dollar, which exhibited postwar strength; with the end of World War I, the US dollar replaced the British pound (and for Switzerland the French franc) as the leading international currency (see Figure 4.4). The French and Belgian francs were initially still linked to the Swiss franc through the Latin Monetary Union. A large inflow of French and Belgian silver coins, which had to be accepted by the SNB at par according to the rules of the Union, forced Switzerland to restrict the import of such coins from October 1920, and finally to completely suspend acceptance of Union silver coins by the end of 1920. De facto, this ended Swiss membership in the Union. Officially, however, the Union was terminated only through cancellation of the Union Treaty by the end of 1926.

Most extreme was the decline of the German mark, which emerged in spring 1919 and ended in hyperinflation, economic chaos, and the total decay of the German currency in the early 1920s. At the peak of this hyperinflation, one US dollar was valued at more than 4 trillion marks. This process came to its end only with the German currency reform of October 1923 and the replacement of the mark with the – quantitatively clearly limited – "Rentenmark."[11] In Switzerland, these developments quickly led to complaints from the exporting sector and calls for the SNB to act to relieve this situation. The SNB's Board, however, (correctly) argued that nominal franc appreciation would soon be compensated by a corresponding increase in German goods prices, and that this would correct the initial disadvantage at which Swiss exporters were placed.

The postwar decline in the Swiss price level was seen by the SNB as a normalization of preceding price increases caused by wartime conditions. In this sense, it was favorably viewed by the SNB. The postwar crisis was seen – fundamentally correctly – as a general international phenomenon and not as a specifically Swiss problem. This view made the SNB relatively immune vis-à-vis public demands for a relaxation of its monetary policy. Yet, between April 1921 and August 1922, the discount rate was reduced in several steps, reaching a low of 3 percent (previously reached only once, in February 1909, as shown in Figure 4.5).

---

[11] The Rentenmark was in turn replaced (or, more precisely, supplemented) by the "Reichsmark" in August 1924.

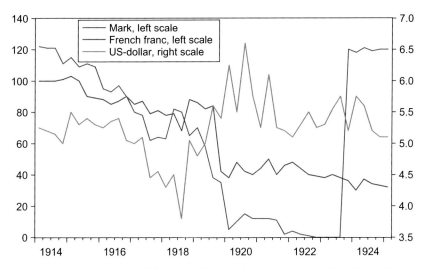

Figure 4.4: Exchange rates of the mark, the French franc, and the US dollar, in Swiss francs, 1914–1925

Note: Monthly averages; CHF/100 Mark, CHF/100 FF, CHF/1 USD. October 1923: German currency reform, introduction of Rentenmark.

Data sources: Ruoss (1992), p. 133; Bordo and James (2007), p. 49

The National Bank's responsibility for the economic crisis of the early 1920s was very controversially discussed at the time. A federal commission mandated explicitly to investigate the question came to a verdict exonerating the SNB in 1923. The SNB, it was argued, did not lower banknote circulation immediately before the outbreak of the crisis; hence it could not be held responsible for the crisis. The Free Economic League, on the other hand, again raised sharp criticism of the SNB: After having caused inflation during the war, it was held accountable for having caused deflation and recession after the war. The League now called for an increase in note circulation aimed at supporting the level of consumer prices. From a modern point of view it is clear that the SNB must assume responsibility for the development of prices in a period when it was not constrained by the rules of a metallic, fixed exchange rate currency regime. On the other hand, we must also realize that the SNB and postwar Switzerland were successful in avoiding both the extremes of complete currency decay (as in Germany) or an overly drastic fiscal consolidation and deflation regime (as in Great Britain and the United States). Of course, Swiss starting conditions, due to the country's neutrality during the war, were somewhat better than those of the previously belligerent countries.

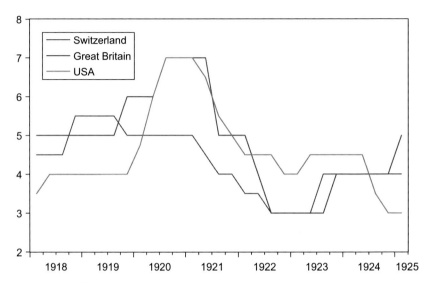

Figure 4.5: Official discount rates in Switzerland, Great Britain, and the United States, 1918–1925 (in %, monthly averages)
Data source: Ruoss (1992), p. 124

Switzerland – together with Great Britain, the Netherlands, Denmark, Sweden, and Norway – belonged to a small group of countries which were able to stabilize their currencies in the course of the 1920s at prewar parity to either gold or the US dollar. The SNB had upheld this goal throughout the war and the postwar period. In November 1924, it announced its intention to henceforth stabilize the dollar within the gold points of 5.16 and 5.21 Swiss francs, respectively. With this, the prewar parity was de facto reestablished. In May 1924, the Swiss franc was adopted by the Principality of Liechtenstein, bordering Switzerland to the east, as its official means of payment.[12]

The return to fixed exchange rates was made possible by a stabilization of international finances after the end of the German hyperinflation and the limitation of German reparation payments through the so-called Dawes Plan, and also by the prospect of Britain's forthcoming return to the prewar gold parity of the pound. The latter was officially announced in April 1925. Shortly afterwards, on June 17, 1925, the SNB formally

---

[12] In 1980, a formal monetary union regulated by a treaty between the two states was created.

reaffirmed its decision to fix the Swiss franc at its prewar parity. The temporary phase of flexible exchange rates officially came to its end. Over the year 1925, upward pressure on the Swiss currency repeatedly forced the SNB to buy US dollars.

THE INTERNATIONAL GOLD EXCHANGE STANDARD AND RESTORATION OF GOLD CONVERTIBILITY

From 1925 to 1929, foreign exchange markets remained fairly stable; the Swiss franc stayed close to parity with the US dollar. International conditions were defined by the international gold exchange standard created at an international conference held in Genoa, Italy, in 1922 to discuss global economic and financial affairs after the war. In the course of the 1920s, most European states joined the system created by this standard. It allowed countries to maintain their monetary reserves in the form of either gold or foreign currencies which were themselves directly exchangeable for gold. Including foreign exchange as part of a country's monetary reserves had to some extent been practiced before; a more systematic use of this method was now seen as a means to limit the monetary demand for gold, which was expected to grow in view of a widespread shift back to gold standard conditions, and thereby relieve the expected upward pressure on the price of gold resulting from this shift.

Economically, this was a period of boom. Average real growth in Switzerland for the years 1925 to 1929 amounted to roughly 4 percent; unemployment fell to low levels. Consumer prices fell by a total of about 4 percent between 1925 and 1929, mainly due to declining food and resource prices, transmitted to Swiss domestic prices through the fixed exchange rate (Ruoss, 1992, p. 183).

Up to 1929, the SNB was still not required to redeem its notes in gold; banknotes officially continued to be "legal tender," with no redemption obligation for the SNB. Formally, thus, Switzerland did not yet satisfy all the rules defining the gold standard (in contrast to most other countries at the time). The SNB always had the firm intention to return to full gold convertibility, but for quite a while it thought its reintroduction would be premature. A redemption obligation was reintroduced in Switzerland through parliamentary decision only in December 1929, and full gold convertibility thus re-established – shortly before the international gold exchange standard, as a result of the forthcoming world economic crisis, broke down again. Henceforth, the SNB could redeem its notes in either gold or "gold currencies" (i.e., foreign currencies subject to equivalent redemption obligations). From this time, silver ceased to serve as a monetary metal.

The SNB's monetary policy in this phase was mainly aimed at maintaining the Swiss franc exchange rate at its parity level. Between 1925 and 1929, this created no particular problems. For the first time since the outbreak of World War I, public criticism of the SNB subsided. This was related to the remarkable stability of Swiss interest rates at low levels: The discount rate was lowered from 4 to 3.5 percent in December 1925 and left unchanged at this level throughout this phase. Short-term market rates stayed close to the discount rate, and long-term rates receded from 5 to about 4.5 percent.

In international comparison, the level of Swiss interest rates was remarkably low – lower than in most other countries (including Great Britain and, since 1928, also the United States). The Swiss franc interest rate bonus, which was to be characteristic of most of the subsequent twentieth century, made its first appearance. This reflected confidence in Swiss monetary authorities and their policies, and in the political stability of the country overall. It offered the SNB a certain – although very limited – independence in its interest rate policies and its efforts at exchange rate stabilization through foreign exchange intervention. In this regard, the SNB (like other central banks of the time) did not always play strictly according to the rules of the international gold exchange standard.

In monetary policy, the discount rate no longer played the central role that it had done in the classical gold standard before 1914. Instead, foreign exchange interventions and – especially up to 1926 – fixing the conditions for placing *Bundesreskriptionen* back on the market (a kind of open market operation) were increasingly used. Keeping the discount rate unchanged for a long period of time reflected intentions to maintain low and stable short-term interest rates. Over time, trade with gold coins and gold exports was liberalized again, yet the instrument of gold transactions as a policy means did not regain the position it had held under the classical gold standard prior to the war. Influencing banks and market participants through moral suasion and gentlemen's agreements also gained some importance.

The international gold exchange standard did not have a long life. As early as the beginning of the 1930s, it broke down again: in September 1931, after the onset of the world economic crisis, Great Britain suspended convertibility and devalued the pound sterling relative to the US dollar by about 30 percent. Some responsibility for the standard's failure is usually given to central banks and their lack of commitment to the rules of the game – for example, their efforts to neutralize international gold flows through compensatory open market operations and their prevention, for domestic reasons, of adjustments in money circulation required by the balance of payments. However, the central reason for the system's demise was in all likelihood that, due to the difficult and unstable situation of many participant states and the world overall, a sufficient degree of confidence in the stability of the new system had not been present from its very beginning. In particular, after the war, the Bank of England and the British pound never regained the absolute confidence of the international markets that they had held in the era of the classical gold standard before 1914. The 1920s were also marked by a crisis of the agricultural sector following the large-scale reloca-tion of agricultural production during the war, and, especially, by the tensions and conflicts resulting from the reparation payments imposed on Germany and its associates by the Versailles Treaty,[13] as well as the war debt accumulated by the Allied countries vis-à-vis the United States.[14] The stock market crash of 1929 and the great economic crisis of the subsequent years inflicted a blow to this fragile system which it was unable to survive.

---

[13] Criticized by Keynes in his well-known treatise *The Economic Consequences of the Peace* (Keynes, 1919).

[14] In connection with the organization of German reparations, the Bank for International Settlement (BIS) was established in Basel in 1930.

5

From the Great Depression to World War II
(1929–1945)

The global economic crisis of the 1930s was an incisive event of historic proportions – economically, socially, politically – that shapes our thinking in many ways to this day. The crisis began with the stock market crash of October 1929 in the United States, but soon came to embrace the entire world. The stock market crash was followed by a massive disruption in national and international banking and finance and an unprecedented decline of the real economy throughout the world. Industrial production and income fell dramatically, large-scale unemployment and poverty spread, and world trade shrank drastically. Deflation pressure resulting from the international monetary regime, protectionist measures, and a wave of competitive devaluations further aggravated the situation.

A phase of economic boom and unbridled speculation had preceded this period, often referred to as the "Roaring Twenties." The stock market exuberance and the rapid growth of debt experienced during those years were subjects of concern for monetary authorities in the United States but also in other countries, including Switzerland. The Federal Reserve raised the discount rate by 1 percentage point, to 6 percent, in August 1929, but without much effect on the markets' mood. Only the crash of October 23 put a sudden stop to the party.

THE GREAT DEPRESSION AND THE GOLD STANDARD

The dramatic impact of the world economic crisis is best illustrated by a few statistics. From 1929 to 1932, industrial production declined by 46 percent in the United States and by 41 percent in Germany. In Great Britain the decline over the same period was a comparatively modest 11 percent. The declines experienced by France and Switzerland were somewhere between the two extremes (Switzerland's production declined by 21 percent from 1929 to 1932). In most countries, the bottom was reached in 1932; subsequently the situation slowly improved again. In 1937, the world economy was roughly back to the production levels of 1929. France and Switzerland were exceptions, however, experiencing a new, strong setback in 1935 and 1936 after a weak recovery from 1932 to 1934 (Zurlinden, 2003, p. 88).

Prices also fell strongly during the Great Depression. In the initial phase, until 1931 – when the fixed exchange rates of the gold standard still applied – deflation as measured by wholesale price movements remained more or less uniform across countries. After 1931, when Great Britain devalued the pound sterling, prices stabilized first in Great Britain and later in the United States and Germany. In France and Switzerland, on the other hand, the decline in prices continued for another three years. In France, the decline amounted to 44 percent from 1929 to 1935; the corresponding figure in Switzerland was 36 percent (Zurlinden, 2003, pp. 88–9). Price deflation, combined with relatively sluggish money wages, led to increasing real wages and, as a result of emerging deflation expectations, to high real interest rates, contributing to a further aggravation of the economic situation. Unemployment throughout the world increased dramatically. In the United States and Germany it reached average levels of 25–30 percent of those employed in 1932/3. In Switzerland, the number of registered unemployed rose from about 8,000 in 1929 to an average of 93,000 in 1936.

An extensive literature dealing with the Great Depression, and especially with the experience of the United States, points to a number of competing – although not mutually exclusive – factors of explanation, among them the role of bank failures and financial distress, the excessive burden of international indebtedness (a legacy of World War I and the Versailles Treaty), the increasing protectionism in trade, and – especially important from our point of view – the role of central bank policy and the international currency system.[1]

Up to the devaluation of the British pound in 1931, the gold exchange standard was in place. Confidence in this system and its future was steadily fading, though. More and more often, the pursuit of domestic policy objectives (price stability, employment) was seen to be in conflict with the established rules of the international currency system. An erosion of confidence in the maintenance of the old gold parities led central banks to

---

[1] Important references are, among others, Friedman and Schwartz (1963), Temin (1978), Bernanke (1983, 1995, 2000), Eichengreen (1992) and Romer (1992).

exchange foreign exchange reserves for gold,[2] introducing a scarcity of gold and a deflationary tendency into the world economy. A coordinated devaluation of all currencies relative to gold (i.e., a joint increase in the gold price of all currencies) might have neutralized this deflationary pressure (Eichengreen, 1992). However, this did not happen; the major participants were not able or willing to commit to a common course. Instead, a series of uncoordinated devaluations followed, while some players took resort to foreign exchange controls and capital market restrictions. Many countries still linked their currencies to gold in one way or another, but the gold standard as an international system of coordination and regulation was finished. Still, even after 1931, many central banks remained fundamentally attached to the gold standard and tried, in various ways, to retain its traditions.

The wave of devaluations started in September 1931 when the British government, after a serious decline in market confidence in its commitment to maintain the gold parity, suspended convertibility. The pound reduced strongly in value. The other members of the Commonwealth, as well as the Scandinavian countries, followed the British example. Even before this, the currencies of Germany and Austria had come under great pressure in the wake of the German–Austrian banking crisis in May 1931. In this situation, the German government – instead of giving up gold parity – decided to introduce administrative controls of foreign exchange and capital markets. Many Central and East European countries, particularly Austria and Hungary, followed Germany in adopting exchange and capital market controls. In autumn 1931, the US dollar came under pressure. The Federal Reserve first reacted – still under the spell of old gold standard rules – by raising the discount rate. While this did calm currency markets, it also prolonged and aggravated the general economic and financial crisis. After the election of Franklin D. Roosevelt, US monetary policy changed course: In March 1933, convertibility for banknotes was suspended and the export of gold prohibited. In April 1933, the dollar was allowed to float. It declined strongly over the subsequent months; in January 1934, it was stabilized at 59 percent of its previous value in gold.

Switzerland joined France and a few other countries – Belgium, the Netherlands, Italy, and Poland – in July 1933 to form the so-called "gold block," committing to continued maintenance of the old parities to gold. Given the preceding devaluations of the British pound, the US dollar, and

---

[2]   According to Nurske (1944), the share of foreign exchange in total central bank reserves declined markedly between 1929 and 1933.

numerous other currencies, this amounted to a strong real appreciation and a corresponding deterioration of the competitive position in international trade for the gold block countries. In principle, this could have been compensated by an internal deflation of wages and prices. A policy of domestic wage deflation was strongly opposed by labor unions and other interest groups, though, and therefore not really feasible. Not surprisingly, speculative attacks on gold block currencies arose out of this situation. Belgium finally devalued in spring 1935 and France in September 1936; shortly afterwards, the Netherlands and Switzerland followed suit (by 30 percent in the case of the Swiss franc). In practically all cases, devaluation was followed by an economic recovery. This indicates that monetary factors and monetary policy are among the important determinants of the economic crisis and that Switzerland's long commitment to the old parity, in view of a drastically changed international environment, was a decisive policy mistake.

SWITZERLAND DURING THE GREAT DEPRESSION

From a Swiss point of view, the great economic crisis of the 1930s was caused by external events, transferred quickly to the Swiss economy through the fixed exchange rates of the gold standard regime. The exporting sector became the first victim of these events, with declining foreign demand hitting internationally exposed firms hard. Deflation and expectations of deflation pushed up real wages, real interest rates, and the real burden of nominal debt. Over time, the domestic economy, which was only moderately affected at first, began to suffer too. The situation turned critical with the devaluation of the pound and Germany's transition to foreign exchange and capital market controls in 1931. Subsequently, Switzerland suffered from an overvaluation of its franc, further reinforced by the devaluation of other currencies, especially the US dollar in 1933/4, and by the disruptions caused by the increasing restrictions on international capital flows and trade.

In the initial phase of the crisis, though, perceived currency weakness and devaluation expectations abroad caused large amounts of capital to flow into Switzerland. As a result, monetary aggregates in Switzerland never fell below the levels reached in 1929/30, in contrast to many other countries. Within eight months of the British devaluation of 1931, Swiss gold and foreign exchange reserves increased from 1 billion to 2.4 billion francs. In 1932 and later, however, when international exchange markets calmed down and eventually turned, devaluation expectations affected the

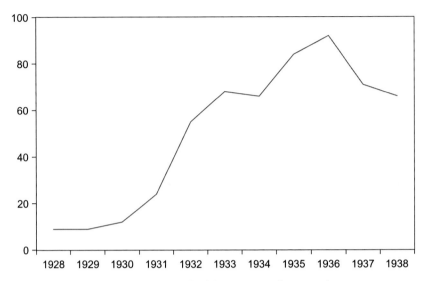

Figure 5.1: Unemployment in Switzerland (in 1,000, yearly average), 1928–1938
Data source: Zurlinden (2003), p. 94

Swiss franc too. In the period to 1936, Swiss international reserves fell by about 1 billion francs. Nevertheless, Swiss authorities continued to maintain their commitment to the gold standard and the old parity of gold for a long time. The country's large gold reserves made them believe in the feasibility of this course. Only the devaluation of the French franc in 1936 finally changed their mind.

Zurlinden (2003) has summarized in detail the development of the Swiss economy and its major macroeconomic indicators during the Great Depression; for a few illustrations see Figures 5.1–5.7. A recent publication edited by Halbeisen, Müller, and Veyrassat (2012) provides interesting additional information.[3]

Unemployment hit Switzerland very hard, as was the case for most other countries at this time. The number of officially registered unemployed, which was about 8,000 in 1929, steadily rose over the following years – with the exception of 1934 – to reach an average of 93,000 in 1936, with a monthly peak of 124,000 in January 1936. This corresponds to rates of unemployment of about 0.4 percent in 1929 and 4.8 percent in 1936, with a peak value of 6.4 percent in January 1936. From today's point of view,

---

[3] See, in particular, the contribution by Halbeisen and Straumann (2012).

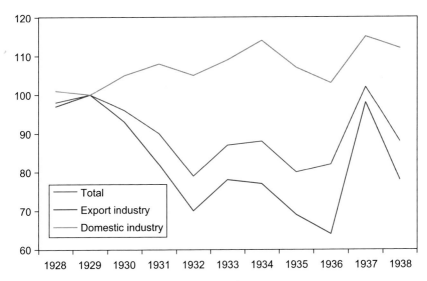

Figure 5.2: Industrial production in Switzerland, 1928–1938
Source: Zurlinden (2003), p. 95

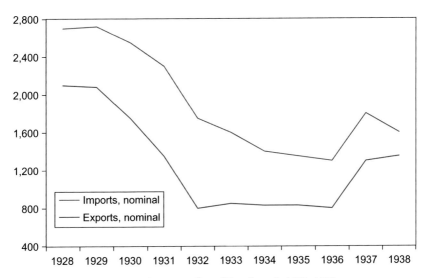

Figure 5.3: Swiss exports and imports (in million francs), 1928–1938
Data source: Zurlinden (2003), p. 96

(a)

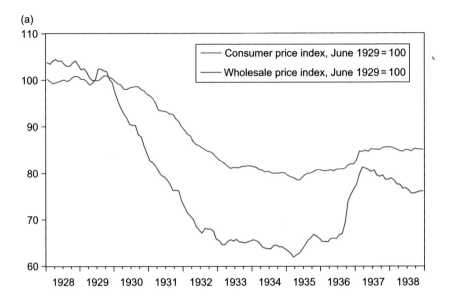

(b)

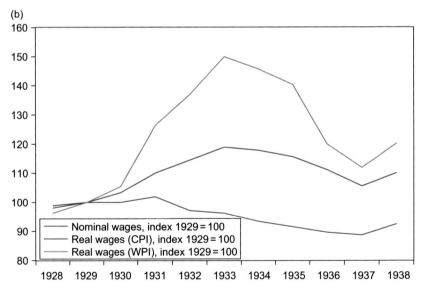

Figure 5.4: Prices and wages in Switzerland, 1928–1938
Source: SNB Monthly Statistical Bulletin, CPI, Table O11, www.snb.ch/de/iabout/stat/statpub/
statmon/stats/statmon; Swiss economic and social history database: nominal wages, Table G18;
WPI, Table H9a, www.fsw.uzh.ch/hstat/nls_rev/overview.php

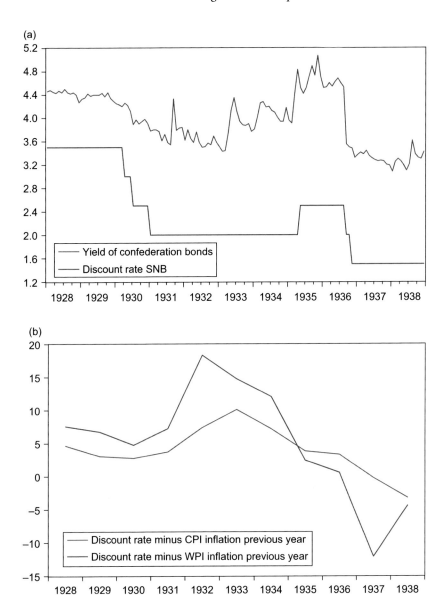

Figure 5.5: Swiss interest rates, 1928–1938
Source: SNB Historical Series, 4, T3.2L, T1.1L, www.snb.ch/de/iabout/stat/statrep/statpubdis/id/
statpub_histz_arch#t3

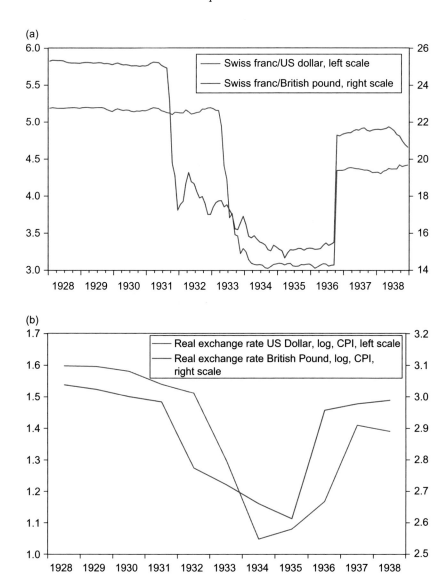

Figure 5.6: Swiss franc exchange rates, 1928–1938
Source: SNB Monthly Statistical Bulletin, Table G1, www.snb.ch/de/iabout/stat/statrep/statpubdis/
id/statpub_statmon_arch_xls_de

these numbers may seem relatively low for a crisis period. However, it
must be noted that in the absence of any obligatory unemployment
insurance, the incentive for those not finding work to register was low.
Official numbers, therefore, are likely to seriously underestimate effective

(a)

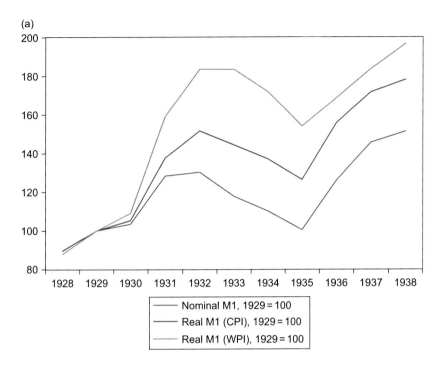

(b)

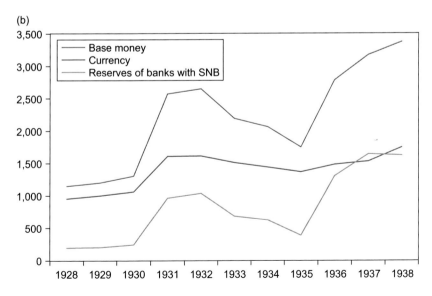

Figure 5.7: Swiss monetary aggregates, 1928–1938

Data source: Swiss economic and social history data base: M1 1851–1907 (Table Q3), www.fsw.uzh.ch/hstat/nls_rev/overview.php

unemployment, and comparisons with modern unemployment statistics are not very informative. Estimates based on populations covered by (voluntary) unemployment insurance lead to considerably higher rates: 14.6 percent on average for 1936, with a peak of 20.9 percent in January 1936 (Zurlinden, 2003, p. 95).

Industrial production fell by about 21 percent between 1929 and 1932. Subsequently, a moderate recovery set in until 1934, only to be followed by a renewed contraction in the years 1935 and 1936. The devaluation of 1936 finally turned things around for good. Especially hit by the global depression were the strongly export-oriented sectors, such as the textiles, machine, watch-making, and chemical industries. Nominal exports declined by about two thirds from 1929 to 1932. This was partly due to the decline in world market prices, but additionally, in volume terms – measured in tons – exports fell by about 50 percent. The share of exports in net social product declined from roughly 22 percent in 1929 to 10 percent in 1932.

Wholesale prices declined by almost 40 percent from 1929 to 1935. After the franc devaluation in 1936, they increased again, but not nearly to the level of 1929. Consumer prices followed a more sluggish and moderate course, falling by a bit more than 20 percent from 1929 to 1935. In contrast to prices, nominal wages declined only modestly during the depression years. Until 1931 they actually rose slightly; afterwards, they declined slowly until 1936, by a total of about 10 percent compared to 1929. As a consequence, real wages increased substantially, especially over the first years of depression. Attempts to reduce nominal wages met strong political resistance. In 1933, a proposal by parliament and the federal government to temporarily cut federal employees' wages by 7.5 percent for the years 1933 and 1934 was decisively defeated in a public referendum vote. (It was enacted through emergency legislation a few months later anyhow.) Rising real wages was a common experience of all the gold block countries.

The SNB's discount rate was lowered, in three steps, from 3.5 to 2 percent between April 1930 and January 1931, and then left at this level for the following four years. In May 1935 the SNB raised it to 2.5 percent in view of a weakness of the Swiss franc at the time. Shortly before the devaluation of September 1936, it was reduced again to 2 percent, and after the devaluation it was reduced to as low as 1.5 percent – its lowest value up to this time. Capital market rates roughly followed this pattern, moving in a corridor of about 4 to 5 percent. Given price deflation and corresponding deflation expectations, real interest rates until 1936 did increase substantially.

Real exchange rates were strongly influenced by the international sequence of devaluations. Between 1931 and 1936, a massive overvaluation of the Swiss franc occurred, vis-à-vis first the British pound and later also the US dollar (and the currencies following them). The exchange rate of the German Reichsmark was of lesser importance, as trade with Germany (and Eastern European countries) was governed by exchange controls and mutual clearing arrangements. The nominal exchange rate of the French franc was unchanged until 1936; in view of slightly higher French inflation, some real Swiss franc appreciation occurred vis-à-vis France, too.

The Swiss banking sector, like many other nations' financial sectors, suffered severely from the world economic crisis. While there was no epidemic blaze of banking failures and financial panic comparable to developments in the United States, Germany, and some countries in Central and Eastern Europe, a number of Swiss banks found themselves in a very precarious situation, and the stability of the banking and financial sector became an issue of great concern for politics and for monetary authorities. These difficulties were caused by credit losses due to the general decline in economic activity, but even more so by massive losses resulting from the liquidation of blocked claims against debtors in Germany and other countries in Central and Eastern Europe after 1931. The big banks with strong international exposure were particularly affected by the latter problem. Some institutions had to be restructured or even liquidated. Two banks, the *Schweizerische Volksbank* and the *Banque d'Escompte Suisse*, had to request government support. The *Banque d'Escompte Suisse* was liquidated in 1934 anyhow. The *Schweizerische Volksbank* only survived due to capital support of 100 million francs from the Confederation.

In response to the banking crisis and the resulting vulnerability of the financial sector, in 1931 the SNB relaxed its conditions for central bank discount credit. The federal government and the SNB agreed that, beyond general liquidity assistance, emergency help and, especially, capital support to individual banks were, in principle, tasks for the government rather than the central bank. Against this background, the *Eidgenössische Darlehenskasse* was created in 1931, an institution of government support extending credit to distressed banks in exchange for blocked and illiquid foreign claims. The *Darlehenskasse* was capitalized partly by the federal government (75 percent) and partly also by the banking sector (25 percent); beyond that, it could refinance its activities with the central bank. As an additional response to the banking crisis, a new banking law was enacted in 1934, introducing new regulations concerning bank creditor protection and the processes governing banks' payment difficulties. An extensive literature exists dealing with the situation of Swiss banks and with Swiss authorities' policy response to the banking crisis in the interwar period; see, e.g., Halbeisen (1998), Perrenoud et al. (2002), and Baumann (2004).

THE DEBATE ABOUT DEVALUATION

For many contemporaries, the Great Depression began in 1929/30 as an ordinary economic slump following a stock market disruption, of a type the preceding century had seen many times. As the crisis continued and gradually worsened, awareness slowly grew that this was a disaster of a special kind. Critical for Switzerland was the year 1931, when the British pound and other currencies went off gold. This was reinforced by the devaluation of the dollar in 1933/4. For Swiss authorities, the question in this situation was whether Switzerland should also follow the path of devaluation or whether it should attempt to adjust to the new environment, and reestablish the Swiss economy's price competitiveness, by pursuing a policy of domestic wage and price deflation. Switzerland opted for the second route. Formally, the federal government was responsible for this fundamental policy decision, not the SNB. However, the SNB was one of the important actors determining this course, and it explicitly supported it for a long time.

For many years, the devaluation option was not seriously considered by the Federal Council and the SNB. One argument which was repeatedly advanced was that for the strongly import-dependent Swiss economy, devaluation would only lead to price inflation and thus would not really help. More fundamental, however, was another point: Devaluation was seen as a breach of faith in times of turmoil and distress. Gold and the commitment to the established parity of gold were viewed as anchors of stability which should not willfully be given up in an increasingly uncertain and unstable world. Great Britain's suspension of convertibility in 1931 was still viewed as a regrettable temporary measure, which would before long be reversed. An important role was also played by Switzerland's large gold reserves, which had authorities convinced that maintaining the old gold parity was feasible as an objective.

As it turned out, the policy of internal deflation was much more difficult to enforce than its proponents had originally thought, and doomed to be a failure. Although the SNB was successful in defending the external value of the franc and its parity to gold to the end, the decline of domestic prices (relative to exchange rates and foreign prices) was too slow, and the decline in money wages far too weak. Measures of internal deflation met strong political resistance and were violently opposed by labor unions and other groups of interest. The real exchange rate of the franc and real wages persisted at excessive levels, prolonging the depression.

The tenacious Swiss insistence on the old gold parity has occasionally been related to the interests of the Swiss banking and financial sector in a strong and stable currency, or to other specific interests and structural characteristics of the Swiss economy. This does not seem particularly convincing, though, in view of the strong response of the entire economy, including the financial sector, when devaluation finally came in autumn 1936. It is much more likely that it was the idea of the gold standard as such – the proven monetary system with a long and successful tradition – which stayed strongly embedded in peoples' minds and remained persuasive.[4]

It is interesting to note that leading representatives of the exporting sector, for example, from the chemical and the machine industry – and the influential Swiss Chamber of Commerce and Industry, the *Vorort*, itself – strongly supported official policy and argued against devaluation.[5] A frequent argument was that the products of the Swiss exporting industry were only moderately price-elastic, hence a devaluation of the franc would only lead to higher costs of import goods and higher wage demands. An

---

[4] The great power of conviction that gold standard orthodoxy was able to maintain over a long time is documented in a detailed and careful study on "Gold Standard Mentality" and its influence in Switzerland in the 1930s by Allgoewer (2003). Straumann (2010, pp. 129–30) also supports this view. On this issue see also Tanner (2000), who emphasizes the influence of a growing Swiss tendency in the 1930s to retreat to national traditions and go separate and independent ways regardless of international developments (*Mythos Gotthardstaat*). While this may be valid for other areas of public policy, it is utterly unconvincing as an explanation of Swiss policies in the monetary area. The international gold standard, whose rules Swiss authorities – and those of the other gold block countries, including France – tried to maintain up to the bitter end, is the perfect example of a truly international order. In fact, Switzerland was one of the "Last Mohicans" of this dying world of uncompromising commitment to common rules. All others – those who had devalued early, such as Great Britain and the United States, and those who had taken resort to administrative control of exchange and capital markets, such as Germany – had abandoned this global order in favor of national objectives and independence long ago.

[5] According to Bosshardt (1961), a group of business leaders from eastern Switzerland differed from this opinion, however. Publication of a speech he gave at a confidential meeting of this group on June 8, 1936, in St. Gallen was made impossible at the time as a result of lack of approval by the Federal Council and the SNB (Bosshardt, 1961, pp. 117–19), he says, and did not become possible until 1961 (Bosshardt, 1961, pp. 120–54).

important role was also played by the fact that trade with Germany and the countries of Central Europe was ruled by bilateral clearing arrangements and administratively fixed exchange rates; in consequence, it would not have been influenced much by devaluation of the Franc vis-à-vis gold. In any case, representatives of industry arguing for devaluation remained a clear minority.[6]

Nevertheless, an intense political debate about the currency regime and devaluation took place, which became more and more heated as time went on. This debate found its climax in June 1935 in a public vote on a popular initiative launched by the political left in favor of a public employment programme, the so-called *Kriseninititative* ("crisis initiative"). Opponents of the initiative – which was defeated by the voters – feared that it would weaken confidence in the stability of the franc and in authorities' ability to defend the ruling gold parity. Some academic economists, such as Eugen Böhler from ETH Zürich and Paul Keller from the University of St. Gallen, argued for credit expansion in support of the economy and employment, and referred to other countries' positive experiences with devaluation, but yet without recommending a similar step for Switzerland (Böhler and Keller, 1935). Even the political left refrained from demanding devaluation, at least up to the defeat of their crisis initiative.

After this vote, public statements favoring devaluation became more frequent. Notable examples were Edmund Schulthess (who had retired from the Federal Council in spring 1935) and Paul Rossy (formerly deputy governor in the second department of the SNB, after his resignation from the SNB in October 1935). Official policy, and the federal government's willingness to stick to this course, were now also discussed controversially within the SNB. The Governing Board was divided. The chairman, Gottfried Bachmann, stuck to his view and remained consistently opposed to devaluation until the end. The vice chairman, Charles Schnyder von Wartensee, favored internal discussion of a devaluation policy; in the case of a French devaluation, he wanted to follow France and devalue by the same extent. Ernst Weber, the head of the SNB's third department, advocated devaluation by 40 percent, independent of the course chosen by France (Bordo and James, 2007, p. 67).

Among the most ardent opponents of the SNB and official monetary policy was, once again, the Free Economic League (*Freiwirtschaftsbund*), which had already during the preceding decades consistently criticized the

---

[6]   See, e.g., Halbeisen (2005); Bordo and James (2007), pp. 52–3.

gold standard system and advocated a transition to a "manipulated currency" aiming at internal price stabilization.[7] During the entire period of depression, it demanded devaluation and an end to the Swiss franc's linkage to gold. The Free Economic League always remained outside the political establishment, though. Its adherents were never taken completely seriously – even if, from today's point of view, their ideas on devaluation and the choice of currency system seem rather reasonable. This owed not least to the fact that they also advocated some very extreme policy positions, including the prohibition of private property of land, the abolition of interest, and the idea of "stamp money" (a tax or user's fee on money holdings aimed at preventing money hoarding), as proposed by Silvio Gesell. Generally, they were viewed as difficult, sectarian, and missionary. For this reason, they may even have been counterproductive as an influence in the political debate over devaluation.[8] This does not change the fact, however, that their instincts in this debate proved superior to those of the official policy actors.[9] When devaluation finally came in 1936, it was – obviously – welcomed by the Free Economic League. However, the League continued its critique: Devaluation did not solve the fundamental problem, in its view. It did not represent a definitive parting from the gold standard, only setting a new gold parity at another level.

The actual change in policy followed the French decision to devalue. One day after this step was taken by France, on September 26, 1936, the Federal Council decided to devalue the Swiss franc relative to gold (and thereby other currencies) by 30 percent. At the same time, it suspended the SNB's obligation to redeem its banknotes in either gold or foreign exchange. One day later, the president of the Federal Council, Albert Meyer – who had himself opposed devaluation in the Council's deliberations – announced the decision in a public radio speech. "A franc remains a franc" was the somewhat euphemistic phrase he employed in an obvious effort to reassure the Swiss people and preserve confidence in the nation's currency.

Given the French devaluation, an unchanged policy by Switzerland would undoubtedly have further weakened the – already weak – economy of the country. Also, the risk of speculative attacks on the Swiss franc appeared likely to become substantial under these new conditions. These

---

[7] See Chapter 4. [8] Allgoewer (2003), pp. 17, 158–9.
[9] On the Free Economic League and their ideas see, e.g., Schmid (1948/69), Hoffmann (1982), Schärrer (1983).

insights led the Federal Council and the SNB to finally change their views. Theirs was a decision motivated by acceptance of the hopelessness of an unchanged course, not by personal conviction and belief. Fundamentally, the Federal Council and the SNB were still strongly attached to the gold standard and its rules. Devaluation, in their view, meant a violation of legal obligations. But risking the SNB's (still substantial) gold reserves for a fight which appeared desperate to begin with seemed overly hazardous. Also, it was difficult to deny that the deflation policy of the past had not been a success. Expectations of a renewal of international currency cooperation through tripartite negotiations between the United States, Great Britain, and France also played a certain role at the time, but proved to be in vain.

The devaluation of the franc was undoubtedly an incisive moment in Swiss monetary history, with far-reaching effects. Nevertheless, it did not represent a fundamental change in the country's monetary order. Maintaining gold parity – at a newly established level – and gold coverage of the franc continued to be central elements of the country's currency system and were considered key factors for ensuring monetary stability. The policy instruments of the central bank and the relationship between government and central bank were not affected, either. Important as the devaluation was, it was much less fundamental than the transition to flexible exchange rates, after the breakdown of the system of Bretton Woods a few decades later, would be.[10]

An interesting shift in monetary thinking in comparison to the nineteenth century may be noted, though. Then, the adoption of the monetary standards of important neighbor countries, notably France, was in the foreground as the guiding principle of Swiss monetary policy. Now, the view became dominant that monetary stability was a value "as such," and that this value would be best ensured by firmly linking the franc to gold – even if this should mean sacrificing a fixed exchange rate. When France was forced to devalue again in July 1937, Switzerland did not follow and the SNB argued that, at that moment, floating the franc vis-à-vis other currencies was preferable (Bordo and James, 2007, p. 70).

The devaluation was welcomed by representatives of commerce and trade and by the Swiss public overall. The financial sector, which recovered quickly, was particularly positive. A minor political debate followed concerning ownership and distribution of the 538 million-franc profit resulting from the revaluation (in terms of francs) of the SNB's gold

---

[10] Roth (2007), pp. 44–5.

reserves. At first, this sum was used to finance a fund for managing exchange market interventions (*Währungsausgleichsfonds*). In 1940, however, when public sector wartime expenditures sharply rose, 475 million francs were distributed to the Confederation and the cantons.[11]

Ex post facto, the long defense of the old gold parity by Swiss monetary authorities and the real upward valuation of the Swiss franc that it caused were classified by most observers as important policy mistakes. Given the international conditions Switzerland faced – which it could not influence itself – an earlier devaluation would in all likelihood have allowed the country to live through the crisis years with less damage.[12] Bordo and James (2007), using counterfactual simulations of the Swiss economy based on a small open economy macro-model, clearly support this view. In one of their (counterfactual) scenarios, they assume that the SNB unexpectedly switched from a gold peg to a peg against the British pound until 1938 (at the average Swiss franc/pound sterling rate of 1931) after the UK went off gold in 1931. In a second scenario they alternatively assume that the SNB unexpectedly switched from a gold peg to a peg against the dollar until 1938 (at the average 1932 Swiss franc/dollar rate) after the US went off gold. The exchange rates to other currencies were calculated using concurrent cross-rates; the changes in policy regime were assumed to be accepted by market participants as credible and durable. Both devaluation scenarios indicate clearly that an earlier devaluation would have stimulated output as compared to its actual path, would have brought about a turnaround from deflation to inflation at an earlier date, and thus would have ended the Swiss depression more quickly.

An earlier devaluation would probably have dampened the net inflows of gold and foreign exchange from which Switzerland benefited after 1931. Under the assumption that the SNB refrained from sterilized foreign exchange interventions, this would have reduced the direct positive effects of an earlier devaluation (because money supply would have increased less and interest rates would have been higher). Bordo and James use robustness tests to argue that the positive devaluation effect would, in all likelihood, have dominated nevertheless. Only under very extreme conditions could this have been reversed.[13]

---

[11] A further revaluation of the SNB's gold reserves in 1940 led to an additional gain of 100.9 million Francs. After World War II, 100 million Francs from this fund were used for a Swiss payment to the Allied Powers as a result of the Washington Agreement of 1946.

[12] See, e.g., Ritzmann (1973), pp. 100–1.   [13] Bordo and James (2007), pp. 55–9, 93–6.

WARTIME ECONOMICS: FOREIGN EXCHANGE CONTROLS AND SNB GOLD TRANSACTIONS

The economic depression of the 1930s was soon followed by an even greater human catastrophe – the outbreak of World War II. Switzerland was fortunate enough to be spared the sad fate of those directly involved in its horrors. Nevertheless, the war unavoidably and strongly influenced economic and monetary developments and actions in Switzerland, too.

Between the devaluation of 1936 and the outbreak of the war, the global economy, and with it that of Switzerland, regained some strength. However, the forthcoming political and military tragedy cast a major cloud over this recovery. Especially in Germany and in Italy, but increasingly also in other countries, economies were restructured in preparation of war. The armaments industry and sectors related to it benefited strongly from these developments. In Switzerland, the real economy quickly recovered after the devaluation. Industrial production and foreign trade both grew again. The number of unemployed declined to about 40,000 up to 1939. The burst of inflation expected as a result of devaluation turned out to be moderate: Consumer prices rose by about 5 percent in 1937, but remained more or less constant afterwards. The banking and financial sector stabilized quickly. Share prices, especially bank shares (which had suffered severely before), recovered strongly.

After the war broke out, the domestic sector of the Swiss economy and its international relations in trade and finance were increasingly trimmed to wartime needs and requirements. Ensuring adequate provision of vital supplies to the Swiss population became a central motivation of policy choice. A growing dependence on the belligerent parties constrained Swiss policy options in this. Nevertheless, the conversion to wartime economics took place without major frictions. The rising expenditures of the central government were financed through the capital markets and new taxes; in contrast to the experience of World War I, government finance through central bank support did not become a major issue.

The geographic isolation of Switzerland after the Axis powers' early military success created a precarious situation for the country. Trade with Germany and its allies by necessity became very intense. Trade relations with Germany resulted in large net exports and corresponding net clearing claims; in 1944, these amounted to about 1 billion Swiss francs. Switzerland was also a net creditor to Italy. From 1940 onwards, the SNB had to absorb substantial amounts of foreign exchange. Surpluses in the balance of payments and gold sales by foreign central banks to the SNB (reflecting a high demand for Swiss francs on the part of both the Axis powers and the Allies) caused a strong increase in liquidity provision and the potential for rising inflation (Bordo and James, 2007, p. 76). The SNB in part attempted to neutralize these effects through a sterilizing operation involving gold sales to the government. An agreement concluded with the commercial banks with the objective of restricting the exchange of US dollars for Swiss francs served the same purpose (Gentlemen's Agreement between the SNB and the commercial banks of September 17, 1941; see Schweizerische Nationalbank [1957], p. 124).

With this agreement, the exchange market was split into a market for "commercial dollars," where dollars were traded for francs at the gold parity rate, and a market for "financial dollars," in which dollars were traded freely at a deep discount. For Swiss exports sold for commercial dollars, quotas were set. The commercial dollar rate also applied to transactions involving the Swiss diplomatic services and transactions of a humanitarian nature. The introduction of comprehensive exchange market controls was considered, but eventually dismissed.

As Bordo and James noted, the period of World War II, in contrast to that of World War I, was marked by surprisingly little controversy about the SNB's monetary policy actions. During the previous decades, the SNB had been the focus of considerable debate, as we have seen. "Perhaps because of the increasingly threatened geo-political position of Switzerland, the central bank increasingly became part of a consensus about national institutions" (Bordo and James, 2007, p. 92).

The SNB's gold transactions during World War II, on the other hand, proved to be highly controversial. While the gold deals of the SNB during World War I had never been a subject of special critique, those of World War II were under dispute almost from the beginning. A thorough reconstruction and investigation of these transactions took place only in the 1990s, in the course of a general debate about Switzerland's role during World War II, driven not least by political pressures from abroad. The problematic nature of these transactions derives in essence from the doubtful nature of the German Reichsbank's legal title to large parts of the gold it sold to the SNB at this time.[14]

During World War II, the SNB acquired large amounts of gold from both sides of the conflict. The German Reichsbank sold gold to the SNB amounting to 1,231 million Swiss francs; in addition, it sold gold to Swiss

---

[14] On this subject see, e.g., Fior (1997), UEK (1998), Crettol and Halbeisen (1999), Grossen (2001), Bordo and James (2007), and Klauser (2007).

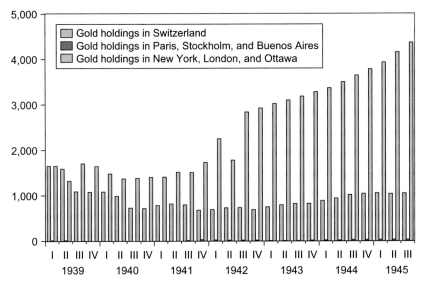

Figure 5.8: Gold holdings of Switzerland (SNB, Confederation, Fund for Exchange Market Intervention), 1939–1945 (in million francs)
Data source: Crettol and Halbeisen (1999), p. 49

commercial banks for 244 million francs. From the United States, the SNB bought gold worth 1,529 million francs; from Great Britain, gold worth 669 million francs. All these transactions reflected both war parties' strong desire for foreign exchange in the form of Swiss francs, and for the supplies which could be obtained in exchange for it. From the Swiss perspective, the purchase of gold reflected the country's determination to adhere to the gold standard and its rules and, consequently, the necessity of having command over sufficient gold reserves. On the development of Swiss gold holdings see Figure 5.8.

A substantial part of Swiss gold holdings remained blocked abroad during the war, however, especially in the United States.[15] During the war the SNB made attempts to concentrate the market for gold in its own hands, in order to improve its control over domestic gold reserves. From autumn 1941, the German Reichsbank was advised to sell gold to the

---

[15] Most of the foreign gold holdings of Switzerland were in the Allied countries of the United States, UK, and Canada. Only a nearly negligible share of this stock was held in Argentina, France, and Sweden.

SNB only. For gold coins and bullion, price ceilings were set to prevent commercial banks benefiting from gold price increases. Gold imports and exports were subject to official approval.

The main critique of the SNB's wartime gold transactions concerns its purchases from the German Reichsbank and the Reichsbank's legal title to the gold it sold. A frequent reproach is that the volume of the German gold sales to the SNB exceeded estimated German prewar gold reserves by a considerable margin, even with Austrian prewar holdings included.[16] Beyond such calculations, there were early indications that the gold sold by the Reichsbank derived partly from dispossessed holdings of other central banks, especially those of Belgium and the Netherlands, and that it may also have included gold expropriated from private individuals, including gold plundered from the victims of the Holocaust in Central and Eastern Europe.

The SNB apparently disregarded these doubts, despite being aware of them from an early stage. Its motivation, at least initially, seems to have been the argument that its gold policies were a "normal" and necessary part of its efforts to maintain the Swiss franc as a convertible currency, and that this in turn was crucial for ensuring Swiss independence and preventing a German attack ("by providing financial services, Switzerland could buy freedom from attack": Bordo and James, 2007, p. 77). To prove its good faith, it seems, the SNB later felt obliged to maintain this position and to continue its transactions with the Reichsbank up to the very end of the war, in spite of increasing pressure by the Allies to abandon these deals. Nevertheless, there was apparently some disagreement on this question within the SNB. The chairman of the Board of Governors, Ernst Weber, emphasized the importance and necessity of gold purchases under the ruling gold standard system. Gottlieb Bachmann, the President of the Bank Council (and Weber's predecessor as chairman of the board), on the other hand, was afraid of the political risks of these transactions.

After the war, Switzerland paid the Allies 250 million Swiss francs – 100 million of this sum being contributed by the SNB – as a result of the Washington Agreement of May 1946. In exchange, the Allies renounced all

---

[16] This is not entirely clear, however. According to some sources, the published figure for the prewar gold reserves of the Reichsbank considerably underestimated its true holdings, the latter effectively being nearly equivalent to the total gold purchases by the SNB over the entire period of war. See, e.g., Lambelet (1999), pp. 115–16, especially fn. 16.

further claims against Switzerland related to Swiss purchases of gold from Germany during the war. In spite of this, the issue was raised again and became the subject of a highly emotional (domestic and international) debate half a century later, in the 1990s, in the context of a general discussion about Switzerland's role during World War II.

6

Switzerland under the System of Bretton Woods (1945–1973)

The international monetary order that was to rule the first three decades after World War II was established at an international conference that took place even before the war had ended, in 1944, at Bretton Woods, New Hampshire. It was named the United Nations Monetary and Financial Conference, later known simply as the Bretton Woods Conference. It was a conference of the Allies, and forty-four nations were among the participants. Switzerland, as a neutral country, was not part of this circle. The purpose of the conference was to build the foundations of a new international order for trade and monetary relations after the war. The guiding motivation was to ensure that the troubles and confusions of monetary and commercial disintegration which had marked the interwar period, with competitive devaluations, balance of payments crises, import restrictions, and exchange market controls, should not spoil the future too. All in all, the conference was successful in this ambitious and tedious task. The monetary order established at Bretton Woods was a system of fixed but adjustable exchange rates based on both gold and the US dollar, known as the gold dollar or gold exchange standard.

THE BRETTON WOODS CONFERENCE, THE GOLD EXCHANGE STANDARD, AND SWITZERLAND

The architects of the Bretton Woods arrangements had in mind two objectives. The first was to liberalize world trade and get rid of impediments to international payments. Restrictions on international capital movements were not excluded, though, and were even considered to be desirable. The second was to restore a reliable and functioning international currency system based on fixed exchange rates. In support of these objectives, two new international institutions were created, the so-called Bretton Woods Institutions: the International Monetary Fund (IMF), and the World Bank or International Bank for Reconstruction and Development (IBRD).

Switzerland was initially rather skeptical about the negotiations and results of Bretton Woods.[1] In particular, the combination of a liberalized world trade with government-controlled capital movements did not fit Swiss preferences.[2] There were also fears that the IMF could declare the Swiss franc a "scarce currency," and that this in turn could serve as a justification for trade restrictions vis-à-vis Switzerland. In fact, the Federal Council decided against Swiss membership of the Bretton Woods institutions. It was not until 1992 that Switzerland officially joined the IMF and the World Bank – long after the monetary system established at Bretton Woods had broken down. Yet, for all practical purposes, Switzerland did effectively participate in this system from 1945.[3]

The centerpiece and reserve currency of the Bretton Woods monetary system was the US dollar, which was firmly linked to gold. More specifically, the system was defined by the following elements:

- The fixed parity of the US dollar at 35 dollars per ounce of gold.
- The fixed parity of all other member currencies in terms of the US dollar.
- The obligation for all member countries – except for the United States – to keep the exchange rate of their currencies within 1 percentage point of the dollar parity rate through interventions in the market for foreign exchange.
- The obligation for the United States to buy/sell gold at the fixed rate of 35 dollars per ounce from/to the monetary authorities of all other member countries.
- In case of "fundamental balance of payments imbalances" – but only in this case – an adjustment of the parity rate was to take place. Parity changes exceeding 10 percent of the original rate would require IMF approval.

---

[1] Bordo and James (2007), pp. 87–9.
[2] Even if administrative controls of exchange and capital markets did play a certain role in Swiss economic policy during the 1940s: see below.
[3] The Swiss aversion to capital market controls and a certain willingness to live with a floating exchange rate, based on the country's experiences in 1936/7, may not have been internationally fashionable in 1945, and were viewed by others as an expression of backward thinking ("a curious relict of the nineteenth century"). Yet this would become "the prevailing view among international economists and central bankers from the 1970s onward" (Bordo and James, 2007, p. 91).

• Member countries had to deposit monetary reserves with the IMF according to fixed country quotas. In the case of temporary balance of payments imbalances, they were entitled to receive IMF credit (which, depending on credit volume, could be tied to conditions).

In contrast to traditional gold standard rules, central banks in the system of Bretton Woods were not obliged to buy and sell gold in the private market at a fixed price. Insofar as this was the case, national currencies were unredeemable paper money. Economically, however, the system required that the market price of gold for the different currencies stayed near its (implied) parity rate. Otherwise, Gresham's law would have caused difficulties. Central banks as a group had to buy or sell gold in the free market at the parity rate "much as if the gold standard rules had been legally binding" (Niehans, 1978, p. 158).

Basically, the rules of the gold exchange standard applied symmetrically to all participants. In principle, all countries except for the United States could define their parity rates either in gold or in US dollars. As the dollar, the base currency of the system, was the equivalent of one thirty-fifth of an ounce of gold, this choice did not matter. Switzerland maintained a fixed value of the franc in terms of gold. An economically relevant asymmetry was created by the fact, however, that the US dollar, in addition to gold, served a central role as an instrument of international reserves.

Bretton Woods' gold exchange standard shared certain similarities with bimetallism, as several authors have pointed out:[4]

"Just as the private sector under bimetallism holds currency in the form of gold and silver coins, so the associated central banks held their reserves in gold and dollars. Just as the government under bimetallism guarantees a fixed exchange rate between silver and gold, so the United States guaranteed a fixed exchange rate between the dollar and gold. Just as under bimetallism fluctuations in the relative demand and supply of gold and silver can be absorbed, within limits, by shifts in the composition of the monetary circulation, so fluctuations in the relative demand and supply of gold and dollars could be absorbed, within limits, by shifts in the composition of international reserves ... [This] gave the gold / exchange standard a flexibility and a margin of freedom for national monetary policies that a pure monometallic standard does not have." (Niehans, 1978, p. 159).

---

[4] See, e.g., Aliber (1967), Niehans (1978, chapter 8) and Kugler (2016).

However, the gold exchange standard suffered from certain intrinsic weaknesses, which led to its early demise at the beginning of the 1970s. The major problems of the system discussed in the literature were these:[5]

- *The "nth country problem."* The United States, as the system's reserve currency country (the "*n*th country"), enjoyed a preferred position in the sense that it alone did not have to subordinate its monetary policy to exchange rate stabilization (there are only *n*-1 independent exchange rates in a system with *n* members), but instead could direct it toward domestic policy objectives. This implied a special responsibility of the United States to maintain a policy of long-run monetary and fiscal stability. Otherwise, long-run survival of the system was unlikely, as the credibility of the dollar – the system's reserve currency – and thus of the system itself would become doubtful. From the 1960s on, the United States no longer did justice to this special role, but increasingly succumbed to the temptations of an inflation policy.
- *The lack of a clear rule for exchange rate adjustments in case of "fundamental" disequlibria in the balance of payments.* Countries with structural balance of payments deficits, as well as those with structural surpluses, often resisted the required adjustment, for domestic reasons. A delayed need for correction contributed greatly to the destabilization of the system.
- *Retaining capital flow restrictions as an important pillar of the system.* In an increasingly globalized and free economic world, these restrictions proved to be difficult to enact and unable to stabilize the system in view of diverging national policy preferences.
- *Using gold as the system's anchor without willingness to accept temporary deflation.* A growing real demand for money (resulting from economic growth) would have required an increase in the real price of gold and thus – given a fixed nominal price of gold – acceptance of a declining price level, that is, temporary deflation. This was not politically feasible, however. Rather, the real price of gold continuously declined due to inflation – a development that, in the long run, would have led to a complete substitution of gold by the dollar, and thus would have robbed the system of its anchor.[6]

---

[5] For a variety of views on the monetary order of Bretton Woods see, e.g., the contributions in Bordo and Eichengreen (1993).

[6] Kugler (2016).

OVERCOMING ISOLATION IN EXTERNAL RELATIONS

The decade leading up to World War II, and World War II itself, were characterized in Switzerland and in the world overall by exchange market controls, bilateralism, and many restrictions on international trade and payments. For Switzerland, the blockage of Swiss assets, including those of the SNB, in the United States and Great Britain was an incisive experience.

Liberating international economic relations from this corset of restrictions became a central challenge for policymakers in Switzerland – and elsewhere – in the postwar years. The path back to less restricted relations in international trade, payments, and capital markets proved to be very tedious and rough, though.[7] Initially, bilateral treaties on mutual credit extension played an important role in easing the way.

Relations between Switzerland and the Allies, especially the United States, were tense after the war, due to the extent of Swiss trade with Germany during the war and the SNB's gold transactions with the Reichsbank. This did not make it easier for Switzerland to restore unencumbered external relations. The Washington Agreement of May 1946, signed after long negotiations between Switzerland and the Allies, constituted a crucial step in the normalization of relations with the United States. Other important marks in the effort to overcome Swiss isolation in trade were as follows:

- The Currie Agreement of March 1945 between Switzerland and the Allies, which allowed a relaxation of existing Allied states' import restrictions. Switzerland's intact industrial base and the country's ample currency reserves were of considerable help in these negotiations.
- Bilateral treaties with Great Britain, Belgium, and the Netherlands in 1945 and 1946 on trade and payments in exchange for credit extension.
- The restoration of bilateral trade relations with almost all European countries by early 1947.

ADMINISTRATIVE CONTROL OF THE FOREIGN EXCHANGE MARKET

After the war, Swiss authorities initially had high hopes for a return to a full-fledged gold standard, recalling the experiences after World War I.

---

[7] A detailed description of this phase in Swiss monetary history is given by Bernholz (2007). See also Spahni (1977), Durrer (1984), and Halbeisen and Straumann (2012, pp. 1023–51).

As a consequence, maintenance of the Swiss franc's fixed gold parity became a fixture of Swiss monetary policy until 1973.[8] Increasingly, a second central motivation of Swiss monetary policy was to maintain stable consumer prices. As the Swiss balance of payments in the 1940s was marked by permanent surpluses, a conflict between these two objectives soon arose. The SNB wanted to admit neither a change in the gold parity nor inflation. Instead, it attempted to resolve this conflict by splitting the market for foreign exchange, especially the US dollar market, and by introducing administrative controls with the aim of restricting capital inflows into Switzerland.[9]

As we have seen, the splitting of the US dollar market had been introduced during the war, three months after the US blockage of Swiss assets, with a gentlemen's agreement between the SNB and the commercial banks in September 1941.[10] This policy of a two-tier dollar market continued until 1949. The freely tradable financial dollar fluctuated strongly in value and, in certain periods, dropped far below the official parity of 4.31 Swiss francs per US dollar. The low was reached in 1944, at 2.29 Swiss francs; after the war, the financial dollar recovered substantially, but always stayed below the official parity rate (see Figure 6.1).

More specifically, the two-tier dollar market and the policy of administrative controls installed by the Swiss authorities included the following elements:

- Quotas for exports which could be sold for commercial dollars (i.e., the proceeds of which could be exchanged at the official parity rate).
- Exclusion of "noncommercial" transactions from the "official" market: Only "commercial" transactions were admissible for exchange at the official parity rate; all other transactions had to be conducted at floating exchange rates (below parity) through the free market for financial dollars.
- Enforcement of import financing at the official (parity) dollar rate: The financing of imports in the free market (which would have been of advantage to importers) was prevented.
- Partial freezing of export revenues: 50 percent of all dollar revenues from exports was blocked for three years on accounts at the SNB

---

[8] Formally, it was only abandoned with the revision of the federal constitution of the year 2000.

[9] Bernholz (2007, p. 112), following Salin (1964), refers to this policy as *Devisenbann-Wirtschaft* ("policies to repel foreign exchange") or *inward exchange controls*.

[10] See Chapter 5.

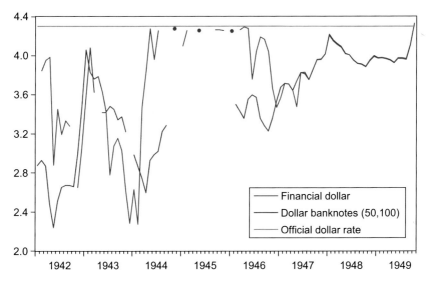

Figure 6.1: Official US dollar exchange rate and exchange rate for financial dollars and dollar notes, 1942–1949
Data source: Bernholz (2007), p. 121

(in an attempt to restrict the effects of SNB dollar purchases on the money supply and consumer prices); only the residual 50 percent was paid out immediately in Swiss francs.

The policy of administrative controls and a split market for foreign exchange required a large amount of bureaucracy and resources, in the form of personnel. The distinction between "commercial" and "noncommercial" transactions was naturally fuzzy. Requests for exceptions and attempts at evasion became daily business. To prevent or limit effects of central bank dollar purchases on the money supply and on inflation, the SNB sold gold against Swiss francs in the market and to the federal government. These sales lasted from 1943 until September 1947; the government's peak holdings of gold were reached in September 1947 at 1,258 million Swiss francs.

For a limited time, this policy was successful in keeping Swiss inflation moderate. In the longer run, however, it turned out to be a failure. Demands to abandon all these bureaucratic measures and restrictions, both from domestic sources and from foreign countries – especially the United States – became increasingly urgent. Among Swiss economists, a lively debate developed about the pros and cons of the two-tier dollar market. Eugen Böhler from ETH Zurich, Walter Adolf Jöhr from the University of St. Gallen, and Valentin Wagner from the University of Basel favored the split dollar market system, while Hugo Sieber and Fritz Marbach from the University of Berne took a stand against it.[11] The SNB itself viewed this system with increasing doubt. From 1947 onward, it relaxed exchange market restrictions step by step, and on September 23, 1949 – following a devaluation of the pound sterling and other currencies, which implied an effective revaluation of the Swiss franc,[12] easing the SNB's policy dilemma – the two-tier dollar market system was officially ended. Restrictions concerning the import and export of gold were only relaxed in 1951 and totally abandoned in 1952, however.

A certain inclination toward a policy of administrative controls and defensive measures, for example, in the form of a ban on Swiss franc deposits by foreign-based individuals or negative interest rates on their Swiss franc claims, or in the form of limitations of credit growth, continued to play a role in Swiss monetary policy for quite a while, even beyond the transition to full convertibility within Europe (which was to follow in 1958), and even beyond the breakdown of the Bretton Woods fixed rate system in the early 1970s, up to the currency crises of the late 1970s.[13]

RESTORATION OF FOREIGN EXCHANGE CONVERTIBILITY

The way out of bilateralism in trade and exchange market controls in Europe was strongly influenced by the United States' Marshall Plan and the resultant foundation of the Organization for European Economic Cooperation (OEEC) in 1948, and particularly the European Payments Union (EPU) created under its auspices after lengthy negotiations in 1950 among eighteen nations.[14] The EPU immediately helped to liberalize a considerable part of international trade. The liberalization of capital movements would follow only later, though. The central feature of the EPU was the multilateral settlement of balances on bilateral trade or current accounts (in units of account corresponding to a US dollar). Each country was allocated a quota, which was divided into five tranches. The first tranche was financed fully by credit extension; subsequently, the proportion which

---

[11] For references, see Bernholz (2007), p. 131, fn. 34.
[12] The fact that Switzerland did not follow this devaluation illustrates the continuity of Swiss stability culture. As mentioned before, 1936 represented no break in this respect.
[13] See, e.g., Schiltknecht (1970).
[14] On this and the following, see Bernholz (2007), pp. 135–8 and 144–5; see also Kaplan and Schleiminger (1989), Schwerdtel (1992).

had to be paid in gold or dollars increased with every tranche. Balances exceeding the quota had to be settled fully in gold or dollars. The system was tailored such that on average, with full utilization of quotas, a 60:40 ratio between credit financing and payments in gold or dollars resulted. Later, the share of gold/dollar payments was gradually increased. The Bank for International Settlements (BIS) in Basel was assigned the task of administering the resulting banking operations.

Switzerland and the SNB were initially hesitant about the EPU and its efforts. They were afraid of possible discrimination against important Swiss export items, such as watches or tourism, as "nonessentials." More importantly, they feared that an undesirable (from the Swiss point of view) automatism in international credit extension might result. In consequence, a certain preference existed on their part for bilateral credit agreements, which were seen as an asset in international trade negotiations. Yet, at a fundamental level, the rationality of the EPU's objectives, and the potential benefit of these efforts for Switzerland, could not be denied. After negotiations establishing an upward limit for the Swiss credit extension at 600 million Swiss francs, Switzerland formally joined the EPU on November 1, 1950.

Subsequently, Switzerland was an active member of a group of creditor countries (including Germany, Belgium, and the Netherlands) which pushed for an increasing proportion of gold/dollar settlements and a reduced role for automatic credit extension, thereby easing and accelerating the return to full convertibility. The return to convertibility was driven in particular by Great Britain. In 1955, following difficult negotiations, a European Monetary Agreement (EMA) was drafted, providing for convertibility for non-residents at fixed exchange rates in the event of the EPU being abolished and for the creation of a European fund as a safety net for countries with weak currencies. However, the transition to full convertibility under the EMA and the discontinuation of the EPU were again delayed for several years (due to a deterioration of the UK's balance of payments). Finally, in December 1958, the EMA was signed, with Swiss participation (after initial hesitations).

MONETARY POLICY UNDER BRETTON WOODS: CAPITAL INFLOWS AND INFLATION PRESSURE

During the 1960s, Swiss monetary policy was shaped by the country's commitment to defend the gold (and thus dollar) parity of the Swiss franc and by the evolution of the Swiss balance of payments; this period was characterized by speculative inflows of capital and resulting inflation pressure. Not before its liberation from these constraints with the breakdown of the Bretton Woods system at the beginning of the 1970s would the SNB gain the freedom to pursue an autonomous policy course aimed at price level stability.

The 1960s marked the end phase of the international system of fixed exchange rates established at Bretton Woods. At this time, and partly even before, an intensive international debate about the pros and cons of fixed versus floating exchange rates had developed, with participation from those in both academic and policy circles. Central topics of this debate were the dangers of destabilizing speculation under flexible rates, on the one hand, and the increased independence in cyclical stabilization and inflation policies that such a system would allow, on the other. Economically, it had always been clear that a fixed exchange rate system could thrive and survive only if its major participants were able to agree on mutually consistent monetary policy paths. This came to be crucially important for Switzerland and a few other European countries, especially Germany.

In Switzerland and in Germany, policy preferences throughout the postwar period were strongly marked by a desire for low inflation. The fashion of multiple objectives for monetary policy and possible trade-offs between unemployment or growth and inflation, which strongly influenced policy debates elsewhere at this time, never gained much influence in Switzerland and Germany. The view persisted that a regime of price stability was, over the longer run, conducive to real economic stability and growth, and that multiple (and possibly inconsistent) monetary policy goals meant overburdening central bank policy with impossible tasks. The clear preference for a price stability goal was made easier for Switzerland, of course, by the fact that Swiss unemployment remained extremely low throughout this period.

At the same time, however, Swiss monetary policy was strongly determined by the idea of a firm currency linkage to gold and a fixed parity of the franc to gold and other leading currencies. This represented no major problem as long as the important players of the Bretton Woods system – in particular the United States, as its reserve currency country – remained committed to a policy of monetary stability. Up to the early 1960s, this was more or less the case. It is true that Switzerland had to struggle with speculative capital inflows and potential inflation pressure in phases throughout the 1940s and 1950s, and that it tried to fend off this threat through the use of administrative controls as described above. However, the objectives of internal and external stability of the franc really began to clash over the course of the 1960s, when US monetary policy shifted more and more toward an inflationary course intended to favor employment and growth and to keep interest rates low (the latter not least in view of the financial needs of the public sector caused by the Vietnam war and other government programs).

The results were a decay in international confidence in the US dollar and, under Bretton Woods' fixed exchange rate system, chronic deficits in the US balance of payments. Mirroring these were massive capital inflows, an expansion of liquidity, and imported inflation in Switzerland (and other countries attempting to protect themselves from these inflation tendencies in similar ways, in particular Germany). The SNB had to buy large quantities of dollars to maintain the fixed dollar exchange rate. As a consequence, there was an undesired increase in the supply of money and corresponding inflation pressure. In the long run, attempts to counter these developments with restrictive monetary policy measures had no chance of succeeding under the fixed exchange rate system of Bretton Woods, as the interest rate increases resulting from such measures would only have induced further capital inflows and led market participants to bet even more highly on an ultimately unavoidable upwards revaluation of the Swiss franc.

Swiss monetary policy in the 1960s was strongly marked by the attempt to solve this policy dilemma through the use of non-market, administrative instruments of control. In the long run, these instruments were doomed to be failures, too. Yet, it took Swiss authorities a decade to come to this conclusion. Reconstituting convertibility thus did not bring an end to the policies of administrative control that had been implemented during the preceding two decades. Rather, a whole arsenal of additional tools was developed, all aiming to restrict the inflow of foreign capital or to neutralize its effects on the money supply and liquidity provision. These instruments were introduced partly through gentlemen's agreements between the SNB and the banks, partly through federal emergency legislation. They included a series of measures meant to restrict "the inflow of foreign money," such as the prohibition of interest payments, or even negative interest rates (administrative charges), on foreign deposits at Swiss banks; conventions limiting the level or the growth of credit extension by banks; freezing bank reserves through reserve requirement increases, including reserve requirements on incremental deposits; and monitoring consumer price increases. Not surprisingly, these measures had no lasting success.[15]

---

[15] See Schiltknecht (1970).

The problem of imported inflation persisted, because its fundamental cause was not removed. In the early 1970s, Swiss inflation rose beyond 7 percent, with a (lagged) peak of 9 percent in 1973 and 10 percent in 1974.

Political resistance toward formal participation in the Bretton Woods system and a certain mistrust of its institutions persisted throughout the 1950s, 1960s, and beyond. But although Switzerland was not formally a member of the Bretton Woods institutions until 1992, it took part in numerous forms of international cooperation undertaken to prevent or limit international currency crises, for example, through participation in the currency loan arrangements of the Group of Ten (a group of ten leading industrial countries) or in the so-called London Gold Pool (cooperation between central banks to keep the market price of gold near its official price of 35 US dollars per ounce).[16] Not surprisingly, these efforts were in vain, since they did not remove the basic inconsistency between diverging national monetary policy preferences and the system of fixed exchange rates.[17]

Reacting to a new wave of speculative capital inflows, on May 9, 1971 the Swiss government decided to revalue the Swiss franc by about 7 percent, supplementing this decision (once more) with new administrative controls (through emergency legislation) to keep foreign money out. On August 15, 1971 the US government suspended the gold convertibility of the dollar, and on December 18, 1971 an international realignment of the exchange rates of the most important currencies in the context of the Smithsonian Agreement took place. For the Swiss franc, this rearrangement resulted in an additional revaluation of 6.4 percent.

However, as this exchange rate realignment was again not linked to effective coordination of monetary policies between the involved nations, international currency markets were only temporarily calmed. In summer and autumn 1972, markets were in turmoil again, once more creating severe upward pressure for the Swiss franc.

On January 23, 1973, the SNB, with the consent of the federal government, decided to cease its foreign exchange purchases in the market. From today's perspective, after forty years' experience with flexible exchange rates, the dramatic nature of this decision may be difficult to appreciate. It was made by the acting authorities with great reluctance – more with a

---

[16] For detailed information on Swiss participation in these international collaborations, see Bernholz (2007), pp. 155–60.
[17] For an international perspective on these developments, see, e.g., Coombs (1976), Solomon (1977), and Toniolo (2005).

view to the inevitability of this step than by conviction. Fixed exchange rates were simply no longer a credible option, given the enormous level of speculative capital flows. Thus, Switzerland's era of fixed exchange rates came to an end. Initial expectations that a return to fixed exchange rates would soon become possible once again proved to be wrong. The era of flexible exchange rates had run its course.

7

The Era of Flexible Exchange Rates
(1973–present)

The transition from fixed to flexible exchange rates in January 1973, after
the breakdown of the Bretton Woods system, marks the most important
turning point in the history of Swiss monetary policy since the creation of
the SNB. It was this fundamental change in monetary regime that gave the
SNB the freedom to pursue an autonomous policy of inflation control.
Prior to 1973, the commitment to maintain fixed parities vis-à-vis other
currencies had made this impossible. The global surge in inflation during
the 1960s and early 1970s had resulted in huge capital inflows, excessive
monetary growth, and accelerating inflation in Switzerland as elsewhere.
For the SNB, as for other central banks, this regime change meant a
massive increase in status and power. The opportunity to pursue a more
independent monetary policy was used decisively by the SNB. This was not
particularly surprising given that – much as in Germany – a broad
consensus existed in Switzerland at the time in favor of a policy of inflation
control. The deeply rooted traditions of political and fiscal stability characteristic of the country provided favorable conditions for establishing
such a course.

Together with the Deutsche Bundesbank, the SNB was a pioneer in the
use of money growth targeting and employed it successfully to reduce
inflation to levels consistent with price level stability during the 1970s.[1]

---

[1] In this, the SNB as well as the Bundesbank were strongly influenced by monetarism, a
school of thought in monetary theory and policy that stresses the role of money in the
control of inflation and economic activity. Monetarism, which originated in the 1960s
and reached its peak intellectual influence during the 1970s and 80s, also emphasized the
role of expectations (largely disregarded by the early Keynesians) for understanding
macroeconomic fluctuations and recommended steady money growth and a commitment to rules-based economic policies in general. Leading monetarists included Milton
Friedman, Karl Brunner, Allan Meltzer, and Phillip Cagan, among others. For the SNB

Swiss inflation, measured by the increase in the consumer price index (CPI), fell from 9 percent in 1973 and 10 percent in 1974 to levels between 0 and 2 percent in the period 1976–8. Over time, the SNB's conceptual framework for policymaking gradually shifted in response to changes in the monetary environment and developments in monetary theory and research. From 1975 to the end of the 1980s, the SNB's policy was based on yearly money growth targets; in the 1990s, the yearly targets were replaced by a medium-term money growth objective defined over periods of five years. At the beginning of the year 2000, finally, a new policy concept was introduced based on inflation forecasts and a clear definition of price level stability.[2]

CONSCIOUS DECISION FOR FLOATING AND MONETARY AUTONOMY

As pointed out at the end of Chapter 6, the transition to flexible exchange rates resulted more from the obvious inevitability of such a step than from preference and conviction on the part of the responsible authorities. Many, including representatives of the SNB and politics, considered it dangerous and initially entertained expectations of a return to fixed rates in the not too distant future. Yet we can say that Switzerland and the SNB accepted floating by conscious decision and with due consideration of its advantages and disadvantages, once it became clear that a return to a credible, broad-based international system of fixed exchange rates was prevented by the heterogeneity of the major international players' monetary policy objectives.[3]

Switzerland could have pegged the Swiss franc to another – preferably stable – currency, as many other small and medium-sized countries have often done and still do.[4] The obvious candidate for such a peg would have been the German mark. In principle, this would have been possible by unilateral decision, without formal agreements. Proposals of this kind were

and the Bundesbank, the Swiss-American economist Karl Brunner was of special importance.

[2] SNB policy in the flexible exchange rate era is reviewed in more detail in Baltensperger (2007); see also Baltensperger (1985) and Rich (2007).

[3] See, e.g., Schiltknecht (1994) for a summary of the considerations leading Switzerland to this path.

[4] Straumann (2010) analyzes in detail why some small and medium-sized European countries have historically opted for fixed rates and others for floating.

repeatedly advanced in public and scholarly debates, for instance in connection with the formation of the European "currency snake" in the early 1970s or with the European Monetary System (EMS) initiated in 1979, and even more after the creation of the Economic and Monetary Union (EMU) at the end of the 1990s.[5]

What was always decisive in this question for Swiss authorities was the fact that, for all practical purposes, such a policy would have meant abandoning the country's monetary autonomy and delegating it to the Bundesbank or, after 1999, to the European Central Bank. This would not only have implied giving up the option to pursue an independent monetary policy aimed at the specific needs of the Swiss economy, but would also almost certainly have led to the disappearance of the Swiss franc interest rate bonus, which was firmly established in the markets by this time. After the experiences of the preceding decades, such a course could not really be considered an attractive, serious alternative for Switzerland. As Bordo and James have noted, the experience of 1936/7 had "led to a certain skepticism about a fixed rate system and a willingness to live in a world with floating currencies" in Switzerland (Bordo and James, 2007, pp. 90–1). The politically caused isolation of the war and postwar years further strengthened the Swiss inclination to insist on an independent course of autonomy. Beyond this, Straumann (2010, pp. 278–80) rightly points to the strength of the Swiss commitment to open international capital markets, which authorities did not want to sacrifice to a fixed exchange rate system.[6]

Bernholz (2007, p. 172) has argued that with a policy firmly linking the Swiss franc to the German mark (or the EEC currency snake and later the euro), Switzerland could have avoided the large exchange rate fluctuations experienced under its actual policy course without having to accept higher

---

[5] Participation in the currency snake was discussed intensively during the early 1970s. In 1973, the Federal Council and the SNB were skeptical of the idea. In 1975, nevertheless, negotiations were opened. They led to no results, however, with a negative attitude on the part of France playing a major role on the side of the EU (or, to be more precise, the European Economic Community, or EEC, as it was at the time). See Halbeisen (2006), Bernholz (2007, p. 172), and Straumann (2010, pp. 288–91).

[6] Straumann (2010, chapter 7) stresses Swiss non-membership in the EU (EEC) as another important factor in the Swiss decision to adopt flexible rates, since this non-membership made it difficult, or even impossible, to participate in the European currency snake. Note, however, that EU non-membership reflects the same basic preference for national autonomy as does the decision for monetary independence; in this sense, both are expressions of the same fundamental attitude.

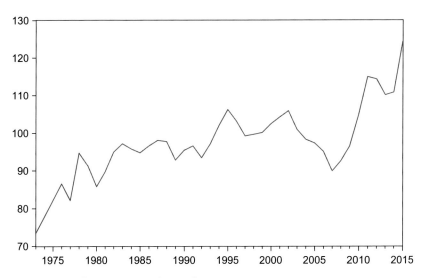

Figure 7.1: Real appreciation of Swiss franc, 1973–2015

Effective exchange rate index of Swiss franc against euro era, increase indicates real appreciation.
Data source: SNB data, https://data.snb.ch/de/topics/ziredev#!/cube/devlanda

inflation. This is questionable, however. The tendency toward real appreciation which has characterized the Swiss franc and the Swiss economy since 1970 (see Figure 7.1) would in all likelihood have prevented price level stability in Switzerland under a policy of pegging the D-mark (and later the euro), even if the Bundesbank (and later the ECB) were maintaining low inflation in Germany or Europe, respectively. With a fixed nominal exchange rate, this real appreciation trend would very likely have manifested in the form of a higher rate of inflation in Switzerland. Given the high priority that Swiss monetary policy and the SNB were internationally known to place on price stability, it is highly probable that a policy of pegging the D-mark and the euro would as a result have suffered from a severe problem of credibility and resulting speculative capital flows (Baltensperger, 2007, p. 637; in more detail Baltensperger et al., 1999, pp. 42–5).[7]

---

[7] Participation in the block-floating of the currency snake could have suffered from the same problem. For this reason it is not clear how successful and enduring such a participation would have been, had it really been attempted.

TRANSITION TO MONETARY TARGETING AND
RETURN TO PRICE LEVEL STABILITY

The SNB did not hesitate to use its new freedom. After the regime change of 1973, a sharp course of monetary restriction was adopted at first. The two-digit rates of growth of central bank money and the money stock M1 attained in the preceding years were suddenly and drastically reduced. As early as 1973, the growth rate for M1, which had reached 17.9 percent the previous year, was lowered to 2.3 percent. Central bank money even declined by 4.4 percent in 1973, after having grown by 18.7 percent in the preceding year.[8] In 1974, M1 stayed roughly unchanged, while central bank money was just allowed to make good on its 1973 decline. Even if these numbers reflected a reaction to the enormous growth of monetary aggregates in the years before 1973, they obviously also represented an abrupt change from a very expansionary to an extremely restrictive monetary policy. Correspondingly, from 1973 to the end of 1974, the SNB allowed a strong appreciation of the Swiss franc and, apart from one action in February 1973, completely abstained from exchange market intervention. This allowed it to absorb a large part of the excess liquidity which had been created by previous interventions.

For the year 1975, a money growth target – for the money stock M1 – was announced by the SNB for the first time. Making this target public was an important element of the SNB's strategy: Market expectations should be guided in accordance with the central bank's long-run objectives. Target growth rates of 6 percent for M1 were announced for 1975 and 1976, while for 1977 and 1978 the targets were set at 5 percent. In view of declining inflation expectations, these rates of money growth were held to be consistent with the SNB's anti-inflationary policy course. Up to (and including) 1977, these targets were met quite closely. According to expectations, this money growth policy was successful in lowering the rate of inflation to comparatively very low levels: from 9 percent in the year 1973 and 10 percent in 1974 to less than 2 percent in 1976 and 1977 and just about 1 percent in 1978. Linked to this was a marked reduction in nominal interest rates. In 1978, money market rates fell below 1 percent, and the yield on federal bonds was just slightly above 3 percent. This shows that the drastic reduction of money growth to a level more consistent with price stability had succeeded in breaking the inflationary expectations prevalent

---

[8]　Monetary base adjusted for banks' end-of-month fluctuations in bank reserves (which served window-dressing purposes).

during the early 1970s. By 1978, nominal interest rates presumably no longer contained much of an inflation premium.

The SNB's policy after 1973 thus succeeded, within a remarkably brief time, in reestablishing price level stability in Switzerland. This fast success, which came as a surprise to many observers in Switzerland and abroad,[9] was due to the quick and decisive adoption of a new policy course in the context of a clearly recognizable change in currency regime. This allowed the SNB to build up a high level of credibility and reputation within a short span of time. The Bundesbank used the same opportunity in a similar way in Germany. The central banks of both countries played a pioneering role in monetary policy at this time.

This success in the fight against inflation was accompanied by a sharp decline in real economic activity, however. In 1975 and 1976, Swiss GDP declined in real terms – in 1975 by no less than 7.4 percent. Although declines were experienced by most industrial countries at that time as a consequence of the first oil shock, the decline in Switzerland was considerably more pronounced than those in practically all other countries. Given the sharply restrictive monetary policy of the SNB in the preceding years, this is no great surprise.

On the other hand, judged in terms of unemployment statistics, Switzerland appeared to have no notable difficulties during this period. Only in 1975/6 did the measured unemployment rate rise slightly above the levels usually experienced before, reaching the (still very low) levels of 0.4 and 0.7 percent. This had to do with the fact that, due to a very high mobility of labor between Switzerland and adjoining European countries, Swiss unemployment statistics included little information content at that time. Compulsory unemployment insurance did not yet exist. The number of foreign workers, which accounted for no less than 26 percent of the total Swiss labor force at that time, fell from about 850,000 in 1973 to 630,000 in 1978, mostly due to a decline in the number of seasonal workers and *Jahresaufenthalter* (one-year residents). This reduction in the foreign labor force reduced both potential output and aggregate demand.

It is important to note, however, that this reduction of the foreign population, and thus of the Swiss economy overall, happened to coincide

---

[9] In a contribution in 2007, Mishkin noted that the US Federal Reserve was overly tolerant of inflation in the 1970s due to an overly pessimistic evaluation of the chances and costs of anti-inflation policies, and revised this assessment only after the successful disinflation policy of Paul Volcker in the early 1980s (Mishkin, 2007). The Swiss and the German central banks were ten years ahead of the Federal Reserve, and most other central banks, in this regard.

with a large part of the Swiss voting population's clear desire to reduce the country's reliance on foreign labor, as manifested by a new and more restrictive stance toward immigration and the inflow of foreign workers. To a certain extent, therefore, this reduction was probably politically unavoidable in any case. This observation does not lessen the magnitude of the Swiss recession of 1975, but it is part of the picture that explains why it was politically feasible for the SNB to follow such a tight course of monetary policy. It also implies that it is not very informative and somewhat misleading to compare the levels of Swiss GDP reached in the late 1970s and 1980s with an extrapolated trend of Swiss GDP prior to 1975.

EXCHANGE MARKET TURBULENCE AND TEMPORARY ADOPTION OF AN EXCHANGE RATE TARGET

While the problem of reducing high inflation to levels more consistent with a stable financial environment was at the forefront of Swiss monetary policy in the years after 1973, this objective had more or less been reached by 1977/8. At the same time, labor market conditions were fairly satisfactory in 1977/8, given the tighter conditions set by the Swiss policy vis-à-vis foreign workers and immigration. In the years after 1977/8, therefore, the SNB's monetary policy was increasingly dominated by the question of how to maintain these favorable conditions in view of various kinds of external disturbances, notably exchange rate changes and energy price fluctuations.

The main problem in 1977, and even more in 1978, was an enormous appreciation of the Swiss franc relative to all important currencies. The markets' belief in the seriousness of the SNB's commitment to price level stability, in the context of an international environment still characterized by monetary expansion and high inflation, led to a dramatic speculative inflow of capital and a strong appreciation of the Swiss franc. In real terms, in 1978 the franc appreciated by almost 15 percent vis-à-vis the D-mark and by more than 26 percent vis-à-vis the US dollar; in terms of an export-weighted average relative to the most important trading partners, the real revaluation was 16.6 percent. Although this strong revaluation had relatively little effect on trade flows and the current account balance at first, it assumed dramatic proportions in summer 1978 and threatened to severely damage the Swiss real economy.[10] The SNB had always reserved the right to deviate from its previously announced targets in cases like this and, in

---

[10] Not before summer/autumn 2011 would Switzerland experience a similarly dramatic exchange rate appreciation, as a consequence of the European debt crisis.

view of these developments, decided to tolerate a temporary increase in the money supply far beyond the target previously set. For 1979, it chose not to set a money growth target. Finally, in October 1978, after long internal discussions, it announced its decision to temporarily return to an exchange rate target and to keep the Swiss franc price of the German mark "clearly" above 80 per 100 mark; see, e.g., Schiltknecht (1994, p. 64); Rich (2007, p. 298). The result was strong overshooting of the money growth target for 1978. In the six months between September 1978 and March 1979 alone, central bank money rose by 17 percent and M1 by 11 percent.

In spring 1979, exchange markets calmed down and the SNB started to withdraw the liquidity created during the crisis. The SNB hoped that a purely temporary deviation of money growth from the longer-run expansion path deemed consistent with price stability – understood as a temporary accommodation of a massive increase in the international demand for Swiss money – would not have serious consequences for domestic inflation. This hope was only partially fulfilled, however. In the years after 1978 inflation rose again, from 0.6 percent in 1978 to 4.4 percent in 1979 and 6.6 percent in 1981. Even if the second oil price shock that occurred at that time did also play a role, this development was, first of all, a consequence of the immense liquidity created in the previous years. Due to the recurrence of inflation, the policy shift of 1978 has often been questioned *ex post facto*. According to Schiltknecht (1994, p. 65), after his retirement from the SNB in 1985, chairman Fritz Leutwiler declared the policy change of 1978 to have been a major mistake in retrospect. In our view (and that of Schiltknecht), this conclusion is not justified; the decision for monetary accommodation was appropriate at the time. Given the enormous appreciation of the Swiss franc, a policy of non-accommodation would very likely have caused great damage to the real Swiss economy. What is true, however, is that in 1979 and 1980 the SNB was too reluctant and overly tardy in eliminating the liquidity overhang remaining from the crisis years (Baltensperger and Böhm, 1984, p. 72; Baltensperger, 1985), partly because it underestimated the forthcoming cyclical expansion (Kugler and Rich, 2002, p. 266), thereby creating the foundations for the subsequent surge of inflation.

RETURN TO ANNUAL MONEY GROWTH TARGETS AND TO MONETARY STABILITY

For 1980 and the subsequent years, the SNB returned to its policy of targeting money growth. In contrast to the years before 1979, when it had used targets for M1, its target variable was now central bank money adjusted for month-end fluctuations in bank reserves (the "monetary base adjusted"). This change was justified by the observed instability in the money multiplier relating the monetary base to M1.[11] For 1980 and 1981, the SNB announced a growth target of 4 percent. In both years, however, its policy turned out to be clearly more restrictive than initially announced; central bank money declined in both 1980 and 1981. The motivation for this was an acceleration of inflation dynamics – to peak levels beyond 7 percent in 1981 – which had not been sufficiently anticipated when the targets were set.

The disinflation policy of the early 1980s in Switzerland took place under somewhat different, and in a sense more difficult, conditions than those of the 1970s. In the earlier period, many other countries had followed a policy of expansion at a time when Swiss monetary policy had turned restrictive. In the early 1980s, in contrast, most of the important industrial countries were also following a rather restrictive course. Aided by a considerable Swiss franc appreciation, success in the fight against inflation in the 1970s thus was comparably quick and easy, while in the early 1980s the effect on the inflation rate, partly due to a weakening franc, was slower and weaker.

The events of the years between 1978 and 1981 strongly influenced the SNB's and the public's view of the role of the exchange rate in monetary policy. Henceforth, the SNB kept a close eye on the exchange rate in policy setting. Its pragmatic response to the exchange rate shock of 1978 established a long-lasting market opinion that the SNB would not tolerate a violation of the .80 Swiss franc floor for the price of the German mark.

The subsequent years, 1982 to 1986, mark a quiet period for Swiss monetary policy. Inflation declined to the 2–3 percent range and stayed more or less at this level. Money growth targets – which were set at 3 percent for the period 1982–5 and at 2 percent for 1986 – were met rather closely. The renewed decline in inflation was preceded by a cyclical contraction in the period 1981–3. Business conditions picked up again after 1983, however. In the United States, 1983 marked the conclusion of the disinflationary policy under Paul Volcker. Although exchange rate fluctuations gave rise to occasional concerns, in comparison to the experiences of the preceding decade, they remained moderate overall.

---

[11] See Chapter 9 for more on this, especially Figures 9.4 and 9.5 and Tables 9.5 and 9.6.

THE LATE 1980S: INSTABILITY OF RESERVE DEMAND AND UNINTENDED MONETARY EXPANSION

These favorable conditions came to an end in the period 1987–90 with developments which were to put a strain on the SNB's policies for the next decade. For 1987, the SNB had again set a money growth target of 2 percent. Actually, it tolerated a monetary expansion beyond this mark, mainly in view of the Swiss franc's strong tendency to appreciate, and signs of weakness in the international economy. The Swiss domestic economy remained robust nonetheless. The stock market crash of October 1987 and the resulting widespread fears of a slump in the world economy further induced the SNB to postpone the policy tightening which would otherwise clearly have seemed advisable. For 1988, the SNB even raised its money growth target to 3 percent. By mid-1988, however, it became increasingly obvious that the feared downturn in world economic conditions would not materialize. It was the clear intention of the SNB to tighten its policy in response to these developments.

At this time, however, Swiss monetary policy was severely complicated by two important institutional changes in the Swiss financial system, which the SNB found highly challenging: the introduction of a new, electronic interbank clearing system (Swiss Interbank Clearing SIC) and an overhaul of the liquidity requirement regulations for Swiss banks. Both changes together led to a massive reduction in banks' demand for central bank money. The SNB was well aware of this change, but found it extremely difficult to reliably estimate its extent and its realization over time. In lowering money growth, the direction of its response was, in principle, correct. By severely underestimating the size and the speed of the banks' adjustment in reserve demand, however, the SNB was led on a policy course which, in retrospect, turned out to have been far too expansionary. It is true that these developments were difficult to judge at the time. Nevertheless, a stronger reliance on interest rate signals would probably have allowed a superior response. In this sense, the concentration on money growth characteristic of the SNB's policy approach at that time was not particularly helpful. Also, the SNB found it increasingly difficult in this period to communicate its policies to the public.

In December 1987 the SNB declared that, given the unclear situation just described, it might ultimately have to undershoot its 1988 target (central bank money growth of 3 percent). In fact, central bank money shrank by almost 4 percent in 1988. Interest rates remained very low, however, and it became increasingly clear during 1988 that the monetary policy stance had been, and still was, too expansionary, given the dwindling demand for bank reserves. The consequence was an excessive supply of money and, with the usual lag of two to three years, a reacceleration of inflation. In 1989, the SNB started to effectively tighten its policy. For both 1989 and 1990, it kept money growth below the targets originally set, realizing that the Swiss economy was fully overheated and marked by a major speculative real estate boom. However, on the inflation front, the damage had already been done by this time. Inflation reached levels between 5 and 6 percent in 1989 and 1990, hitting a peak of 6.6 percent by the middle of 1991. The central bank and other economic observers were repeatedly surprised by the strength and persistence of the developing inflation dynamics.

TRANSITION TO MEDIUM-TERM TARGETS FOR MONEY

The developments of the late 1980s led the SNB to undertake a major modification of its policy framework. The repeated and sizable deviations of money growth from the originally announced targets had seriously damaged the effectiveness of annual growth objectives as a credible instrument with which to inform the public about the SNB's policy intentions. Nevertheless, the SNB continued to rely on a money growth objective. However, after 1991, instead of announcing annual growth targets, it relied on a medium-term objective. In December 1990, it announced its intention to increase central bank money to approach a medium-term expansion path. This expansion path was defined by an evolution of central bank money that the SNB considered to be consistent with price stability and with full resource utilization in the economy. In 1990, the SNB estimated that an average 1 percent growth of central bank money would be in line with this requirement. The length of the target period was left unclear at first, but was soon specified as three to five years. The purpose of this strategy shift was to allow the SNB more flexibility in its year-to-year policy course and to pay attention to different indicator variables, notably interest rates, the exchange rate, and business cycle conditions, while still reasserting its clear long-term commitment to price level stability.

The years 1991–3 were marked by the SNB's efforts to restore price stability in Switzerland. These efforts resulted in a sharp stabilization crisis, with strong corrections in the real estate market and heavy losses to banks. The real estate bubble burst, and a severe mortgage and banking crisis developed. The Swiss banking sector's accumulated mortgage credit losses in this period were estimated at 40–60 billion francs – an order of magnitude comparable to worldwide bank credit losses during the recent financial crisis if upscaled accordingly. Overall, the Swiss banking sector managed to handle this crisis with relative ease, relying on its ample capital reserves (held largely in the form of hidden reserves at the time). Nevertheless, the crisis came as a major shock to the Swiss population and increased risk aversion in real estate and mortgage market behavior for the next two decades. One (small) bank failed, the *Spar- und Leihkasse Thun*, and several other banks in jeopardy were taken over by larger ones. A number of cantons, among them the cantons of Berne, Geneva, and Vaud, had to bail out their cantonal banks using taxpayers' money.

At first, the SNB's medium-term growth target seemed to perform its role as a policy indicator relatively well. While actual money stayed clearly below the target path, this was consistent with a below average level of money demand caused by high interest rates and low economic growth. In contrast, the medium-term money growth path signaled that, once inflation and nominal interest rates had returned to normal levels and output to full capacity, money would have to grow faster again to catch up with the increase in money demand resulting from these normalizations.

In 1991 and 1992, in the course of the German reunification, the German mark became very strong and the SNB, somewhat reluctantly, tightened policy. At this state inflation was still running at almost 5 percent. After mid-1992, however, as the real economy remained weak and the exchange rate had stabilized, the SNB returned to a more relaxed policy stance. By 1994, inflation had declined to about 2 percent and economic indicators slowly started to improve. However, doubts about the recovery persisted. The Swiss franc was on the rise again.

MISJUDGMENT OF THE BUSINESS CYCLE AND MONETARY OVERRESTRICTION: 1994–1995

What followed was one of the most controversial phases in Switzerland's recent monetary history. Rarely over the past few decades has the SNB been under such public pressure and exposed to as much criticism as was the case in these years. The level of central bank money was still well below the medium-term target path, signaling a need for lower interest rates and a more expansionary policy. Nevertheless, the SNB initially continued to follow a course which left interest rates unchanged at the level reached at the end of 1993. The main motivation for this was the fear of reigniting inflation in view of an expected cyclical recovery and the introduction of a new value added tax. It turned out that the strength of the recovery was overestimated, by the SNB as well by others, for 1994, and then again for

1995. With hindsight, it therefore became clear that the policy course pursued by the SNB was too restrictive.

In the spring of 1995, the SNB began to correct this error, motivated by renewed weakness in real economic activity and employment and the increasing strength of the Swiss franc. It let money market rates decline significantly and allowed central bank money to approach the target path from below. The latter had been extended for another five-year period by the beginning of 1995, but with a starting point that had been shifted downwards somewhat compared to the previous target path (to reflect a downward revision in the SNB's estimate of the economy's demand for central bank money).

The SNB was strongly criticized for its policy in 1994 and 1995, both at the time and afterward.[12] While this criticism is justified for 1994 – its policy was clearly too restrictive in retrospect – inspection of the facts shows that for 1995, it is not. The SNB first began to relax its policy at the end of 1994, and continued to loosen it decidedly after the spring of 1995. Contrary to a view often circulated in the media, thus, the policy change was also in effect in 1995, not only in 1996. Of course, results would have been better had the SNB changed its course in the summer of 1994.[13]

Many critics blamed this error on the monetary targeting framework to which the SNB still adhered at the time. The SNB was admonished for being a slave to its "monetarist" convictions and traditions. This criticism has no basis in this case, however. In fact, in 1994 the SNB's money indicator (being far below its target value) gave the appropriate signal (pointing to the need for a more expansionary policy), but was overruled in the SNB's decision process by other indicators supporting a different course (Rich, 2007, p. 320). Decisive motivations in this were a misjudgment of the cyclical developments of the economy – the business cycle expectations of the SNB and most other forecasters were too optimistic – and the fear of reigniting inflation. The latter fear, again, was not totally ungrounded at the time. The influence of the new value added tax has been mentioned. In addition, the experience of 1980/1 – when the SNB had been too tardy in switching to a restrictive stance, thus sparking a reacceleration of inflation – was still well remembered by many observers, and expected inflation in 1994 was thus not firmly anchored at a low and stable level.

---

[12] See, e.g., Ettlin and Gaillard (2001).
[13] For a detailed discussion, see Baltensperger (2007), pp. 592–6.

The SNB's policy of 1994 without doubt bears part of the responsibility for the extended weakness of the Swiss economy during the 1990s. Monetary policy was only part of the picture, however, and has often been blamed too exclusively for all Switzerland's economic woes in this period. Lagging structural reform in many areas of public policy – notably the consolidation of public finances and various social policy programs, and the removal of domestic and international barriers to market access – were at least as important, in all likelihood. Also, we should not forget that the origin of the problems of 1994/5 was the monetary overexpansion of the late 1980s. Had this overexpansion not occurred, the subsequent surge in inflation and the resulting need for monetary correction, with its stabilization and banking crises, including the difficulties of 1994/5, could have been avoided. This correction was no mistake: It was painfully needed. But, as with all such corrections, it had its costs.

RETURN TO NORMALITY AND TRANSITION TO A NEW MONETARY POLICY FRAMEWORK

The years after 1996 up to the end of the decade were marked by a gradual return to normality for the Swiss economy and the SNB's monetary policy. Inflation, interest rates, and the exchange rate all returned to levels consistent with long-run experience. Growth and employment remained weak for some time; by the end of the decade, however, full employment was more or less restored. The worldwide boom of the late 1990s, with its technology and stock market exuberance, was helpful in this, of course. In terms of monetary policy, these years were unproblematic, apart from occasional temporary turbulence created by the Asian and Russian crises in 1997/8 (which, obviously, was not specific to Switzerland).

Given the difficulties experienced over the 1990s, the use of money as the main indicator variable for monetary policy decisions was increasingly questioned, both inside and outside the SNB. While actual money had persistently stayed below the target line in the first phase of medium-term targeting (for reasons which could be explained), it was allowed to grow far beyond this line in the second phase, apparently without causing inflation pressure or other problems (for reasons which were much more difficult to identify this time). The demand for central bank money had become highly unstable, and explaining and predicting its movements and its information content increasingly difficult. The medium-term target path consequently proved less and less useful as a guide for monetary policy decisions. Beyond this, it was also less and less successful as a communication device.[14] In view of the large and prolonged deviations of actual money from the target path set, it became increasingly difficult to convince the public that the target line was really a meaningful and effective constraint on monetary policy and carried information about the future course of monetary policy.[15] At the operational level, in this period the SNB increasingly moved from control of aggregate bank reserves to policy implementation via the control of a short-term interest rate (in accordance with usual central bank practice).

These developments caused the SNB to investigate alternative frameworks and procedures for its policy analysis and actions. In December 1999, it announced its decision to abandon monetary targeting and change to a new policy concept, effective January 2000.[16] The new approach was centered on inflation forecasts as the major indicator for monetary policymaking. It was based on three central elements:

- First, price stability continued to be the primary objective of monetary policy. Price stability was defined as an increase in the CPI of "less than 2 percent." As deflation was explicitly excluded as undesirable, a reasonable interpretation of this formulation defines price stability as an inflation rate between 0 and 2 percent. In this respect, the new concept represented a continuation of the old approach. For the SNB, the monetary target had never been an end in itself, but had always been considered an instrument in the pursuit of its ultimate objective: price stability.

- The second element was the quarterly publication of a broad-based inflation forecast over a horizon of up to three years, to be used as the SNB's main indicator in its policy decisions. If the forecast indicated a violation of the price stability range under current policy conditions, monetary policy was to be reviewed. The SNB never reacted mechanically to the inflation forecast, however, but always took into account the general economic situation in determining its policy reaction. The

---

[14] Rich (2007, pp. 313–19) presents a detailed and careful analysis of the SNB's medium-term targeting approach and its role in the SNB's policymaking and communication.

[15] One rather ironic aspect of this period is that, at a time when the SNB's main communication problem involved explaining to the public the deviations of actual money growth from its money growth target path, it was frequently criticized for being a prisoner of its allegedly purist "monetarist" beliefs.

[16] For detailed discussions of the SNB's monetary policy "concept 2000" see, e.g., Baltensperger et al. (2007) or the contributions in Swiss Society of Economics and Statistics (ed.) (2010).

SNB continued to consider the price stability goal as a medium- to long-term commitment; for the short term, it reserved the right to respond flexibly.

- Third, at an operational level, the SNB now implemented its policy by fixing and announcing a target range for three-month Libor in Swiss francs (the most important money market rate for Swiss franc investments). Normally, this range had a width of one hundred basis points. A more restrictive monetary policy meant raising this target range, and vice versa. Additionally, the SNB determined and announced in which area of this fairly wide band it wished Libor to remain. This generally tended to be the mid-point of the announced target range. The SNB regularly reviewed its target range in view of its inflation forecast.

The SNB's new policy concept was based on what may be called the core ideas of inflation targeting – an approach to monetary policy-making that was pioneered by the Reserve Bank of New Zealand and successfully adopted over the 1990s by a number of other central banks, among them the Bank of England. However, the SNB adopted these ideas in a moderate and flexible form only. It consciously avoided the "narrow" adoption of such an approach – characterized by short-term inflation targets fixed from year to year and by a complete neglect of monetary aggregates in monetary policy decision-making – practiced by numerous central banks, for example, the Bank of England, at the time. The SNB, instead, wanted to stress a medium- and longer-term horizon and its continued interest in observing monetary aggregates as potentially relevant information variables for its inflation forecasts. Beyond this, it wanted to emphasize its responsibility to itself define, within its legal mandate, the concrete meaning of "price stability" – similar to the ECB, but in contrast to, e.g., the Bank of England, to which the inflation target was annually given by the government. For these reasons, the SNB consciously refrained from using the term "inflation targeting" to characterize its new framework. Generally, it wanted to stress the continuity of its policy in the context of a changed strategy.

One particularity of the SNB's approach was the use of a (fairly wide) target range for its operational interest rate target. The justification for announcing a range, rather than a point target, was that it allows the SNB to react flexibly to shocks, especially foreign exchange market shocks or problems regarding liquidity distribution, without signaling a change in its basic policy perspective. Such flexibility was deemed indispensable for a small open economy with an internationally important currency and financial market. Another peculiarity of the SNB's approach to interest rate control was the use of a three-month rate for unsecured loans, rather than the risk-free overnight rate, which the SNB can control directly. Again, this allows short-run flexibility, implying "automatic" reactions in the overnight rate in cases of disturbed money market conditions and resulting variations of risk premiums.[17]

The development and introduction of the SNB's new monetary policy framework coincided with a reform of the constitutional and legal foundations of the National Bank and its policies. On January 1, 2000, a reform of the Swiss federal constitution became effective which, among other things, changed the constitutional article on money and currency. The new article (article 99 of the revised constitution), and a new act on currency and payment instruments based on it *(Währungs- und Zahlungsmittelgesetz* of May 2000), rescinded the – up to this point formally still valid – official gold parity of the Swiss franc and the corresponding gold coverage regulations for the SNB. By doing so, the article and act legally sealed the Swiss franc's separation from gold, which had, for all practical purposes, already taken place in January 1973.[18] This also freed the way for a revaluation of the SNB's gold reserves, and for the subsequent sale of an important part of these gold reserves in the context of a rescaling and diversification of the country's international reserves. The new constitutional article also established, in a formal way, the SNB's independence from government and private interest groups. A new National Bank Act (*Nationalbankgesetz* of May 2004), based on the new constitution, spelled out a clear mandate for the central bank, obliging the SNB to maintain price stability as its prior objective while taking account of cyclical developments. As a counterpart to the SNB's independence, its accountability to the public and politics was explicitly stipulated.

A CHANGED MONETARY ENVIRONMENT: FORMATION OF THE EUROZONE

The introduction of the euro at the beginning of the year 1999 marked an important change in the international environment for Swiss monetary policy. In the phase leading up to the EMU, and even more so after its actual inception, numerous commentators predicted that the SNB would

---

[17] Kohli (2010, p. 428) speaks of an "automatic stabilizer" property of the system in this context.

[18] Up to the year 2000 formally based on "emergency legislation."

gradually lose its ability to pursue an autonomous monetary policy in view of the growing importance of the euro. The newly created common European money would establish itself as a parallel currency in Switzerland before long and eventually displace the Swiss franc altogether, many argued. Impressed by the sheer size of the European economic space, they thought an independent role for the Swiss franc would become impossible. Up to now, these fears have been proven wrong.

In fact, over the first ten years of its existence, the euro did establish itself as a reliable and stable currency, thanks to responsible, stability-oriented policies on the part of the newly created European Central Bank (ECB). The euro's international role as an investment and reserve currency strongly grew in importance. However, no major disadvantages for Swiss monetary policy resulted from these developments. Quite the reverse – if anything, a stable euro, and in particular the disappearance of highly unstable former partner currencies like the Italian lira, made the SNB's task less difficult. Age-old experience was reconfirmed that an established currency is not easily displaced as a domestic means of payment unless it suffers from extreme weakness itself, and that "small" currencies can well survive next to much "bigger" ones without being subject to automatic erosion. The use of currencies is strongly influenced by "network effects," and multiple currencies are linked to high costs.

Much more challenging to Switzerland is the reverse problem, caused in the more recent past by increasing instability of the eurozone. The high economic and social heterogeneity of eurozone member countries represented major risks and potential structural tensions for the eurozone from the beginning. These dormant problems fully revealed themselves with the European debt crisis of 2010/11. In the course of this crisis, the ECB increasingly became subject to political pressures originating from fiscal and other woes of eurozone member states, casting a shadow on the ECB as an institution and doubt on the euro as a currency. As a consequence, the Swiss franc came under immense upward pressure – the biggest challenge to Swiss monetary policy at the moment, and probably for some time to come.

In the year 2000, shortly after the introduction of the SNB's new monetary policy concept, increasing inflationary pressures reflected in its inflation forecast and strong signals of cyclical acceleration induced the SNB to tighten its policy. It raised the mid-point of its target range for Libor in several steps, from 1.75 percent to 3.5 percent, in June 2000. This policy adjustment allowed the SNB to maintain inflation below the critical mark of 2 percent. At the same time, it enabled it to demonstrate its willingness and ability to pursue an autonomous policy vis-à-vis the newly created ECB.

In the following year, the situation changed drastically, first as a result of the stock market decline in the spring and summer of 2001, and then even more so with the terrorist attacks of September 11 and the political turbulence that followed. This caused the SNB to reverse its policy by lowering the mid-point of its interest rate target band in several steps. The deterioration in worldwide economic conditions and its dampening effect on inflation prospects, including the discussion of fears regarding deflation in the United States and elsewhere, led the SNB to make additional interest rate cuts, resulting in a Libor target band of 0.0–0.75 percent, with a target value around 0.25 percent, in March 2003. This extremely loose monetary policy was maintained until mid-2004. In summer 2004, the SNB started to slowly normalize monetary conditions; however, with the economy still weak, this process was soon interrupted again. In early 2006, with economic conditions clearly improving, the SNB began to raise the mid-point of its target range, bringing it up in several steps to 2.75 percent in September 2007. This level was maintained throughout most of 2008, in the face of growing signs of an impending global financial crisis.

INTERDEPENDENCE OF MONETARY, FISCAL, AND POLITICAL STABILITY

There is no question that overall, the SNB's policy approach and performance during the flexible exchange rate phase, from 1973 up to the outbreak of the financial crisis in 2008, has been remarkably successful. The SNB's inflation record across this entire period is outstanding among the major central banks. There were extended periods in which inflation consistently remained low, such as between 1982 and 1988 – at a time when this was not the case in many other countries in the industrialized world – and then again from 1993 to the present (see Figure 7.2). The SNB has successfully managed to establish an environment of confidence and credibility. Together with the stability of the country's political system, this has been a major force in creating financial tranquility and a level of nominal and real interest rates which has consistently stayed below that in other currency areas (Figure 7.3).

Nevertheless, the SNB's monetary policy over this period was also marred by a number of failures, and turned out to be quite controversial in certain phases, as we have seen. In particular, there were surges of inflation in 1980-1 and then again in 1988-90. In both cases, this

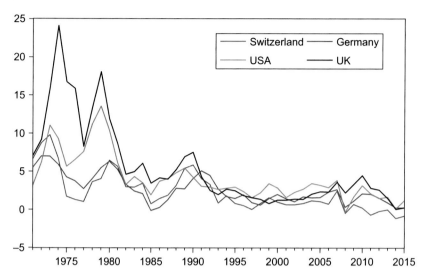

Figure 7.2: Inflation 1971–2015 (yearly averages, in %)
Source: SNB data, https://data.snb.ch/de/topics/aube#!/cube/iukpaus

necessitated subsequent phases of monetary tightening and consolidation, with the usual resulting stabilization costs. In the early 1990s, especially, this – together with tardy structural reforms in areas of the real economy – contributed to economic recession and sluggish growth. In 1994, the SNB's exaggerated insistence on monetary restriction prolonged economic weakness. By the end of the 1990s, however, the SNB had successfully managed to shift its policy to an approach based on inflation forecasts and policy implementation via the control of a short-term money market rate. Experiences with this approach, up to the financial crisis, have been very positive. The outbreak of this crisis, however, changed policy conditions on a worldwide scale, Switzerland being no exception.

The comparative success of the SNB's monetary policy and that of the Swiss franc on the exchange market is strongly dependent on the political stability of the country and the fact that the Swiss population has supported a system of fiscal stability and moderation over a long period of time. Monetary, fiscal, and political stability are mutually dependent. A sound monetary order can hardly arise and survive under unstable economic and political conditions. Disordered currencies, conversely, damage the efficiency of the economic system and can lead to economic and political decay in the extreme. Switzerland has been fortunate in this respect. Apart from a brief encounter with fiscal pressures on SNB policy

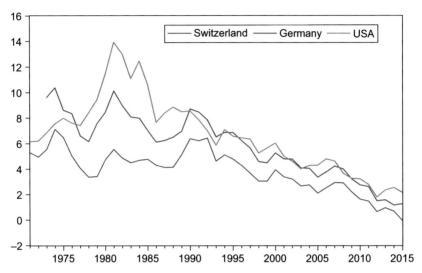

Figure 7.3: Yields on government bonds (10 years), 1970–2015
Source: SNB Monthly Statistical Bulletin, Table E4, www.snb.ch/de/iabout/stat/statrep/statpubdis/id/
statpub_statmon_arch_xls_de; Deutsche Bundesbank, Zeitreihe Umlaufsrenditen, www.bundesbank
.de/statistik/statistik_zeitreihen.php?lang=de&open=zinsen&func=row&tr=WU8612; FED, Selected
Interest Rates, www.federalreserve.gov/releases/h15/data.htm; SNB data, https://data.snb.ch/en/
topics/ziredev#!/cube/rendoblid

during World War I, fiscal dominance of monetary policy has never been a
serious concern over the past hundred years. Swiss voters have shown great
respect for fiscal responsibility and soundness in economic policy in
general. Taxation and government debt have stayed comparatively moderate, with the latter even formally constrained through a constitutional
"debt brake" introduced at the federal level in 2001, after a brief flirtation
with fiscal irresponsibility and overextension during the 1990s. The political institutions of direct democracy have been a major force in creating
these conditions and, as a consequence, an environment permitting the
SNB to successfully pursue its course of monetary stability.

MONETARY POLICY IN THE FINANCIAL AND EURO CRISES

In autumn 2008, when financial market conditions dramatically worsened
and a collapse of the international banking and finance system appeared
imminent, the SNB, in line with other important central banks, changed
course quickly and decisively. In view of an impending breakdown of

worldwide interbank lending markets, its measures were initially concentrated strongly on ensuring functional money markets and an adequate provision of liquidity to the economy. As the crisis went on, preventing a sharp decline in real economic activity – and another Great Depression – became of paramount importance. In 2010/11, the European debt crisis – with payments crises in Greece, Ireland, and Portugal, and possible contagion to other highly indebted nations, particularly Italy and Spain – entered the scene as an additional source of disruption.

The near-collapse of the international financial system also meant that industrial countries' central banks became involved, in a way unknown since the 1930s, in efforts to save and stabilize banks and ensure financial stability. In Switzerland, a spectacular intervention by the Confederation and the Swiss National Bank in support of the globally active big bank UBS took place in October 2008. The Confederation injected 6 billion Swiss francs of fresh capital, and the SNB set up a fund with the purpose of absorbing up to 60 billion US dollars' worth of bad assets from UBS.[19] Given the economic significance and the international interconnectedness of UBS, the necessity and urgency of this measure was generally accepted in Switzerland. Yet, great uneasiness prevailed among the public; the fact that the central bank had to intervene on such a scale in a bank saving measure was understood to be a deficiency and led Switzerland to assume a tough stance in forthcoming discussions of "too big to fail" regulation.

Between October 2008 and end-2008, partly in coordination with other central banks, the SNB reduced its target Libor band, in several steps, to 0–1 percent, a reduction of its target rate of 225 basis points. In March 2009, the target band was narrowed to 0–0.75 percent and the target rate set at 0.25 percent. In August 2009, finally, the target range was further reduced to 0–0.25 percent, with a target rate "as close to zero as possible." As time went on, these interest rate measures were supplemented by substantial "quantitative easing" – direct central bank purchases of assets in the markets – in the Swiss case mostly in the form of foreign exchange acquisitions. In the first half of 2010, the SNB bought euro assets for more than 100 billion Swiss francs – an operation which met strong public criticism later on due to the accounting losses that resulted from it.

Fundamental weaknesses of the euro, and simultaneously of the US dollar, increasingly put upward pressure on the Swiss franc, which was increasingly viewed by investors as playing a pronounced "safe haven" role in these

---

[19] In November 2013 the SNB sold this fund back to UBS, thus bringing an unorthodox and challenging measure to a successful and profitable end.

uncertain times (while it had been valued relatively weakly in the years before 2008). A massive wave of franc appreciation in the summer of 2011, of a magnitude and speed unknown in recent times – at the end of 2009, the euro had been valued at about 1.50 francs; in August/September 2011 it was temporarily down to almost parity – caused the SNB to declare a lower limit of 1.20 Swiss francs for the euro on September 6, 2011. This exchange rate floor, which the SNB announced it would enforce by all available means, subsequently shaped Swiss monetary policy for over three years, until mid-January 2015. The SNB's justification for this step was that a policy of non-intervention would have implied sharply tightened monetary conditions and a great risk of irreversible damage to the Swiss real economy. The SNB was careful to set the floor on the euro at a level which, in fundamental and purchasing power terms, still represented a very high valuation for the franc. By firmly defending the 1.20 floor, the central bank provided a minimum level of security in planning for Swiss enterprises and stability for the Swiss economy. For these reasons, the policy received strong public support, which was crucially important for its credibility and effectiveness.

In the first year of its new course, the SNB had to enforce the 1.20 floor by actually intervening in the market on a large scale. In spring and summer 2012, the euro crisis intensified, aggravating the weakness of the euro. In the second and third quarters of 2012, the SNB had to acquire foreign exchange for about 180 billion Swiss francs. The SNB's unconditional enforcement of the 1.20 floor was soon successful, however, creating high credibility and acceptance in the market. For an extended period of time – until December 2014/January 2015 – there was no need for further large-scale intervention. The real Swiss economy developed well, generating high employment and growth, with inflation staying very low or even slightly negative.

The exchange rate floor was explicitly adopted by the SNB as a temporary measure in view of a highly disoriented and uncertain global exchange market situation, not as a permanent change in its fundamental monetary policy course. It was never understood by the SNB as a departure from its tradition of monetary autonomy. Rather, it represented the SNB's view of the optimum response such autonomy permits in an international environment of extreme monetary turbulence.

On January 15, 2015, in an announcement that took the markets completely by surprise, the SNB declared the end of its minimum exchange rate policy. Over the weeks preceding this decision, a new wave of euro-zone problems centered on Greece, combined with the expectation of massive euro liquidity creation through ECB purchases of member country government bonds, had forced the SNB to absorb large amounts of foreign exchange once again in defense of its 1.20 euro rate floor. In December 2014, reacting to a similar measure by the ECB, the SNB had already announced the introduction of a negative interest rate on sight deposit account balances (in excess of a certain exemption threshold) at the SNB. On January 15, 2015, it set this interest rate at –0.75 percent. At the same time, it lowered its three-month Libor target band to –1.25 percent to –0.25 percent.

The discontinuation of the SNB's minimum exchange rate policy caused strong reactions both in the markets and in public discussion. The Swiss franc appreciated sharply against all other currencies. Although a considerable short-term overshooting was soon corrected, the franc remained very highly valued, at least vis-à-vis the euro. Public opinion was split between massive disapproval on the one hand – especially on the part of representatives of the export sector, trade unions, and the political left – and applause on the other – particularly from those who had always expressed a preference for a monetary policy more distant from that of the eurozone. It is clear that the abolition of the exchange rate floor was a major shock to the Swiss economy and that the resulting exchange rate conditions presented a difficult challenge for Swiss enterprises and policymakers. Obviously, however, medium- to long-term developments – including changes in relative levels of nominal prices and wages, in addition to nominal exchange rates – will be much more decisive than immediate, short-term market reactions.

In our opinion, the SNB had good reason to abandon its exchange rate floor policy in January 2015. The international monetary environment had changed strongly since the time that it was introduced. In 2011, both Europe and the United States were widely considered to be in a very weak state. At times, the debate about the US federal government's debt ceiling assumed nearly apocalyptic dimensions. Consequently, not only the euro but also the dollar tended toward pronounced weakness – the dollar frequently even against the euro. The Swiss franc was viewed by many as the only remaining safe currency and became an object of desire and wild speculation, losing all relationship to the real Swiss economy that it represents. With its exchange rate floor, the SNB had to set a firm mark for completely dysfunctional currency markets.

In early 2015, the situation was once again very different. The United States had overcome its main problems and managed, to a considerable degree, to return to economic stability and success. A normalization of US monetary policy was widely expected, and the US dollar had refound a position of strength. The world was again much closer to a state in which international capital flows are driven by interest rate differentials and other economically comprehensible factors, rather than merely by phobia and rumors. Rationally viewed, given relative interest rate conditions, the dollar was the more interesting currency for investors in 2015 than the Swiss franc. Under similar conditions, the SNB would hardly have taken resort to a minimum exchange rate policy in 2011. In Europe, on the other hand, the ECB increasingly turned to an extremely expansionary and risky policy aimed more or less openly at a weakening of the European currency. Terminating Swiss monetary policy's unconditional dependence on ECB policy thus became almost imperative for the SNB. The minimum exchange rate policy became increasingly unsustainable. Had the SNB maintained it for longer, it would have run a high risk of losing long-term control over its balance sheet, and thus over future monetary conditions in Switzerland.

Additional support for the introduction of the exchange rate floor in 2011 and its abandonment in early 2015 is provided by our econometric analysis of the trend in the real exchange rate given in Chapter 11 (see Figures 11.2 and 11.5 and Table 11.4). If we use the trend-adjusted PPP model documented there in order to calculate long-run equilibrium exchange rates for late summer 2011, we obtain values of 1.39 for the euro, 1.08 for the dollar, and 1.65 for the pound, respectively. The actual exchange rates were 1.12 (euro), 0.78 (dollar), and 1.28 (pound), indicating a very strong over-valuation of the Swiss franc against all these currencies at that time. Conditions in late 2014, in comparison, were completely different: The pairs of actual versus equilibrium exchange rate values were 1.20 and 1.26 for the euro, 0.97 and 0.99 for the dollar, and 1.55 and 1.53 for the pound, respectively.

As is the case for most other countries, even without further prolongation of the minimum exchange rate regime, the monetary policy pursued over the crisis years has created huge growth in the SNB's balance sheet and in the liquidity held by Swiss banks and the Swiss economy. The SNB's balance sheet grew from 127 billion Swiss francs at the end of 2007 to 640 billion francs by the end of 2015 – growth of a factor of five. Over the same period, Swiss banks' reserves with the SNB increased from 8.7 billion to 402 billion francs. The SNB's foreign exchange reserves grew from about 50 billion by the end of 2007 or 47 billion by the end of 2008 to 593 billion francs by the end of 2015. Only the future will show whether, and to what extent, central banks will again successfully rein in this huge liquidity without creating inflation, once the situation normalizes and the demand for liquidity recedes to more usual levels. There is no doubt that they possess the instruments necessary for doing so. Whether they will be willing and politically able to use these instruments in due course remains to be seen.

PART III

KEY QUESTIONS AND GENERAL INSIGHTS
FROM SWISS MONETARY EXPERIENCE

Part II of this book reviewed the monetary history of Switzerland from a chronological point of view, describing the circumstances of the Swiss franc's creation as the country's national currency in the nineteenth century and its subsequent ascent, over the twentieth century, to the status of one of the most successful and stable currencies of the world. Part III, as a complement, takes up a number of issues and questions of general interest, looking at them from a more fundamental and analytical perspective. These issues are, first, the Swiss experience with currency and banknote-issue competition in the nineteenth century; second, the stability and structural breaks in Swiss money demand and supply over different monetary regimes; third, the (generally low) level of Swiss interest rates in international comparison (often referred to as the "Swiss interest rate island"); fourth, the behaviour of the Swiss franc's exchange rate under different monetary regimes in the nineteenth and twentieth centuries; and, finally, the contribution of Swiss banks to economic performance and stability, including also the role of capital imports and exports. These central issues of Swiss monetary and financial history are covered in separate chapters in Part III of this book.

In recent years, a number of new statistical series on various financial and economic data have become available, covering the entire period under consideration, or at least important parts of it. Utilizing these and other ("older") data, we are able to provide interesting new information on some of the key questions concerning the history and role of the Swiss franc and the Swiss monetary system. These investigations unavoidably include a certain amount of technical analysis. In consequence, Part III is written at a somewhat more demanding, formal level, in comparison to the preceding Part II of the book.

8

The Swiss Experience with Currency and
Note-Issue Competition 1825–1905

The roles of competition and monopoly in matters of currency and money have been a subject of economic discussion for a long time. Is it advisable to grant government a monopoly in currency, note issue, and their regulation? Or should we, conversely, allow free competition between issuers of money and banknotes? Note that the question of monopoly and competition arises at a number of different levels: first, and most fundamentally, with regard to the definition of the monetary unit and the right of coinage; second, with regard to the issue of paper money in the form of banknotes; third, and finally, in connection with the creation of money in the form of bank (demand) deposits. Swiss monetary experience of the nineteenth century offers a wealth of interesting insights into the first two of these questions.

Historically, the view has become dominant that money exhibits public good-type features, in particular strong network effects, and as a consequence is characterized by a tendency toward centralization and monopoly, justifying government intervention.[1] The majority view among contemporaneous economists clearly coincides with such a position.[2] Swiss monetary history of the nineteenth century, as we will see, is consistent with this view.

THREE PHASES OF CURRENCY AND
NOTE-ISSUE COMPETITION

In 1850, Switzerland decided in favor of a centralized government monopoly at the first level mentioned above, with the creation of the Swiss franc

---

[1] For just one reference, see, e.g., Friedman (1960), p. 8.

[2] Nevertheless, there is also a minority position arguing in favor of competition in the provision of money. The most ardent modern proponent of this view was Hayek (1978).

as the national currency of the new federal state. With regard to banknote issue, on the other hand, Switzerland retained competition until 1905, when the Swiss National Bank was founded. Nevertheless, a crucial break took place in 1881, when the previously unregulated competition in banknote issue became heavily regulated under the new Federal Banknote Act.[3] From the perspective of money and note-issue competition, thus, Swiss monetary experience in the nineteenth century can be divided into three separate and interesting phases:

- The period from 1825 to 1850, a period of "true" currency competition without a single, dominant currency and with free choice of currency denomination in banknote issue.[4]
- The period from 1850 to 1881, a period of unfettered free banking with unregulated competition between a large number of private and public note issue banks, but now with a common, dominant (although not yet legally prescribed) currency, the new Swiss franc.[5]
- The period from 1881 to 1905, a period of limited banking freedom, with the Swiss franc now prescribed as the common currency denomination in banknote issue and strong regulation of the note-issue business (but as yet without a national monopoly in banknote issue).[6]

NOTE-ISSUE COMPETITION WITHOUT A COMMON,
DOMINANT CURRENCY: 1825–1850

Prior to 1850, Switzerland offered a rare example of real currency competition, with free choice of currency denomination in banknote issue, comparable to the blueprint proposed by Hayek in his well-known contribution of 1978. Between 1825 and 1850, eight note-issue banks came into existence in Switzerland: two in Berne (in 1825 and 1834, respectively); one each in Zürich (1836), St. Gallen (1837), Basel (1844), and Vaud (1845); and two in Geneva (1846, 1848). The non-existence of a national currency and the multitude of circulating monies and coins offered these banks great freedom in selecting the currency base of the banknotes they issued.

---

[3]   As far as the creation of money in the form of bank deposits is concerned, Switzerland – like virtually all other countries – has kept a competitive system to date.
[4]   Comparable to Hayek's 1978 proposal.
[5]   In terms of modern deposit money, this is comparable to a banking system with free, unregulated competition in the deposit business.
[6]   In terms of modern deposit money, this is comparable to a banking system with heavily regulated competition in the deposit business.

As Weber (1988) has shown, they chose among the most stable of the currencies in use at the time, that is, they made their notes convertible into one of these at fixed terms. In that period, these were foreign currencies (see Table 8.1 for the currency base of the notes of different banks). Weber interprets this as evidence in favor of Hayek's conjecture.[7] Demand for a bank's notes was dependent on the expected purchasing power and acceptance of these notes, hence on the choice of their currency denomination. In consequence, competition forced banks to link their notes to a currency with large circulation and stable purchasing power, preventing over-issue and debasement of notes. As a result, the paper money issued by these banks was stable in terms of purchasing power. Furthermore, there were no major bank failures or financial crises. In this sense, this experiment can be deemed a success and an example in support of a competitive system.

On the negative side, this positive judgment is counterbalanced by the fact that throughout this period the demand for banknotes remained small, and banks' note-issue business unimportant.[8] Economic agents apparently did not see too much advantage in using banknotes rather than coin. Especially in rural areas and for small, everyday transactions, the banknote remained unimportant as a means of payment. Coins retained their status as the "real" money, with the banknote an imperfect and not overly attractive substitute.[9] The high costs of note issue and circulation, notably the high metal reserves (voluntarily) maintained for reasons of confidence-building, also constrained the growth of the note-issue business. For the Bank in Zürich, according to Bleuler (1913), average yearly metal reserves varied between 35 and 77 percent of its note circulation (see Table 8.2).

UNREGULATED NOTE-ISSUE COMPETITION WITH A COMMON, DOMINANT CURRENCY: 1850–1881

The monetary reform of 1850 brought an important change. After its introduction, the Swiss franc established itself quickly and without

---

[7] It is important to note, however, that the foreign currencies used in Switzerland at the time were backed by foreign government bodies. In this sense, the system was not entirely private, but still based on public authority (though not a Swiss one), in the final analysis.

[8] According to Weber (1992, p. 193), the average shares of banknotes in the balance sheets of Swiss note-issue banks during the decade of the 1830s were 4.4 percent for cantonal banks and 19.2 percent for private banks. In the decade of the 1840s, the corresponding numbers were 3.5 percent for cantonal banks and 25.2 percent for private banks.

[9] Ritzmann (1973), p. 42.

Table 8.1: *Swiss issuers of paper money, 1825–1850*

Issuing bank	Year [a]	Proprietor of bank	Currency unit [b]	Banknote circulation end of year		
				1830	1840	1850
1. Deposito-Cassa der Stadt Bern	1825 1825	City of Berne	Old Swiss franc	88	170	87
2. Kantonalbank von Bern	1834 1834	Canton Berne	Écu	-	217	200
3. Bank in Zürich	1836 1837	Private	Brabant thaler	-	873	1651
4. Bank in St. Gallen	1837 1838	Private	Imperial guilder	-	[c] 598	[d] 1967
5. Bank in Basel	1844 1845	Private	French franc	-		1179
6. Banque du Commerce de Genève	1846 1846	Private	French franc	-	-	2025
7. Banque Cantonale Vaudoise	1845 1847	Mixed public/private	Écu	-	-	350
8. Banque de Genève	1848 1848	Mixed public/private	French franc	-	-	328

Note: (a) first line: year of foundation, second line: year of first issue; (b) 1,000 Swiss franc; (c) average September; (d) average October.
Source: Weber (1988), p. 462, based on Jöhr (1915)

Table 8.2: *Metal reserve ratio of Bank in Zürich, 1838–1850*

Year	r1	r2
1838	-	0.26
1839	-	0.43
1840	0.41	0.61
1841	0.52	0.28
1842	0.35	0.43
1843	0.67	0.33
1844	0.54	0.46
1845	0.53	0.24
1846	0.37	0.46
1847	0.41	0.34
1848	0.65	0.47
1849	0.77	0.74
1850	0.66	0.29

Note: Ratio of metal monetary reserves to banknotes in circulation and checking accounts. r1: yearly average of monthly values; r2: end-of-year values.
Source: Weber (1988), p. 471, based on Bleuler (1913)

difficulty as the new federal state's national currency. The transition from the old chaos of currencies and coins to a common national money obviously reflected a strong public desire for this and helped greatly to improve the efficiency of the Swiss currency and payments system and the strength of the Swiss economy overall.

Legally, Swiss note-issuing banks were still allowed to issue notes denominated in foreign currencies. A few banks did make use of this possibility for some time, in addition to issuing notes in Swiss francs. However, with the Swiss franc now firmly established as the dominant national currency, the demand for foreign currency notes more or less vanished; in consequence, this practice was soon terminated.

The period from 1850 to 1881 thus can be characterized as a period of free, unregulated note-issue competition, but now with a common, dominant currency, the Swiss franc. The authority to license and regulate banks still belonged to the cantons: No federal restrictions existed until 1881. The cantons were liberal in admitting new banks and in regulating their business. As a consequence, a large number of note-issuing banks competing with each other entered the market, some private and some public, the latter in the form of cantonal banks established by the cantons themselves.

In 1881, no less than thirty-six note-issue banks existed.[10] The cantonal banks were not granted a monopoly or other privileges by their cantons,[11] so the note-issue business remained strongly competitive. Banks had to meet some cantonal standards concerning liquidity and capital reserves, but according to all observers these standards were aimed at product safety and customer confidence, and not at preventing competition.[12]

Weber (1992), in an analysis of the Swiss free banking experience before 1881, comes to a favorable verdict as to its results. Note-issue competition, he argues, created a monetary environment that was successful in stabilizing the purchasing power of banknotes at the level of that of metal money while (almost) avoiding financial turbulence and bank failures.[13] There was no over-issue of notes, because in a competitive system the supply of notes with declining purchasing power would not have been successful, forcing banks to stay honest. Increasing costs of note issue prevented the rise of a monopoly, he further argues. The number of issue banks stayed large and the degree of concentration remained low.

Weber emphasizes that under free entry, note issue was guided by benefit-cost considerations. New banks only entered the note-issue business if its expected return was not inferior to that of competing economic activities. Incidentally, the large part of Swiss banks of the period did not issue notes, including important banks such as the *Schweizerische Kreditanstalt* (today's Credit Suisse), founded in 1856. The reason was not that they were not allowed to; rather, they voluntarily decided not to engage in this activity. Some banks included banknote issue in their statutes as a potential field of operation, but never decided to actually take up this option.[14]

---

[10] Jöhr (1915) presented a comprehensive list of all Swiss note-issuing banks between 1825 and 1906; see Table 8.3.

[11] For one exceptional, though unsuccessful, attempt to grant such a monopoly, see note 29 in Chapter 2.

[12] See, for instance, Jöhr (1915), Ritzmann (1973), and Weber (1988, 1992).

[13] Switzerland was not totally exempt from banking problems in this period, though. However, these problems had little to do with banks' note-issue business. In 1870, the Banque Cantonale du Valais failed as a result of the financing of public (cantonal) deficits and bad investments (causing a political scandal involving the resignation of several cantonal government members). The Banque Générale Suisse, founded in 1853 in Geneva after the model of the French Crédit Mobilier, had to suspend payments in 1859 and was liquidated in 1869. The Eidgenössische Bank, founded in 1864 in Berne, had to be restructured at the end of the 1870s.

[14] E.g., the Bank in Winterthur (the predecessor bank of today's UBS).

Table 8.3: *Swiss issuers of paper money, 1825–1906*

Banks	(A)	(B)	Banknotes[a]						
			1840	1850	1860	1870	1880	1890	1900
I Commercial banks									
1 Bank in Zürich	1837–1906	1837–1894	873	1,651	2,154	1,753	4,964	19,873	–
2 Bank in St. Gallen	1837–1907	1838–1907	598	1,967	1,580	1,364	3,986	8,984	17,860
3 Bank in Basel	1844–1907	1845–1907	–	1,179	809	1,277	7,874	19,687	23,825
4 Banque du Commerce de Genève	1846–1907	1846–1907	–	2,025	1,798	3,172	16,214	19,915	23,903
5 Banque de Genève	1848	1848–1899	–	328	927	1,526	4,657	4,820	–
6 Banque Cantonale Neuchâteloise [b]	1855–1883	1855–1883	–	–	1,372	1,982	5,935	–	–
7 Banque Générale Suisse	1853–1869	1857–1869	–	–	58	–	–	–	–
8 Eidgenössische Bank	1864	1864–1882	–	–	–	933	4,883	–	–
9 Banque Commercial Neuchâteloise	1883–1907	1883–1907	–	–	–	–	–	3,352	7,969
II Cantonal banks									
10 Kantonalbank von Bern	1834	1834–1910	217	200	579	1,685	7,644	9,692	19,463
11 Banque Cantonale Vaudoise	1846	1847–1910	–	350	3,666	3,385	5,054	9,874	11,384
12 Aargauische Bank	1855	1856–1910	–	–	250	315	2,610	3,961	5,888
13 Banque Cantonale du Valais	1858–1870	1858–1870	–	–	399	–	–	–	–
14 Solothurnische Kantonalbank [c]	1857	1858–1910	–	–	138	388	2,020	3,984	4,954
15 Basellandschaftliche Kantonalbank	1864	1867–1910	–	–	–	28	713	1,499	1,989
16 St. Gallische Kantonalbank	1868	1868–1910	–	–	–	1,418	5,948	9,982	13,981
17 Zürcher Kantonalbank	1870	1870–1910	–	–	–	1,897	14,042	23,653	29,328
18 Thurgauische Kantonalbank	1871	1871–1910	–	–	–	–	1,289	1,483	4,974

(continued)

Table 8.3 (continued)

Banks	(A)	(B)	Banknotes[a]						
			1840	1850	1860	1870	1880	1890	1900
19 Graubündner Kantonalbank	1870	1873–1910	-	-	-	-	1,988	2,976	3,923
20 Caisse de la dette public Fribourg[d]	1868–1893	1874–1893	-	-	-	-	746	1,468	-
21 Luzerner Kantonalbank	1850	1877–1910	-	-	-	-	984	1,985	5,694
22 Appenzell A.-Rh. Kantonalbannk	1877	1877–1910	-	-	-	-	1,978	2,976	2,979
23 Ersparniskasse des Kantons Uri	1837	1878–1910	-	-	-	-	261	498	1,450
24 Nidwaldner Kantonalbank	1879	1879–1910	-	-	-	-	175	497	995
25 Banque Cantonale Neuchâteloise	1883	1883–1910	-	-	-	-	-	2,962	7,981
26 Schaffhauser Kantonalbank	1883	1883–1910	-	-	-	-	-	1,495	2,462
27 Glarner Kantonalbank	1884	1884–1910	-	-	-	-	-	1,489	2,481
28 Obwaldner Kantonalbank	1887	1887–1910	-	-	-	-	-	493	983
29 Kantonalbank Schwyz	1890	1890–1910	-	-	-	-	-	500	2,974
30 Zuger Kantonalbank	1892	1893–1910	-	-	-	-	-	-	2,967
31 Banque de l'Etat de Fribourg	1893	1893–1910	-	-	-	-	-		4,948
32 Basler Kantonalbank	1899	1900–1910	-	-	-	-	-		-
33 Appenzell I.-Rh. Kantonalbank	1900	1900–1910	-	-	-	-	-		-
III Regional banks									
34 Deposito-Cassa der Stadt Bern [e]	1826	1826–1869	170	87	9	-	-	-	-
35 Banque Cantonale Fribourgeoise	1850–1910	1851–1910			330	378	1,677	996	1,246
36 Thurgauische Hypothekenbank	1852–1908	1852–1908			470	322	735	963	983
37 Bank in Glarus	1852–1912	1852–1882			492	657	1,275	-	-
38 Bank in Luzern	1857–1912	1857–1907			125	216	1,969	3,987	4,977
39 Banque Populaire de la Gruyère	1853	1857–1892			-	65	168	173	-
40 Banca Cantonale Ticinese	1861–1914	1861–1908			-	168	2,119	1,952	1,894

	(A)		(B)				
41 Bank für Graubünden	1862	1863–1882	-	108	693	-	-
42 Bank in Schaffhausen	1862	1863–1908	-	136	667	1,989	3,424
43 Toggenburger Bank	1863–1912	1864–1907	-	350	987	990	978
44 Banque Populaire de la Broye	1864	1865–1882	-	18	18	-	-
45 Caisse Hypothécaire du Canton de Fribourg	1854	1865–1882	-	115	22	-	-
46 Crédit Agricole et Industriel de la Broye	1866	1867–1910	-	70	216	799	994
47 Leihkasse Glarus [f]	1863–1884	1870–1884	-	92	292	-	-
48 Banca della Svizzera Italiana	1873	1874–1907	-	-	1,395	1,996	1,991
49 Crédit Gruyérien	1873	1874–1892	-	-	163	170	-
50 Credito Ticinese	1890–1914	1891–1907	-	-	-	-	2,231
51 Banca Populare di Lugano	1888	1898–1910	-	-	-	-	1,992

Notes: (A) Years of operation, last year only with end of operation before 1914; (B) years of banknote issue.

[a] 1,000 Swiss francs, end of year.

[b] Later Banque Commerciale Neuchâteloise and (new) Banque Cantonale Neuchâteloise.

[c] Until 1886, Solothurnische Bank.

[d] Later Banque de L'Etat de Fribourg.

[e] Note circulation 1830: 88.

[f] Later Glarner Kantonalbank.

Source: Weber (1992), pp. 188–9, based on Jöhr (1915)

The issue of banknotes involved considerable costs: production (printing) costs; personnel costs of bank counter service; and – particularly important – the costs of the metal reserves necessary for reasons of confidence and trust, and the costs of banknote clearing. Note clearing was a central element of concern: The demand for banknotes was dependent on their likelihood of being accepted at full value. With acceptance in doubt, the usefulness of banknotes was limited and costs of information for banknote users became high. This forced banks to conclude agreements on mutual acceptance and led to the formation of clearing networks including entire groups of banks. These arrangements in turn required frequent negotiations, as well as the shipping of metal reserves among banks to settle payments imbalances.

For all these reasons, banks' note-issue business remained rather small and of limited importance throughout most of this period. The average shares of banknotes in the balance sheets of Swiss note-issue banks in the decade of the 1850s were 9.4 percent for the cantonal banks and 20.9 percent for private banks, according to Weber. In the decade of the 1860s, they were even lower, at 6.8 percent and 13.8 percent, while in the 1870s they rose to 10.2 percent and 31.7 percent, respectively.[15] The average length of the period of circulation for banknotes was surprisingly low, according to Mangold (1909): for example, only thirty-six days for the Bank in Basel in the year 1855.[16] Complaints about the complicated nature and the inefficiency of the payments system remained frequent. Several authors, for example, Jöhr (1915) and Ritzmann (1973), stressed this state of dissatisfaction and the inefficiencies causing it and thus, in contrast to Weber, came to a negative assessment of note-issue competition in this period. This competition, they argue, created an untransparent and unmanageable system of payments and therefore was not able to survive.

In a sense, both arguments are right. It is true, as Weber emphasizes, that note-issue competition in this period was consistent with maintaining stable monetary and financial conditions. Contrary to the beliefs of many fundamental critics of note-issue competition, it did not lead to over-issue and monetary overexpansion. In this sense, it was successful. But it is also true that the resulting system of payments was opaque, cumbersome, and not conducive to making the banknote more popular as a means of payment – conditions which set into motion a process aiming to overcome

---

[15] Weber (1992), p. 193, based on Jöhr (1915).
[16] Weber (1992), p. 193, based on Mangold (1909).

these deficiencies by making the banknote more homogeneous and universally acceptable. The Federal Banknote Act of 1881, introducing common standards of quality in banknote issue, was the result of these efforts. However, by successfully introducing such standards, it also created conditions under which competition could no longer perform its disciplinary role, as we shall see.

NOTE-ISSUE COMPETITION WITH A STRONGLY REGULATED NOTE-ISSUE BUSINESS: 1881–1905

The period from 1881 to 1905 can be characterized as a period of (strongly) limited banking freedom: a system with a common, now legally prescribed currency denomination for banknotes and a heavily regulated note-issue business, but still without a centralized government monopoly in note issue. With the Federal Banknote Act of 1881, banks were severely constrained with regard to their liquidity reserves, their equity capital, their banknote redemption, and their issuing policies. Before 1881, they had been more or less free of such restrictions. The regulatory standardization of the banknote enforced by the Banknote Act was successful in promoting the acceptance of notes and the efficiency of the money and payments system. Under these conditions, however, competition could no longer exert its beneficial effects. The result was over-issue of notes and a tendency toward monetary and currency weakness – a state of affairs which would ultimately lead to full nationalization of banknote issue and the foundation of the Swiss National Bank.[17]

Swiss monetary history of this period has been carefully studied by Neldner (1996, 2003), who embedded his analysis in a general discussion of central banking versus free banking in line with British nineteenth-century tradition. Advocates of central banking typically argue that a liberal banking order will tend to be unstable because of an inherent tendency toward over-issue. Justification for this is first and foremost theoretical, but often it is reinforced with empirical references. Empirical experience and its interpretation are controversial, however, and in some cases may also be used in favor of free banking.[18]

---

[17] See Chapter 3.
[18] See, e.g., Selgin (1988, 1994), Selgin and White (1994); for the Swiss case, see Weber (1988, 1992).

Banknote over-issue occurs when banknote supply exceeds note demand at the prevailing price level (at full employment). This comes about when issuing banks increase note issue excessively, but also when they are unwilling or unable to reduce banknote circulation significantly in an environment of rising domestic prices and a depreciating domestic currency – both of these being indicators of an over-supply of money. As a result, the market rate of interest drops below the "natural" rate, domestic prices rise (or are prevented from returning to their previous level), and the domestic currency becomes depressed. In an international fixed exchange rate system, a reserve drain results.

Adherents of free note-issue competition argue that, under competitive conditions, market forces will ensure that over-issue does not occur. An over-issuing bank, as part of reciprocal clearing and due to the fact that customers are redeeming more of its notes, will suffer reserve losses and will be forced to reduce its issue volume. Consequently, they say, there is an automatic check that works against misbehavior.

By contrast, critics of note-issue competition draw attention to an externality in banknote emission: Over-issue by *one* bank and the subsequent tendencies of the domestic currency to depreciate and of reserves to flow out affect *all* banks in proportion to their market shares, they argue.[19] This leads to a tendency for all banks to over-issue. Consequently, the check imposed by banknote clearing and reserve losses is inadequate. All banks are exposed to the temptation to increase their market share through overexpansion. It is important to note, however, that this criticism of note-issue competition is based on the implicit assumption that bank customers consider all banknotes to be of equal value, irrespective of who issued them. In other words, it assumes that users do not perceive any difference in quality between the banknotes of different issuers and therefore see no necessity to discriminate between them.

Neldner sees the Swiss experience, particularly from 1885 to 1905, as a lesson in favor of the arguments and criticism raised by the opponents of note-issue competition. He stresses the rapid note issue and the weakness of the Swiss franc after 1885, as well as the increased redemption of banknotes and the currency metal drain described in Chapter 3. The facts that banknote redemptions and the resulting need for silver imports were concentrated on certain banks, especially banks close to the French border,

---

[19] See, e.g., McCulloch (1831), p. 48: "As all notes ... are equally good in his (i.e., a businessman's) estimation, he sends those in for payment that come first to hand." Longfield (1840, pp. 218–19) makes a similar observation.

rather than on those that were over-issuing,[20] and that banks forced to redeem large quantities of banknotes were unwilling or unable to sufficiently limit their banknote circulation (and their lending), demonstrate the failure of market forces particularly well, he argues. Attempts to alleviate these problems through cartel-type arrangements within a Concordat came too late. Neldner's argumentation here is in line with earlier criticism by Kalkmann (1900), Landmann (1905), and Jöhr (1915).

WAS THE BANKNOTE A HOMOGENEOUS PRODUCT? THE ROLE OF REGULATION OF THE NOTE-ISSUE BUSINESS

While this is convincing as far as it goes, we believe that the argument needs to be refined and completed. As mentioned above, Neldner's critique of note-issue competition – and that of all of his predecessors, back to the Currency School – implicitly assumes that all banknotes are of equal value for users; in other words, that the banknote is a homogeneous product with no perceptible differences in quality. However, if the banknotes of different issuing banks are distinct products, this argument no longer applies and the disciplinary effects of competition can come into play. Quality differences for banknotes are possible along two dimensions:

- the currency denomination of the banknotes (although such differences disappeared in practice after 1850 and legally after 1881, they certainly existed before 1850);
- the quality of the banknotes, in particular as regards their security, their acceptance by potential trading partners, and the nature of bank services linked to the note-issue business.

In principle, great differences are possible along the second of these dimensions, even with a common currency, depending on the quality of the banks' liquidity reserve, capital reserve, clearing, and note-issue policies. This is comparable to bank competition in the deposit business as we know it today. One point is of crucial importance in this context, however: The extent to which quality differences exist and are perceived by bank

---

[20] Between 1892 and 1906, silver imports and silver import costs of the Banque du Commerce de Genève alone made up about 50 percent of the silver imports and silver import costs of all note-issue banks together (Neldner, 1996, p. 185). In the second half of the year 1899, 93 percent of total silver import costs were borne by just five note-issue banks, whose share in total note circulation was just 45 percent (Neldner, 1996, p. 186).

customers is strongly dependent on the nature and extent of regulation of the note-issue (or deposit) business.

In an unregulated banking system (with only the currency prescribed), where banks can stop redeeming banknotes or paying out deposits and can become insolvent, and where banknote holders or depositors can lose their holdings, it goes without saying that customers have strong incentives to monitor banknote qualities and differentiate between the notes of different issuing banks. Such a system has two significant disadvantages, though:

- discrimination between different banknote qualities may cause high information-procurement and monitoring costs for customers; this reduces the attractiveness of using banknotes and the efficiency of the monetary system;
- the possibility that banks may stop redeeming banknotes and potentially fail carries the inherent risk of systemic instability and banking crises.

DESIRE FOR EFFICIENCY AND STABILITY AS MAIN MOTIVATION FOR CENTRALIZATION

This in turn creates strong incentives to eliminate these deficiencies by enforcing common quality standards, for example through the introduction of (common) reserve or capital requirements. This may occur through government intervention and regulation or through measures taken by the banks themselves in the form of cartel-type agreements (concordats). In either case, however, a price is paid in that competition and its disciplinary function in the note-issue (or deposit) business is lost, or at least significantly tarnished. What is involved here is a trade-off between efficiency and stability on the one hand, and the advantages and possibilities of competition on the other. The problem with cartel solutions is that, over the longer term, stability is often difficult to maintain, because there is always an incentive for individual members to break the agreement as long as the others stick to it.

In Switzerland, the note-issue business was regulated along exactly these lines with the Banknote Act of 1881. The externality described by Neldner and others was the result of these efforts. Consequently, Neldner's argument is convincing for the period from 1881 to 1905 – the time to which, in fact, he mainly refers. For the phase from 1850 to 1881, conversely, and most particularly for that prior to 1850, it has little relevance. After 1881, banks' reserve, liquidity, and redemption policies were heavily restricted by legal requirements. The same was true for bank issue levels (rigid issue quotas, fixed issue tax). Before 1881, on the other hand, issue banks were largely free in all these decisions. Although a trend toward standardization of all bank-notes had, to some extent, set in previously, through concordat agreements and similar arrangements, this was the result of voluntary decisions on the part of the banks, which they could have revoked at any time, had they wished to do so. This process was also accompanied by disruptions and resistance. Potentially, until 1881, a great number of differences in the quality of banknotes of different issuing banks were possible.

In this sense, it was not note-issue competition as such that, due to an inherent propensity toward monetary overexpansion, inevitably led to centralization, but rather the quest for efficiency and stability – which was reflected in the Banknote Act and ultimately made the move toward the creation of a central bank unavoidable. Experience suggests that, with regulations enforcing identical banknote quality for all issuers alike, the case for a centralized control of banknote issue becomes compelling, because competition is no longer able to fulfil its disciplinary role.

In this respect, our interpretation differs from that of Neldner, who sees note-issue competition as such as the cause of over-issue and currency weakness, and argues that the latter inevitably result from the former. In a successful, stable banking system, users would soon regard the banknotes of different issuers as perfect substitutes, he maintains. Competitive pres-sure then would inevitably undermine the stability of the system.[21]

Kueng (2007) adopts this interpretation. Analyzing the period prior to the introduction of the Banknote Act (1872 to 1881), he finds it paradox-ical that over-expansion and currency weakness did not also occur during this earlier phase.[22] Both should have been present, he argues, since according to his empirical estimates the note-issue business was profitable at this time. He observes that,[23] even then, banks in many cases were redeeming banknotes reciprocally at par value with no more than minimal deductions (for transactions and transportation costs, etc.), and that there were no significant problems of bank insolvency and failure. Consequently, bank customers had no reason to discriminate between notes from differ-ent issuing banks, he argues. In this respect, the 1881 act did not really change anything, according to Kueng.

---

[21] Neldner (2003), p. 404.
[22] Following a similar discussion in US banking history – see Bodenhorn and Haupert (1996) – he refers to this as a "note issue paradox."
[23] Referring to Jöhr (1915).

However, this argument confuses cause and effect. What is critical for the lack of an externality and of incentives to overexpand is that customers have a motivation to monitor banks, and that banks are aware of this. Before 1881, banks were, in principle, free to deviate from sound policies and behavior. Under such conditions, good behavior on the part of banks and absence of over-issue must be seen as the result of competition and its disciplinary effects.[24] It does not imply that customers do not monitor and, if necessary, discriminate between banks. As long as the quality of all banknotes is sound, customers have no reason to treat different issuers' notes differently. So no paradox needs to be explained. After 1881, by contrast, banknote holders knew that law and regulations enforced that all banknotes had to be redeemed at par. Consequently, they no longer had any incentive to monitor banknote quality.

THE ROLE OF CENTRAL BANKS IN THE METALLIC CURRENCY SYSTEMS OF THE NINETEENTH CENTURY

The history of the SNB's establishment, and the accompanying discussion, contributes to our understanding of the role of central banks in nineteenth-century metallic currency systems.

This role is obviously not identical to the one we see nowadays, within the framework of the fiat money systems that dominate our time, as the core task of central bank policy – to ensure price stability and anchor the value of money. This function was automatically fulfilled by the mechanisms of the gold/metal currency system; in other words, the firm link between money and a good characterized by natural scarcity. There was no need for an active monetary policy establishing the stability of the price level over and beyond this mechanism. This is empirically supported by Figure 8.1, which displays consumer price inflation from 1851 to 1906. Inflation was very volatile, but on average it was close to zero with a sample median of 0.079 percent. The sample mean is slightly higher (0.338 percent), but it is statistically not significantly different from zero (standard error of the sample mean is 1.165).

Why, then, were central banks needed? The oldest central banks, like the Swedish Riksbank and the Bank of England, founded in the seventeenth

---

[24] Otherwise, circular reasoning would be involved: we would simply *assume* that competition must inevitably lead to misbehavior and overexpansion, if absence of the latter were evidence against the possible presence of a workable, disciplining form of the former.

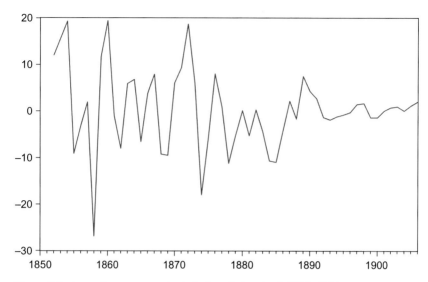

Figure 8.1: Annual consumer price inflation, Switzerland, 1851–1906
Data source: Swiss economic and social history database, Table H17, www.fsw.uzh.ch/hstat/nls_rev/ls_files.php?chapter_var=./h

century, focused mainly on government finances. Their original job was to organize the funding of government expenses and manage government debt, particularly in connection with the financing of wars.

In the nineteenth century, this aspect declined in importance. The main reason for establishing central banks was now linked to the elimination and containment of a number of inefficiencies that were characteristic of the currency systems in place at the time. Central banks offered certain services of a public goods nature which were not readily provided by the market. In this context, Switzerland was a late mover in a process that was taking place in other countries in similar forms. The wave of central bank foundings that occurred over the nineteenth and the early twentieth centuries was mainly a response to the following challenges:

- Overcoming the weaknesses and inefficiencies of a competitive system of banknote issue under a regime of statutory regulation and standardization of the banknote business. This was the challenge just described as the main driving force in the process leading to the creation of the Swiss National Bank. However, all of the following aspects played a role, too.

- Ensuring the stability of the banking and financial system ("financial stability"). Central banks were to prevent, or at least contain, liquidity and banking crises and, if they did happen, alleviate their consequences. This is the role of the central bank as a *lender of last resort*, an agent providing emergency funding to (basically solvent) banks and the banking system overall in times of crisis and stress, thereby preventing panics and system failures. In Switzerland, the crisis of 1870 served as a lasting reminder of the importance of this central bank task.

- Promoting the efficiency of the payment system – the central bank as an agent in the bank clearing mechanism. By coordinating and simplifying payment transactions between banks, central banks helped to improve the efficiency of the monetary system, reduce information and transaction costs, and further economic development. Imperfections in banknote clearing and the need for improved clearing arrangements were constant themes in the Swiss debate surrounding the creation of the SNB.

- Ensuring improved flexibility in the provision of money. Under a pure metallic currency system, with a fixed metal coverage ratio for banknotes and coins, the supply of money was often regarded as being excessively rigid and inelastic. Central banks were to redress this situation and, by varying their coverage ratios, take account of fluctuations in liquidity demand and general economic conditions. Ensuring an elastic provision of money "according to the needs of commerce" was a major task assigned to the SNB. This idea was to become even more important with twentieth-century demand management and business cycle policies. In the nineteenth and early twentieth centuries, the focus was mainly on monetary and financial shocks and disruptions, which were to be corrected and alleviated by the central bank. In the twentieth century this was increasingly supplanted by the idea that the primary task of economic policy is to correct instabilities emanating from the real sectors of the economy. Not until the financial crises of the past two decades was this perception modified anew.

THE DEMAND FOR COINS, BANKNOTES AND SIGHT DEPOSITS: 1851–1906

In this section we supplement our analysis of the supply of banknotes with a discussion of the demand for banknotes and bank deposits as

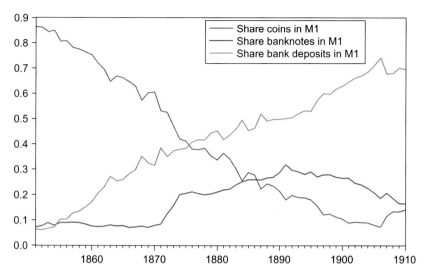

Figure 8.2: Composition of M1 in Switzerland, 1851–1906
Data source: Swiss economic and social history database: M1 1851–1907 (Table Q3), www.fsw.uzh.ch/
hstat/nls_rev/overview.php

means of payment. To this end we use the M1 estimates available for
Switzerland since 1851. Figure 8.2 depicts the development of the shares
of coins, banknotes, and sight deposits in M1 over the period
1851–1906.

The figure shows that Switzerland was a "coin economy" at the time of
the introduction of the Swiss franc: Approximately 87 percent of M1 was
coin in 1851 and the remaining 13 percent was shared equally by banknotes and sight deposits. In the following years we observe a trend decline
in the role played by coin, to 7 percent, whereas the share of sight deposits
increased to 74 percent in 1906. By contrast, the development of the
banknote share is less monotonic: it experienced a strong increase in the
1870s, in the aftermath of the liquidity crisis triggered by the inconvertibility of the French franc during the Prussian-French war. It increased
again after the switch to federal regulation of banknote issue (in 1881) and
reached a peak of 30 percent in 1891. This illustrates banks' incentives to
over-issue, as discussed above. The weakness of the Swiss franc on the
foreign exchange market, and the associated loss of monetary metal and
increasing costs of banknote issue, saw the banknote share decline to
19 percent in 1906.

CONCLUSIONS

Nineteenth-century Switzerland provides interesting examples of the roles of competition and monopoly in the issue of money and banknotes. Overall, the Swiss experience of relatively free banking in the nineteenth century was mixed. To some extent, it tends to support rather than contradict the claims of free banking advocates (for 1820 to 1850, to some degree also for 1850 to 1881). At the same time, however, it also provides backing for major reservations with respect to currency and note-issue competition. It is consistent with the view that although, in principle, competition in note issue can exert a disciplinary effect and may be associated with financial stability, the resulting money and payment system is characterized by inefficiency and high costs – factors which in turn lead to regulatory restrictions and have, in the past, paved the way toward a state banknote monopoly. It is nevertheless remarkable that the process of industrialization in Switzerland in the nineteenth century proceeded extremely successfully without a state banknote monopoly – indeed, without even a uniform currency in the initial stages. We should also recall that our experience with government-run fiat money systems over the past hundred years demonstrates that a state banknote monopoly is no guarantee of monetary discipline and stability either.

The process leading to the introduction of a Swiss central bank and a national banknote monopoly was governed by four main motivations: the quest for efficiency and stability of the monetary system under a regime of statutory regulation and standardization of banknote issue; recognition of the need for the services of a lender of last resort; promoting the efficiency of the payment system; and ensuring adequate seasonal and cyclical flexibility in the provision of liquidity and money.

Finally, Swiss nineteenth-century experience documents and confirms the long-lasting dominance of coin and the slow rise of banknotes and, even later, of bank sight deposits as means of payments in continental Europe.

9

Swiss Money Demand and Supply 1851–2010

This chapter analyses Swiss money demand and supply, and their macro-economic effects over the past one and a half centuries. The changes from a metallic monetary standard to the Bretton Woods system, and finally to a pure de facto paper money standard with flexible exchange rates, naturally led to significant changes in the processes governing money supply. More-over, we should expect a change in monetary dynamics under these different regimes. For instance, domestic prices and nominal income, as well as the money supply, have to adjust under a metallic standard, whereas changes in nominal income, interest rates, and the exchange rate work as shock absorbers under flexible exchange rates. In contrast, there is no strong *a priori* reason that there is a fundamental change in money demand across the different monetary regimes.

This chapter is organized as follows. The first section contains an econometric analysis of Swiss money demand since 1850, focusing on the long-run stability of M1 demand. In the next section, the macroeco-nomic effects of deviations from long-run monetary equilibrium are con-sidered for sub-periods taking into account the breaks in monetary regimes. After this, we provide some results on the development of money supply after the creation of the SNB in 1907. In this context, the stability of the "money multiplier" and the relationship of M1 and the monetary base are analyzed.

SWISS MONEY DEMAND 1851–2010

In this section we provide an analysis of the long-run development of money demand in Switzerland since 1851. We selected M1 as a measure of money for two main reasons. First, data since 1850 are only available for this monetary aggregate. Data for M2 are available since 1907 only, and base money or M0 has only been defined since the foundation of the SNB in 1907. Second, empirical analyses of money demand show that M1, M2, and M3 exhibit a relatively stable money demand function, at least for post-World War I data (Peytrignet, 1996, 2007; Peytrignet and Stahel, 1998), while the same is not true for base money. It is worth mentioning that the SNB gave up on its first attempt to implement monetary targets for M1 in the 1970s, and had ultimately abandoned monetary targeting altogether by the end of the 1990s, not because of the instability of the demand for M1 but because of the instability of the money supply multiplier (SNB, 2007). In addition, the high interest rate sensitivity of Swiss money demand made money supply targets ineffective as a cyclical stabilizer (Rich, 2000; Kugler and Rich, 2002).

Our econometric analysis is mainly based on the following standard partial adjustment money demand function:

$$\log(M1_t) = (a + b_1 log(Y_t) + b_2(i_t))(1 - b_3) + b_3 \log(M1_{t-1}) + \xi_t \quad (1)$$

For data reasons – nominal GDP is available over the entire period, real GDP only since 1890 – we assumed identical long-run elasticities of money demand with respect to prices and real income b_1. In consequence, the hypothesis $b_1 = 1$ imposes itself, given the usual assumption of a unit price elasticity of money demand. The long-run interest rate semi-elasticity is denoted by b_2, and b_3 is the partial adjustment coefficient. We selected the savings deposit rate as an interest rate measure as this is the only interest rate series consistently available since 1850. The data series and their sources are displayed in Figure 9.1. We observe that the money stock and GDP have a visible trend, and even interest rates do not seem to have a constant mean. Such non-stationary characteristics may lead to misleading results if we simply use such variables in regressions without taking into account the properties of the series. A simple device to deal with this problem consists of considering changes or first differences of the series. However, this neglects a possible relationship in levels which we would expect from economic theory for a money demand function. Cointegration analysis provides the statistical tools to test for and estimate level relationships between difference stationary series (indicated as integrated of order 1, or I(1)).

The application of an unit root and a stationarity test to the three series clearly points to I(1) behavior: The null hypothesis of a unit root cannot be rejected and the (trend) stationarity hypothesis is always rejected, at least at

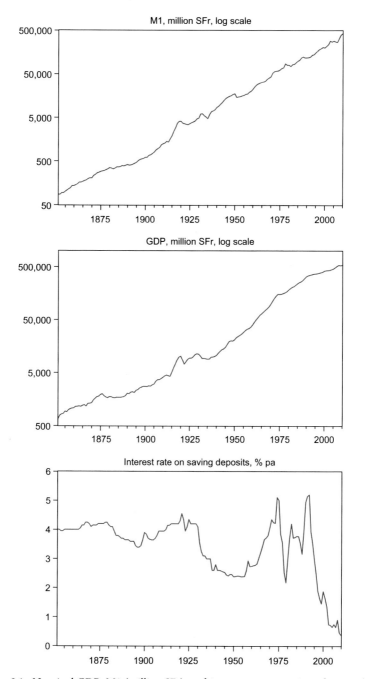

Figure 9.1: Nominal GDP, M1 (million SFr), and interest rate on savings deposits (%), 1851–2010

Data source: Swiss economic and social history database: M1 1851–1907 (Table Q3); GDP 1851–2006 1851–2005 (Table Q16a, b), www.fsw.uzh.ch/hstat/nls_rev/overview.php; SNB historical series: M1 1907–1950 (T1.3) 1950–1975 1975 definition, 1976–2010 1995 definition (T2.1) 1907–1950; all series are converted to the 1995 definition of M1 by chaining using the last overlapping observation. Saving deposit interest rate, 2.4.3 (1851–2006), www.snb.ch/de/iabout/ stat/statrep/statpubdis/id/statpub_statmon_arch_xls_de, all updates using SNB Monthly Statistical Bulletin; www.snb.ch/de/iabout/stat/statrep/statpubdis/id/statpub_statmon_arch_xls_de

Table 9.1: *Regression residual cointegration tests M1 demand, 1851–2010*

$$\log(M1_t) = a + b_1 \log(Y_t) + b_2(i_t) + \varepsilon_t$$

Method	b_1	b_2	R^2	DW	Engle-Granger t	Hansen Test
OLS	1.154***	−0.1762***	0.9780	0.0407	−1.409	
	(0.0281)	(0.0721)				
FMOLS	1.149***	−0.1940***	0.9777	0.0413		2.5738***
	(0.0363)	(0.0764)				
1851–1913	1.571***	−0.1025***	0.9795	0.3929	−3.103	
OLS	(0.0281)	(0.1099)				
FMOLS	1.6239***	−0.0742	0.9791	0.3618		0.7000**
	(0.0501)	(0.0962)				
1914–2010	0.9222***	−0.1819***	0.9904	0.2950	−3.136	
OLS	(0.0197)	(0.0238)				
FMOLS	0.9204***	−0.1937***	0.9903	0.3047		0.0088
	(0.0383)	(0.0285)				

Newey-West standard errors in parentheses
*, **, *** indicate significance at the 10, 5, and 1 percent levels, respectively.

the 10 percent level.[1] Therefore, we tested for cointegration using the regression approaches of Engle and Granger (OLS) as well as Phillips and Hansen (Fully Modified OLS).[2] We selected this approach instead of a multivariate method, such as Johansen's test, based on an error correction system which models the dynamic adjustment of the variables. The reason is simply that the switches in the monetary regime lead to changes in the adjustment dynamics and a constant EC model over the entire sample is clearly mis-specified.

The results presented in Table 9.1 clearly point to the absence of cointegration between the three series analyzed, although the long-run money demand elasticity estimates appear reasonable. First, the Engle-Granger (1987) test does not reject the null hypothesis of no cointegration;

[1] The ADF and KPSS statistics are: −2.76 and 0.140* (logM1), −2.00 and 0.321*** (logGDP), and −1.691 and 0.673** (interest rate, without deterministic trend), respectively.

[2] OLS as well as FMOLS estimates are super-consistent. However, FMOLS corrects for possible endogenous regressors which invalidate statistical tests based on OLS estimates (Hamilton, 1994, pp. 571–629). Alternatives to FMOLS are Dynamic OLS and Canonical cointegrating regression. These two approaches provide essentially the same estimation results as FMOLS in our application.

second, the Hansen (1992) parameter instability test clearly rejects the null hypothesis of cointegration. The inclusion of a deterministic trend in the cointegration regression does not help, as cointegration is still clearly rejected and the estimated coefficients are unreasonably low in absolute value. However, the sub-samples from 1851 to 1913 and 1914 to 2010 show results which are more in favor of cointegration: The residuals are much less positively autocorrelated according to the Durbin-Watson statistic and the rejection of cointegration is much less clear than for the full sample. In particular, the results suggest that we have a break in the income elasticity, which is estimated at around 1.6 before 1913 and 0.92 after.

The results obtained so far suggest that a long-run money demand equation exists, but some of the coefficients exhibit breaks over time. In order to investigate this conjecture, we applied the Bai-Perron (2003) sequential break-point test to the partial adjustment money demand function (1). The results are presented in Table 9.2. The Bai-Perron test for multiple unknown structural breaks is a generalization of the well-known Chow test. The latter approach tests whether a regression exhibits different coefficient estimates for a known sample split, so that we have one break. The Bai-Perron approach allows testing for several breaks at unknown

Table 9.2: *Bai-Perron sequentially determined multiple break points, Swiss M1 demand, 1851–2010*

$$\log(M1_t) = (a + b_1 log(Y_t) + b_2(i_t))(1 - b_3) + b_3 \log(M1_{t-1}) + \xi_t$$

Break test	F-statistic	Scaled F-statistic	Critical value 5%
0 vs. 1 [**]	6.353693	25.41477	16.19
1 vs. 2 [**]	8.292747	33.17099	18.11
2 vs. 3 [**]	6.964083	27.85633	18.93
3 vs. 4 [**]	2.822647	11.29059	19.64

Break dates:		
	Sequential	Repartition
1	1951	1914
2	1914	1951
3	1979	1979

[**] Significant at the 0.05 level, Bai-Perron (2003) critical values Trimming 0.15, Max. breaks 5, Sig. level 0.05, White covariance matrix estimates.

dates. It is essentially a sequential application of the Chow test with varying break dates, taking into account the changed distribution of the Chow statistics.

Table 9.2 reveals three breaks that are statistically significant at the 5 percent level, namely 1914, 1951, and 1979. These dates correspond roughly to the breakdown of the classical gold standard, the adoption of the Bretton Woods system, and the transition to flexible exchange rates. Thus we estimate our money demand function for four sub-periods 1851–1913, 1914–50, 1951–78, and 1979–2010. We use GMM in order to take into account potential simultaneity of M1, GDP, and the interest rate, with two lags of all variables as instruments. The results obtained are given in Table 9.3. Besides the usual regression statistics, we report the specification test suggested by Hansen, which checks the validity of the over-identifying restrictions. Under the null hypothesis of a correct specification, this J-statistic is asymptotically χ^2 distributed with three degrees of freedom.

Table 9.3 indicates a large change in the estimated income elasticity of money around World War I: For the period before 1914 this elasticity is statistically significantly higher than 1 (1.68), while thereafter it is not statistically different from 1. Thus, we get the theoretically expected result for the post-1913 sample with respect to the reaction of money demand to nominal income. The interest rate elasticity is very imprecisely estimated in the first sub-sample. This is not surprising given the lack of interest rate

Table 9.3: *GMM estimates of money demand functions for Switzerland, 1851–2010*

$$\log(M1_t) = (a + b_1 log(Y_t) + b_2(i_t))(1 - b_3) + b_3 log(M1_{t-1}) + \xi_t$$

Sample	b_1	b_2	b_3	R^2	DW	Hansen J-statistic
1851–1913	1.681***	−0.1680	0.9112***	0.9977	1.968	1.094
	(0.1421)	(0.2370)	(0.0440)			
1914–1950	1.017***	−0.3869***	0.3906**	0.9880	1.403	4.183
	(0.0808)	(0.03310)	(0.1914)			
1951–1978	0.9291***	−0.0755*	0.3293***	0.9915	1.431	1.129
	(0.0467)	(0.0373)	(0.1021)			
1979–2010	1.272***	−0.0997***	0.7011***	0.9851	1.584	2.994
	(0.2833)	(0.0319)	(0.221)			

White standard errors in parentheses, *, **, *** indicates significance at the 10, 5, and 1 percent levels, respectively.

variability during this period (Figure 9.1). In the second period we get a highly interest-sensitive M1 demand, which is strongly reduced after 1951 but remains statistically significant. The high interest sensitivity in the sub-sample from 1914 to 1950 is probably related to the worldwide monetary instability during these years. Despite the firm domestic anchoring of the Swiss franc, the instability created by the wars and failed attempts to return to gold in the form of the gold/exchange standard in the interwar period are likely to have had a large impact on market behavior in the highly open Swiss economy.[3]

The high income elasticity of money demand before 1914 is plausibly explained by the fact that Switzerland was mainly a coin economy in 1850. The increased importance of cashless payments is reflected by more than proportionate growth of M1 relative to income. Moreover, we note a very slow dynamic adjustment of money demand of only roughly 10 percent annually during this period. The adjustment speed is much higher for the 1914–50 sample (*c.* 60 percent annually) and the interest rate semi-elasticity is now very high in absolute value. It appears that the drop in interest rates during this period, from around 4 percent to 2.5 percent, led to strong growth in M1. For the Bretton Woods period we report an even faster adjustment (*c.* 70 percent annually) and a lower interest rate sensitivity of money demand. Interestingly, in the last sub-sample we get a break in the tendency toward faster money demand adjustment over time. Since the transition to flexible exchange rates we observe a substantially slower adjustment of M1 demand compared to the Bretton Woods period (*c.* 30 percent annually).

In conclusion, we should stress the constancy of the long-run income elasticity of M1 demand in Switzerland over a very long period of time: For nearly the entire past century, the corresponding parameter estimates are close to and not statistically different from 1. The interest rate semi-elasticity is nearly constant since 1950, but is clearly larger in absolute value in the 1914–50 period. The adjustment speed of money demand, in contrast, has experienced significant variation, showing an interesting U-shaped pattern over time.

To complete this section, we display the deviations from long-run money demand equilibrium as estimated using the results of Table 9.3. Figure 9.2 provides this data set for the entire period from 1851 to 2010.

---

[3] Bordo (1993) and, more recently, Bordo and Redish (2016) discuss the interwar period in relation to the classical gold standard and subsequent monetary regimes; Eichengreen (1992) provides an in-depth treatment of the interwar years.

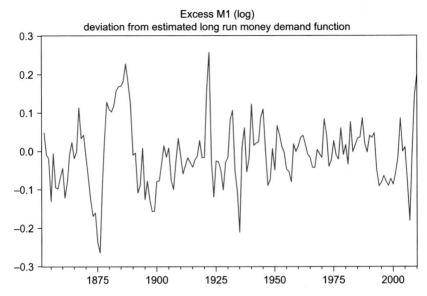

Excess M1 (log)
deviation from estimated long run money demand function

Figure 9.2: Deviations from long-run M1 demand equilibrium in Switzerland, 1851–2010, logs

Deviations from long-run money demand equilibrium are relatively small in the first twenty years of our sample, staying within a +/− 10 percent range. The liquidity crisis of the 1870s led to strong negative deviations of more than 20 percent in absolute value. This pattern is then reversed in the 1880s, where we note an excess M1 stock of the same absolute magnitude. This result is explained by the overissue of banknotes after the federal banknote act of 1881, as discussed in Chapter 8. In the same vein, the silver losses caused by the weakness of the Swiss franc resulted in tighter monetary conditions in the years before the foundation of the SNB. A large "excess money peak" is displayed for the end of World War I. The long-lasting adherence to the old gold parity of the Swiss franc up to 1936 led to strong negative deviations from long-run M1 equilibrium during the Great Depression. The persistently positive deviations from long-run M1 demand during the Bretton Woods years are well visible, too. For the more recent period, we see the persistent tightness of monetary conditions in the mid-1990s as discussed in Chapter 7. This episode was followed by an expansionary monetary policy after the bursting of the dotcom bubble, a tightening of monetary conditions in 2006/7, and a strongly expansionary monetary policy response to the recent financial market crisis.

MONEY DEMAND AND MACROECONOMIC ADJUSTMENT
IN SWITZERLAND 1851–2010

In this section we consider the adjustment dynamics in response to deviations from equilibrium money demand. To this end we estimate error correction (EC) models for the three variables in the money demand equation. The sample has to be split for two reasons. First, we expect different adjustment processes for the different monetary regimes covering metallic standards, Bretton Woods, and flexible exchange rates. Second, we found structural breaks in money demand which correspond roughly to the three seminal changes of the Swiss franc exchange rate regime, namely the breakdown of the classical gold standard in 1914, the operative start of the Bretton Woods system in 1950, and the end of the transition period to flexible exchange rates in 1978. Therefore we estimated the EC model for the corresponding sub-periods. These results are shown in Table 9.4. We report only the estimates of the error correction coefficients and not those of the first difference terms. The lag length for the first differences is determined according to the Akaike criterion. It turns out that we do not need any of these additional variables for the 1851–1913, 1914–50, and 1951–78 samples. For the recent flexible exchange rate period we need a lag length of 3, reflecting a much more complicated adjustment process since 1978.

For the period characterized by metallic standards and (predominantly) by the absence of a central bank, 1851–1913, we find a relatively slow adjustment of all three variables to deviations from long-run money demand equilibrium. The strongest response is found for the interest rate, followed by income and the money stock in the short run. This is what we would expect for a metallic standard, where, in a country without silver and gold deposits, changes in the stock of the monetary metal have to be accomplished by conversion from non-monetary use and imports. Interestingly, this pattern is reversed in the 1914–50 period, characterized by the existence of a central bank and, over extended periods, a de facto paper standard with more or less flexible exchange rates. One third of the disequilibrium is corrected by an adjustment of the money stock, which is supported by a strong reaction of the interest rate, whereas the direct reaction of income is not statistically significant. This dominance of money stock adjustments is increased in the Bretton Woods period, with adjustment of the money stock of *c.* 60 percent within one year. However, interest adjustment is statistically insignificant. This is the pattern of adjustment we would expect in a paper fixed exchange rate regime in a

Table 9.4: *EC model estimates, Swiss GDP, M1 and interest rate for sub-periods, 1851–2010*

$$\Delta m_t = \gamma_1\left(m_{t-1} - b_0 - b_1 y_{t-1} - b_2 i_{t-1}\right) + \Sigma\left(a_{11\tau}\Delta m_{t-\tau} + a_{12\tau}\Delta y_{t-\tau} + a_{12\tau}\Delta i_{t-\tau}\right) + \xi_{1t}$$

$$\Delta y_t = \gamma_2\left(m_{t-1} - b_0 - b_1 y_{t-1} - b_2 i_{t-1}\right) + \Sigma\left(a_{21\tau}\Delta m_{t-\tau} + a_{22\tau}\Delta y_{t-\tau} + a_{12\tau}\Delta i_{t-\tau}\right) + \xi_{2t}$$

$$\Delta i_t = \gamma_3\left(m_{t-1} - b_0 - b_1 y_{t-1} - b_2 i_{t-1}\right) + \Sigma\left(a_{31\tau}\Delta m_{t-\tau} + a_{32\tau}\Delta y_{t-\tau} + a_{33\tau}\Delta i_{t-\tau}\right) + \xi_{3t}$$

Period	γ_1	γ_2	γ_3	R^2 Δm	R^2 Δy	R^2 Δi	se Δm	se Δy	se Δi
1851–1913	−0.0671* (0.03869)	0.0979** (0.0472)	−0.2281*** (0.0699)	0.0478	0.0670	0.1510	0.0377	0.0461	0.0682
1914–1950	−0.3293** (0.1530)	0.0233 (0.1566)	−0.8669*** (0.2603)	0.1169	0.0006	0.2406	0.0862	0.0883	0.1467
1951–1978	−0.5967*** (0.1381)	0.1214 (0.0852)	−0.6643 (0.9896)	0.4179	0.0724	0.0170	0.0532	0.0328	0.3813
1979–2010	−0.6854*** (0.2065)	0.0334 (0.0645)	−1.878 (1.293)	0.5888	0.6407	0.6529	0.0553	0.0173	0.3462

Standard errors in parentheses; the cointegrating coefficients are obtained using Johansen's approach for the sub-samples. These estimates are essentially equal to those reported in Table 9.3.

small country where interest rates are largely exogenous and the money supply has to adjust. The strong correction of the money stock is maintained for the recent flexible exchange rate period, where we get an adjustment of the money stock of nearly 70 percent within one year and, again, a stronger reaction of interest rates. This pattern is what we would expect with a central bank trying to keep monetary conditions stable, as the SNB has done since the 1970s.

We conclude that, in contrast to the relatively high degree of stability of the long-run demand for money, we see strong changes in the monetary adjustment process since 1851. These differences are substantially influenced by changes in the monetary and exchange rate regime. In general, we clearly see over all these regimes a trend toward an increased speed of adjustment of macroeconomic variables to long-run money demand disequilibria. We should point out that this finding does not contradict the result of a slowed-down money demand adjustment since 1978 that was reported in Table 9.3. The latter result was conditional on income and the interest rate, whereas in this section we take into account adjustment of income and interest rates in an error correction framework. Moreover, we include three additional first differences lags in the last period EC model besides the error correction terms, which have a strong influence on the estimates of the dynamic adjustment process.

Finally, we should mention that we estimated the EC model for the GDP deflator and real GDP. For data reasons this is only possible from 1890 onward, and the series for the pre-World War I estimation are rather short. However, the results of this exercise show that the inflation and real growth EC coefficients are statistically not significantly different in all sub-samples. Thus, it appears that we have short-run reactions of inflation and growth to deviations from long-run money demand equilibrium.

M1 AND THE MONETARY BASE IN SWITZERLAND 1907–2010

This section provides an empirical analysis of the monetary base and its relationship to M1. Before the foundation of the SNB, the base for money creation in the form of banknotes and deposits was restricted by the monetary silver and gold stock available in Switzerland. Increases in this stock were possible through two channels only: first, through conversion of non-monetary stocks such as silverware (plates), jewelry, and other precious objects into monetary stocks; second, through imports of silver and gold. Domestic production was not available as an alternative, given the lack of precious metal deposits in Switzerland. Obviously, gold and silver

(a)

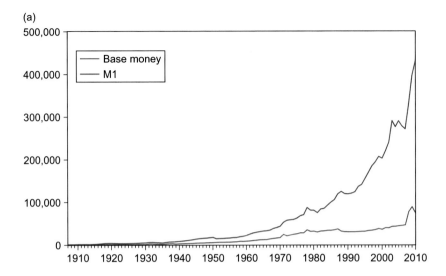

(b) Logs

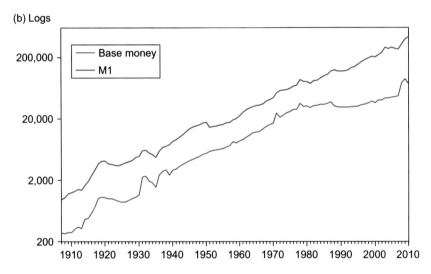

Figure 9.3: Base money and M1 (million SFr), 1907–2010

Source: SNB historical series: M1 1907–1950 (T1.3) 1950–1975 1975 definition, 1976–2010
1995 definition (T2.1) 1907–1950; all series are converted to 1995 definition by chaining using the
last overlapping observation. Base money and currency 1907–1950 (T1.1) 1950–2010 (T1.2) series
are converted to 1950–2010 scale by chaining all updates using SNB Monthly Statistical Bulletin,
www.snb.ch/de/iabout/stat/statrep/statpubdis/id/statpub_histz_arch#t3, www.snb.ch/de/iabout/
stat/statrep/statpubdis/id/statpub_statmon_arch_xls_de

imports had to be financed by a balance of payments surplus on all other transaction. In the short and medium run this could be accomplished via capital imports, but in the long run a current account surplus was needed to this end. Unfortunately, there are no available consistent statistics on the silver and gold reserves of the Swiss banking system which could be related to M1. Therefore we must restrict our analysis to the period since 1907 for which data on base money exist (currency and sight deposits of banks with the SNB).

Figure 9.3 displays the development of base money and M1 since 1907 in absolute and logarithmic scale. It suggests that both money stocks evolve similarly up to 1970. In the past forty years of the sample, this common trend seems to disappear. In order to shed more light on the relation of the two monetary aggregates we calculated the money multiplier, and we show this time series in Figure 9.4. This series seems to exhibit non-stationary behavior. It declined from an initial level of around 4 to a level below 3 during the period from the 1930s to the 1970s. In the following flexible exchange rate period it increased to a level close to 7, before decreasing again. Indeed, the non-stationarity of the money multiplier is confirmed by statistical tests: The unit root hypothesis could not be rejected (ADF = -1.328, with trend) and the stationarity hypothesis has to be rejected at the 1 percent level (KPSS = 0.2671, with trend).

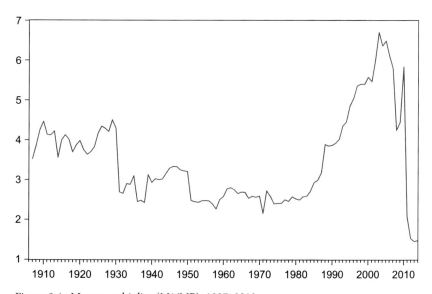

Figure 9.4: Money multiplier (M1/MB), 1907–2010

Table 9.5: *Regression residual tests M1/MB relation, 1907–2010*

$$\log\left(M1_t\right) = a + b_1 log(MB_t) + b_2(i_t) + \varepsilon_t$$

Method	b_1	b_2	R^2	DW	Engle-Granger t	Hansen Test
OLS	0.9359[***]	−0.1159	0.9763	0.1085	−2.1712	
	(0.0578)	(0.0739)				
FMOLS	0.9676[***]	−0.1011	0.9720	0.1166		1.4284[***]
	(0.0384)	(0.0549)				

Newey-West standard errors in parentheses
*, **, *** indicates significance at the 10, 5, and 1 percent levels, respectively.

The non-stationarity of the money multiplier could conceivably be caused by a third I(1) variable entering the relationship between M1 and the monetary base. The interest rate is an obvious candidate as we expect it to have a positive effect on the money multiplier, since a high rate of interest decreases banks' reserve holdings and the use of currency by the public. Therefore we tested for cointegration between M1 and MB including the interest rate. The corresponding results presented in Table 9.5 clearly point to the absence of cointegration: The hypothesis of no cointegration cannot be rejected and the hypothesis of cointegration is clearly rejected. Moreover, the interest rate coefficient has a "wrong" negative sign. In a next step, we checked whether this lack of cointegration result is caused by one or two breaks in the relationship, as with money demand. To this end we tested for multiple breaks, again using the Bai-Perron approach with a 5 percent significance level. This produced estimates for five sub-samples over roughly 100 years, which are shown in Table 9.6. However, the number of breaks is very high and the sub-sample estimates do not make economic sense: Large changes in sign and in the size of the coefficients strongly contradict what we would theoretically expect. Thus, we are forced to conclude that there is no reasonable long-run relation between M1 and the monetary base in Switzerland.

What is behind this striking instability of the money multiplier? In order to shed some light on this question, we consider the changing composition of the use of the monetary base. To this end we plot currency and the monetary base in Figure 9.5 in absolute and logarithmic scale. We see that currency develops relatively smoothly, whereas bank reserves show a very volatile time path. In addition, we know from our previous analysis that

Table 9.6: *Bai-Perron sample split regression partial adjustment M1/MB model, Switzerland, 1907–2010*

$$\log(M1_t) = a + b_1 log(MB_t) + b_2(i_t) + b_3 \log(M1_{t-1}) + \xi_t$$

Sample	b_1	b_2	b_3
1907–1937	0.5315***	0.15750***	0.4134***
	(0.0423)	(0.0325)	(0.0440)
1938–1952	−0.1115	0.3612**	1.0997**
	(0.1426)	(0.1624)	(0.1914)
1953–1975	0.5645***	−0.1122***	0.63910***
	(0.4060)	(0.0227)	(0.0411)
1976–1992	0.7012***	0.0353	0.7960***
	(0.1850)	(0.0215)	(0.0801)
1993–2010	0.3752***	0.0774**	0.4577***
	(0.0431)	(0.0379)	(0.1344)

White standard errors in parentheses, *, **, *** indicates significance at the 10, 5, and 1 percent levels, respectively.

long-run M1 demand, with currency as one component, is relatively stable over the past 100 years. This indirectly supports the view that the volatility of bank reserves is the main reason for a lack of a stable long-run relation between M1 and the monetary base. This is particularly true since 1970 and for the recent financial crisis. This instability is illustrated by the currency share in base money plotted in the last graph of Figure 9.5, which illustrates the volatility of the composition of the monetary base and shows no mean reverting tendency of the currency share in the monetary base MB. This is confirmed by a unit root and a stationarity test. The I(1) hypothesis could not be rejected, whereas the stationarity hypothesis is clearly rejected.

CONCLUSIONS

Our analysis of Swiss money (M1) demand confirms the existence of a long-run relationship between M1 and a small number of key determinants, nominal income, and interest rates, but reveals breaks of the parameter estimates around 1914, 1951, and 1979 – dates corresponding roughly to the end of the classical gold standard, the introduction of the system of Bretton Woods, and the transition to the era of floating rates of exchange, respectively. The long-run income elasticity of money demand changed

(a)

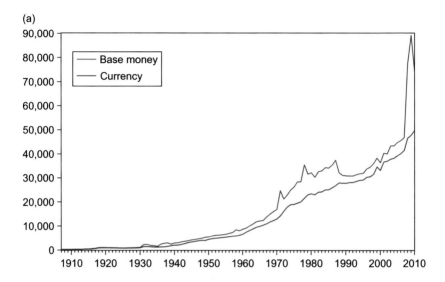

(b) Logs

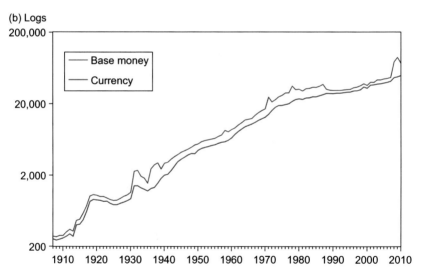

Figure 9.5: Swiss base money and currency (million SFr) (a) & (b); currency share of base money (c), 1907–2010

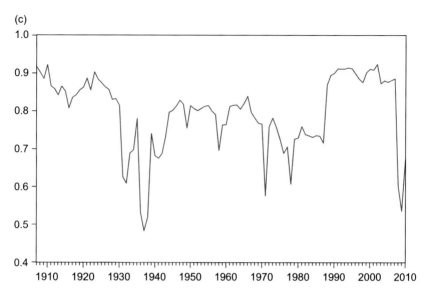

Figure 9.5: (*cont.*)

significantly at the first of these breaks, declining from an estimated value of more than 1.6 in the pre-1914 period to a value of about 1 since. The constancy of this elasticity over the entire twentieth century is remarkable.

The interest rate sensitivity of money demand was significantly negative over the entire post-1914 period, although it declined in size after 1951. For the pre-1914 years, its estimate is very imprecise (not surprisingly, given the lack of interest rate variability during this period). Furthermore, the pre-1914 era was characterized by a very slow adjustment of money demand to its long-run level (only about 10 percent annually). The adjustment speed was considerably higher in the 1914–50 period and under Bretton Woods (60 and 70 percent annually, respectively), and declined again to a level of about 30 percent afterwards.

In contrast to the relatively high degree of stability of long-run money demand, the dynamics of macroeconomic adjustment in response to deviations from equilibrium money demand underwent strong changes over the last century and a half. As expected, adjustment dynamics differed decisively according to the monetary regimes in force in different periods.

The process governing Swiss money supply (as measured by M1), in contrast to money demand, proved to be elusive and subject to much instability. An empirical analysis of the relationship between central bank money (the monetary base) and M1 reveals no clear long-run pattern, the "money multiplier" being highly unstable. The main reason for this was a very high volatility of bank reserves (the other component of central bank money, currency, showing a relatively stable development). This was one of the reasons why the SNB, when introducing monetary targeting as its monetary policy procedure after the breakdown of Bretton Woods, soon abandoned its initial attempt to target M1 and replaced it with a target for central bank money.[4]

---

[4] Although the money multiplier was perceived as a non-stationary variable, it appeared to be rather easily forecastable for eighteen months at the beginning of monetary targeting (Büttler, Gorgerat, Schiltknecht, and Schiltknecht, 1979).

10

The "Swiss Interest Rate Island" 1837–1970

Swiss interest rates appear low compared to those of other countries. For the recent floating exchange rate period, since 1973, the most obvious explanations of this phenomenon that are usually mentioned are a relatively low inflation rate and exchange rate appreciation. However, econometric analysis by Kugler and Weder (Kugler and Weder, 2002, 2005) provides evidence that the inflation- and exchange rate-corrected level of Swiss interest rates was statistically significantly lower than that in foreign countries. In other words, there was a systematic long-run deviation from uncovered interest rate parity for the Swiss franc. This property of the Swiss franc is explained by the exceptional political, economic, and monetary stability of Switzerland,[1] which leads investors to pay a premium for holding Swiss franc fixed income assets. Moreover, the Swiss franc offers diversification benefits (low correlation with other assets in other currencies) which further justify the lower return (Kugler and Weder, 2004).

Note that Swiss banking secrecy and tax benefits offer no convincing explanation for the low level of Swiss interest rates: The low interest rates are also documented for Swiss franc assets created outside Switzerland (i.e., euro currency markets) and most fixed interest rate securities deposited in Switzerland by foreign investors are denominated in foreign currencies.

---

[1] In this context we should recall our discussion of Swiss political and economic development since 1848 outlined in Part I. In particular, we should mention the development of Swiss-style liberal democratic corporatism with peaceful conflict resolution among a heterogeneous population which made Switzerland an early leading industrial nation despite a lack of natural resources. Besides the luck of not being involved in the two World Wars, this was certainly an important pre-condition for reaching and maintaining monetary and fiscal stability over the crisis-prone thirty years from the beginning of World War I to the end of World War II.

These results immediately lead to the question of how Swiss interest rates behaved under the monetary systems of earlier periods, namely Bretton Woods, the interwar gold exchange standard, the classical gold standard, and the different metallic standards before 1880. *A priori*, the stability bonus may be expected for the period since World War I, whereas the diversification benefit is less plausible for fixed exchange rate periods. So far we have only spotty evidence indicating that the period of low Swiss interest rates started after World War I (Kugler and Weder, 2002). Data from before 1914 suggest that in the late eighteenth and early nineteenth centuries, interest rates in Switzerland were higher than in other gold standard countries (see also Bordo and James, 2007, cited in Chapter 3).

This chapter provides an empirical analysis of the level of interest rates in Switzerland in an international perspective for the entire period 1837–1970. These years are mostly characterized by fixed exchange rates of the Swiss franc; periods of flexible exchange rates in this era were considered as transitory episodes. In such a framework, the direct comparison of different currencies' interest rates is meaningful without exchange rate corrections. We consider Swiss interest rates in comparison to those in France, Germany, the Netherlands, and Great Britain. These countries were economically and/or financially important for Switzerland for the period under consideration, and comparable interest rate data are available for them.[2]

DISCOUNT RATE DATA FOR SWITZERLAND, FRANCE, GERMANY, THE NETHERLANDS, AND GREAT BRITAIN

Our empirical analysis relies on discount rate data. This interest rate was the most important money market instrument for most of the period under consideration. Moreover, Homer and Sylla (2005) provide comparable annual (average) data for our five countries. For France, the Netherlands, and Great Britain the discount rate of the de jure or de facto central bank is reported. For Switzerland, the average rate of the banks of issue at four market places (Basel, Geneva, St. Gallen, and Zürich) is taken up to the foundation of the SNB in 1907. For Germany the same procedure is applied for the period before the foundation of the German Reichsbank in 1875. The data series are displayed in Figure 10.1.

---

[2] Some of the materials in Chapters 10 and 11 have also been used by the authors in a discussion of the safe haven status of the Swiss Franc and its historical development, see Baltensperger and Kugler (2016).

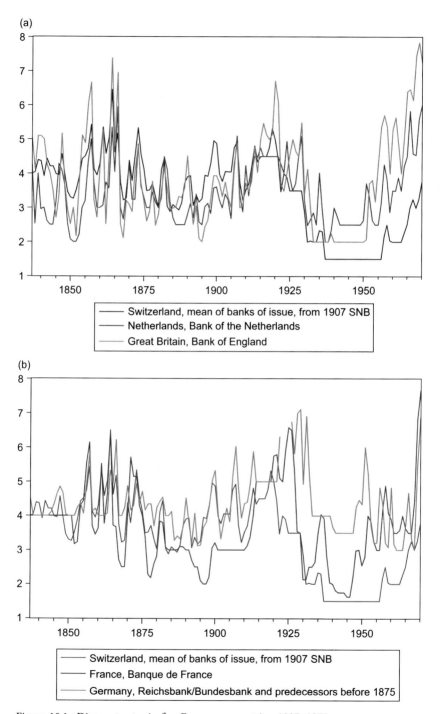

(a)

(b)

Figure 10.1: Discount rates in five European countries, 1837–1970
Source: Homer and Sylla (2005), Tables 23, 27, 29, 33,34, 61, 63, 65, 69, 71
Note: For Germany the interest rates from 1923 to 1925 are omitted because of the German hyperinflation.

Table 10.1: *Descriptive statistics for discount rates in five countries, 1837–1970*

Country	1837–1880		1881–1913		1914–1970	
	Mean	St. Dev.	Mean	St. Dev.	Mean	St. Dev.
Switzerland	4.19 (0.105)	0.697	3.81 (0.110)	0.626	2.56 (0.152)	1.149
France	3.97 (0.145)	0.965	2.96 (0.079)	0.423	3.78 (0.194)	1.463
Germany	4.36 (0.076)	0.504	4.17 (0.131)	0.748	4.45 (0.157)	1.157
Netherlands	3.38 (0.132)	0.875	3.28 (0.118)	0.678	3.58 (0.135)	1.012
Great Britain	3.95 (0.197)	1.306	3.40 (0.119)	0.683	4.01 (0.223)	1.726
ANOVA-test	$F_{(4,215)} = 7.27^{***}$		$F_{(4,160)} = 17.67^{***}$		$F_{(4,277)} = 15.16^{***}$	

Standard errors of means in parentheses, *** indicates statistical significance at the 1 percent level.

A visual inspection of these data series suggests the following pattern: For the first forty years of our sample we note that the Swiss interest rate is higher than the Dutch and the British rate, lower than the German rate, and more or less at the same level as the French rate. This pattern changes around 1880 and we note a premium of Swiss interest rates over all other countries except Germany. World War I appears to trigger the transition to the "Swiss interest rate island," and after 1930 Swiss interest rates are always the lowest among the countries considered.

Table 10.1 provides some descriptive statistics for the data series of Figure 10.1 and three sub-periods, namely 1837–80, 1881–1913, and 1914–70. Moreover, a simple ANOVA test for equality of means is reported.

First of all, we note that we can clearly reject the hypothesis of equality of the five interest rates in all sub-periods by the simple ANOVA test. However, the pattern of differences between the mean interest rates is very different across sub-periods. For the 1837–80 period, the difference is mainly created by the exceptionally low mean Dutch interest level of 3.38 percent. For all other countries, mean rates of approximately 4 percent are reported. Indeed, if we test for equality of means for Switzerland, France, Germany, and Great Britain we cannot reject the null hypothesis. This pattern changes during the classical gold standard. French and British discount rates converge to the low Dutch level of the previous sub-period and are now close to 3 percent, whereas the Swiss and German rate is only marginally reduced. After the breakdown of the classical gold standard in 1914 up to the end of the Bretton

Woods period, we find the "Swiss interest island" pattern. The Swiss discount rate is reduced to a mean of 2.5 percent, whereas all other countries show means relatively close to 4 percent.

Therefore, Swiss interest rates were in no way exceptional for the period 1837–80. Moreover, the introduction of the Swiss franc does not seem to have had a notable influence on interest rates. The only sign of weakness of the Swiss franc is represented by a relatively high interest rate compared to the older currencies with a longer history (British pound, Dutch guilder, and French franc) in the period 1881–1913. This characteristic is, however, shared with the mark, created after German unification in 1871. Thus, the data suggest a "new currency" interest rate premium during the classical gold standard. Moreover, the over-issue of banknotes by competing private and cantonal banks under the strong homogenization requirements of the 1881 federal banking law, which effectively removed the preconditions for competition in bank note issue, contributed to the weakness of the Swiss franc during this period, as discussed in Chapters 3 and 8 above.

The introduction of the Swiss franc did not have a notable average interest level effect. However, it appears that it contributed to a convergence of interest rates in the local markets in Basel, Geneva, St. Gallen, and Zürich, as evidenced in Figure 10.2. We see a strong regional variation of discount

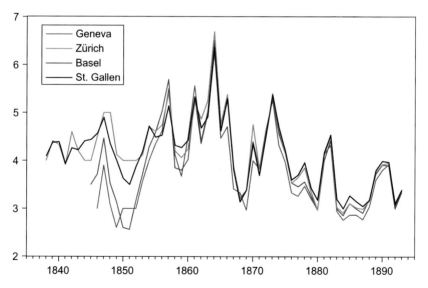

Figure 10.2: Discount rates in Basel, Geneva, St. Gallen, and Zürich, 1837–1893
Source: SNB historical series 4, T1.1a, www.snb.ch/de/iabout/stat/statpub/histz/id/statpub_histz_arch#t3

rates in the 1840s. These gaps are closed in the 1850s, and from 1855 onwards we note only very small differences between the discount rates in the different locations. Of course, the second half of the nineteenth century witnessed the information and transport revolution (telegraphy, railways, and steamships), which led to a higher degree of goods and financial market integration worldwide. The timing of interest rate convergence in Switzerland – within five years after the introduction of the Swiss franc, as displayed in Figure 10.2 – suggests that these trends toward greater market integration were not the primary drivers of this convergence.

ECONOMETRIC ESTIMATES OF MULTIPLE BREAKS IN INTERNATIONAL INTEREST RATE DIFFERENTIALS OF THE SWISS FRANC

The empirical results presented in the preceding section are purely descriptive. Moreover, the sample splits were obtained by visual inspection. These results give some useful first indications but have to be qualified by a more formal approach, given the auto- and cross-correlation of the interest rate series considered. Moreover, even if we had mostly fixed exchange rates during our sample period, the transitory periods of floating exchange rates over the two world wars and some of the interwar years may have led to longer-lasting changes in interest rate differentials. Therefore, this section provides an econometric analysis of the breaks in interest rate differentials of the Swiss franc against French franc, mark, guilder, and pound, taking into account their autocorrelation. To this end we estimate an AR(1) process for the interest rate differential and apply the Bai-Perron (2003) sequential break point test procedure. The estimation results are reported in Table 10.2. The last column shows the long-run level of the interest rate differential implied by the AR estimates.

Table 10.2 confirms the results of our descriptive analysis reported in the last section. It also provides more information on the exact timing and magnitude of changes in the long-run mean interest rate differential for the currencies considered. For the French franc we have no statistically significant intercept estimate for the 1838–88 period. This pattern is replaced for 1889–1913 by a clear long-run interest premium of 1.15 percent, and after 1914 by a 1.47 percent discount for the Swiss franc. The mark displays a slightly positive mean interest rate premium of 0.25 percent before 1921, which increases in absolute value to 2.23 percent in the second half of the sample. The guilder is characterized by an interest discount against the Swiss franc (0.67 percent) up to 1920. Then this pattern is reversed, in two

Table 10.2: *Bai-Perron break regressions for Swiss interest rate differentials, 1838–1970*

$$\left(i_{CH,t} - i_{f,t}\right) = \alpha + \rho\left(i_{CH,t-1} - i_{f,t-1}\right) + \varepsilon_t$$

AR(1) model of the difference of the Swiss to different foreign interest rates, test for breaks in intercept and AR(1) coefficient, $\alpha/(1-\rho)$ is the long run mean of the interest rate differential.

Maximum Number of breaks: 5, Significance level 10%

Country/Period	α	ρ	R^2	se	DW	$\alpha/(1-\rho)$
France 1838–1888	0.112	0.454***	0.773	0.675	1.50	0.205
1889–1913	(1.45)	(4.37)				1.15
1914–1970	0.411***	0.643***				−1.47
	(3.19)	(4.83)				
	−0.334***	0.773***				
	(−2.70)	(8.16)				
Germany 1838–1921	−0.101*	0.602	0.715	0.708	1.80	−0.254
1926–1970	(1.77)	(6.20)				−2.23
	−1.23***	0.448***				
	(−3.99)	(3.81)				
Netherlands 1838–1920	0.334***	0.500***	0.781	0.516	1.95	0.668
1921–1950	(3.80)	(5.38)				−0.816
1951–1970	−0.609***	0.254				−1.70
	(−4.80)	(1.58)				
	−1.31***	0.230				
	(−3.55)	(1.01)				
Great Britain 1838–1914	0.214**	0.373***	0.778	0.770	1.92	0.341
1915–1951	(2.13)	(2.87)				−0.631
1952–1970	−0.420***	0.335**				−3.20
	(−3.12)	(2.21)				
	−1.89***	0.409***				
	(−5.37)	(3.90)				

t-values in parentheses; *, **, and *** indicate statistical significance at the 10, 5, and 1 percent levels, respectively.

steps, to a long-run mean differential of −0.82 percent (1921–50) and −1.7 percent (1952–70), respectively. For the pound we find a similar pattern as for the guilder up to 1951. In the last twenty years of our sample, the weakness of the pound and the associated financial crises and devaluations during the Bretton Woods years are reflected by a very large average interest differential of −3.2 percent.

If we estimate the model for French and German interest rate differentials for the period 1951–70 in order to compare this directly with the Dutch and British results, we obtain a slight reduction in absolute value for Germany (−1.82 percent) and an increase for France (−2.24 percent). Interestingly, the pattern of these mean interest rate differentials from 1950 to 1970 corresponds closely to the mean deviations from uncovered interest rate parity for these currencies reported by Kugler and Weder (2002, table 1) for the years 1980–98, and three-month euro currency rates of −2.41 percent (French franc), −0.83 percent (DM), −1.00 percent (guilder), and −3.01 pound (pound). Thus, at least for money market rates, the change in the exchange rate regime did not have a large impact on the "Swiss interest rate bonus." This suggests that political and economic stability, not diversification benefits, were of utmost importance for short-term interest rates.

CONCLUSIONS

Swiss interest rates are low in international comparison. In the recent period of exchange rate flexibility since 1973, this can partly be attributed to a relatively low inflation rate and exchange rate appreciation. However, analysis by Kugler and Weder (Kugler and Weder, 2002, 2005) shows that these factors cannot fully explain the Swiss interest rate puzzle. Neither can Swiss banking secrecy and tax benefits: The low interest rates are also documented for Swiss franc assets created outside Switzerland, and most fixed interest rate securities deposited in Switzerland by foreign investors are denominated in foreign currencies.

The Swiss interest rate bonus developed over the course of the entire twentieth century. Switzerland's exceptional political, economic, and monetary stability led investors to pay a premium for holding Swiss franc fixed income assets. World War I marks the transition to the "Swiss interest rate island," and since 1930 Swiss interest rates have consistently been among the lowest of all major currency areas.

In contrast to an often held view, our empirical analysis reveals no general interest rate "malus" for the Swiss franc prior to the foundation of the SNB and World War I. We find a mixed picture of the international money market interest rate status of the Swiss franc before and during World War I. In the period 1837–88, Swiss interest rates were in no way exceptional. There is no significant difference from the French franc before 1888, and a slight advantage against the mark. The guilder, the pound, and the French franc (after 1888) had interest discounts of 0.3–1.15 percent until the 1920s. Thereafter, we see the pattern of the Swiss interest rate island develop; it becomes especially pronounced during the Bretton Woods years. This pattern was preserved in the flexible exchange rate period, at least until the most recent zero interest rate policy years.[3] Our conjecture is that it mainly reflects the relative political, economic, and monetary stability of Switzerland during the twentieth century.[4]

Interestingly, the introduction of the Swiss franc in 1850 did not have a notable average interest level effect. However, it contributed to a rapid convergence of interest rates in the local markets in Basel, Geneva, St. Gallen, and Zürich.

---

[3] The near-zero money market interest rates prevalent in many countries in recent years leave little room for a Swiss interest rate advantage. The Swiss interest rate bonus then should be reflected by an expected depreciation of the Swiss franc, which is difficult to create given the high demand for a safe currency in crisis periods.

[4] In this context it is important to note that Swiss interest rate developments cannot simply be attributed to non-involvement in the two world wars alone, as, e.g., the cases of Sweden and Argentina show. Both neutral, these countries suffered from economic and /or political instabilities leading to relatively high interest rates during the twentieth century (Homer and Sylla, 2005, pp. 530–6; 633–7).

11

The Swiss Franc at the Foreign Exchange Market
1850–2010

The Swiss franc is commonly assessed as having been a relatively weak currency up to World War I. On the one hand, this assessment is based on the Swiss money and capital market's dependence on France, the leading country in the Latin Monetary Union formed in 1865. On the other hand, a higher level of Swiss interest rates in the prewar period, compared to other gold standard countries, is cited as evidence (Bordo and James, 2007; Kugler and Weder, 2002). According to this view, the strength of the Swiss franc developed after World War I, as reflected in the internationally low level of real and exchange rate-corrected Swiss interest rates in the twentieth century (Kugler and Weder, 2002, 2004, 2005).

In this chapter we consider direct evidence on the development of the Swiss franc's exchange rate against major currencies under metallic monetary standards from 1850 to 1914 and under the period of transition to a paper monetary standard after World War I.[1] The period from 1850 to 1914 is analyzed in the first section, where the deviations from metallic parities of the Swiss franc against five currencies (French franc, German mark, Dutch guilder, British pound, and Italian lira) are considered. The second section provides an analysis of the development of the real and nominal exchange rate of the franc against the US dollar and the British pound for the period since 1914. The selection of the dollar and the pound is motivated by their international importance in the past century. The pound was the leading international currency before the Great Depression and World War II; thereafter this role was taken over by the dollar, which was clearly the most important currency worldwide under the Bretton Woods system. Moreover, these two currencies experienced a high degree

---

[1] For a related discussion, see Baltensperger and Kugler (2016).

of stability for many years before their decline after the Great Depression and the breakdown of the Bretton Woods system, respectively. For most of the other major currencies of the "long" nineteenth century a long-run assessment is not very meaningful, as they were replaced sooner (mark) or later (French franc, guilder, and lira). However, as the development of the Swiss franc exchange rate against the euro has played a major role in the SNB's monetary policy in the more recent past, we also present an empirical analysis for the real and nominal SFr/Euro exchange rate using quarterly data up to 2014.

DEVIATIONS FROM METALLIC PARITIES OF THE SWISS FRANC BEFORE WORLD WAR I

Before we turn to the data and empirical results, we should recall some basics of exchange rate determination under a metallic standard with and without a central bank. The exchange rate regime between two currencies was determined spontaneously by the internal monetary regime selected by the two countries concerned and by private arbitrage operations. First, for currencies that shared the same metallic standard (say silver or gold) under a regime of full convertibility and free international movement of money and the monetary metal, private arbitrage resulted in an equilibrium exchange rate corresponding to the relative metallic content of the currencies being exchanged.[2] Second, for currencies with a different metallic monetary standard, the arbitrage-equilibrium exchange rate evolved according to the relative price of the two metals.[3] Third, when convertibility was suspended for at least one of the currencies, no arbitrage was possible, and the exchange rate was fully flexible and determined by the volume of fiat money issued. Of course, arbitrage operations were restricted by transaction costs; however, these were reduced greatly by the information and transport revolution of the nineteenth century, which was triggered by the introduction of telegraphy, steamships, and railways.

---

[2] Arbitrage operations involved exchanging the overvalued against the undervalued currency and converting it to the monetary metal, which is then converted again into the overvalued currency, yielding an arbitrage gain.

[3] Arbitrage operations were more complicated in this case than in the case of identical metallic standards: If the exchange rate of, say, the Dutch (silver) guilder against the (gold) pound was higher than the silver-gold ratio, arbitrageurs could buy guilders for pounds, convert them into silver, sell the silver to buy gold, and convert the gold again into pounds, thereby making an arbitrage gain. Thus in the long run, the exchange rate was flexible but followed the relative price developments of silver and gold.

Exchange rate data for the Swiss franc from 1852 onwards are available in the *Handbook of Exchange Rates* by Denzel (2010). From 1842 to 1852 there are quotations of the Zürich gulden, a 9.51 gr. fine silver currency, against a couple of foreign currencies. Therefore we include this data as a "predecessor" of the Swiss franc in our analysis. The exchange rate against the French franc (a bimetallic currency with 4.5 gr. fine silver Ag; 0.2901 gr. Gold Au); the mark (Hamburg, 8.66 gr. Ag; German Empire from 1873 onwards, 0.3905 gr. Au); the Dutch guilder (9.45 gr. Ag, 0.6048 gr. Au from 1876 onwards); the British pound (7.32 gr. Au); and the Italian lira (Piedmont before 1861, 4.5 gr. Ag; 0.2901 gr. Au) is considered. The Swiss franc (and the Zürich gulden) shared metallic standards with all currencies except the pound before Switzerland adopted the full French bimetallic standard in 1865. Therefore the metallic parities were easy to calculate in most cases, given the metallic contents of the currencies given above. For the years before 1865 and the pound we calculated the time varying metallic parity of the silver Zürich gulden and Swiss franc against the gold pound using the data on the London market price of gold and silver that is provided in Officer and Williamson (2013).

The exchange market data is based on bills of exchange drawn between Zürich and the foreign cities (Paris; Amsterdam; London; Hamburg till 1872, Berlin thereafter; Genoa till 1861, Milan thereafter) provided by Denzel (2010, pp. xxii–xlix; 313–26). The exchange rate is quoted in Swiss francs per unit of foreign currency. The data are annual and obtained as averages of monthly observations. Given this market data and the metallic parities, we calculate the deviations from parities in percentage points. This allows us to get some information on the strength of a currency: If it is undervalued with respect to the metallic parity, markets see a risk with respect to its convertibility, or other restraints on arbitrage operations such as capital controls in the future. Thus if the Swiss franc is weak relative to the pound (i.e., the pound is strong), we expect positive deviations of the pound exchange rate from parity. This measure is only meaningful if actual convertibility is given.

These series are displayed in Figure 11.1. From 1842 to 1852 we have data for the Zürich gulden and from 1852 to 1914 for the Swiss franc. The data overlap in 1852 allows us to check the strength of the Swiss franc in comparison to the Zürich gulden.

The graphic representations of these deviations suggest the following observations. First, we note more volatile exchange rates for the years before 1875. This reflects the decrease in transaction costs and the move to the international gold standard in the last quarter of the nineteenth

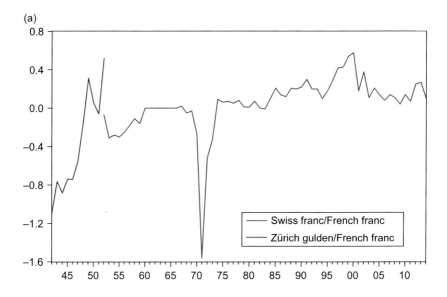

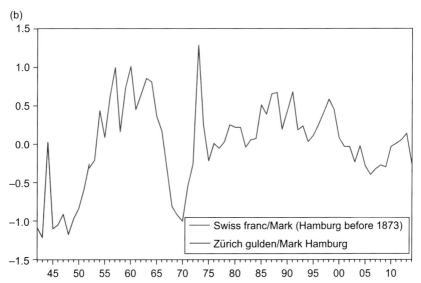

Figure 11.1: Deviations from metallic parity, Swiss franc (1852–1914) and Zürich gulden (1842–1852)

century. Second, we note some large deviations from parity for the Italian lira for the periods of suspended convertibility resulting from excess paper money creation (1866–80, 1893–1905). Moreover, the Swiss franc was generally overvalued against the lira, even for the years with convertibility.

Figure 11.1: (*cont.*)

As a consequence of the suspension of convertibility in reaction to the Franco-Prussian war, even the French franc suffered from this problem (1871–7), albeit to a lesser extent. Third, we note an equal or mostly lower deviation from parity for the Swiss franc than for the Zürich gulden in

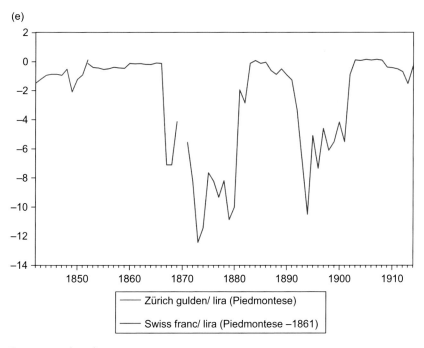

Figure 11.1: (*cont.*)

1852. In this sense the Swiss franc appears as a successful replacement of the Zürich gulden for international transactions. Fourth, we note a mixed picture of over- and undervaluation of the Swiss currencies against the French franc, the mark, the pound, and the Dutch guilder before 1875. Only in the second half of our sample is a consistent undervaluation of the Swiss franc visible.

Table 11.1 reports some descriptive statistics for the deviations from parity. For the French franc and the Italian lira, only years with convertibility were included in the sample. Moreover, Table 11.2 provides some information on the linear relationship between the series obtained by a principal component analysis. We note that on average the Swiss franc is undervalued: The mean ranges from 8.6 bps to 57 bps for the French franc and the Dutch guilder, respectively. Applying a standard *t*-test indicates that all these mean estimates are significantly different from zero. The principal component analysis shows an interesting pattern: The first significant component with high loadings on the mark, guilder, and pound exchange rate represents all non-French influences on the foreign

Table 11.1: *Deviations from parity, Swiss franc exchange rate against five currencies, 1852–1914, in percent*

Exchange rate of Swiss franc	Mean	St. Dev.	Min	Max
French franc 1852–1870, 1878–1914	0.086	0.193	−0.311	0.578
Mark	0.142	0.452	−1.005	1.289
Dutch guilder	0.571	0.634	−0.432	2.069
British pound	0.271	0.461	−0.407	2.102
Lira 1852–1865, 1881–1886, 1906–1914	−0.429	0.644	−2.459	0.160

Table 11.2: *Principal component analysis of deviations from parity, Swiss franc exchange rate against French franc, mark, Dutch guilder, and British pound, 1852–1870, 1878–1914*

Eigenvalues			
Number	Value	Proportion	Cumulative Prop.
1	2.473871	0.6185	
2	1.140736	0.2852	0.6185
3	0.195955	0.0490	0.9037
4	0.189438	0.0474	0.9526

Eigenvectors (loadings):				
Variable	PC 1	PC 2	PC 3	PC 4
French franc	−0.179640	0.879502	0.389886	0.205414
Mark	0.534829	0.401871	−0.730997	0.134538
Dutch guilder	0.577485	−0.223620	0.421499	0.662452
British pound	0.590083	0.122353	0.368742	−0.707716

Correlations:				
	French franc	Mark	Dutch guilder	British pound
French franc	1.000000			
Mark	0.114895	1.000000		
Dutch guilder	−0.423010	0.618063	1.000000	
British pound	−0.138849	0.765971	0.753438	1.000000

exchange value of the Swiss franc. The second component is a French franc factor with a corresponding loading of 0.89. This pattern is reflected by the relatively high correlation between the exchange rates against the mark, guilder, and pound.

In order to check the stability over time and the statistical significance taking into account autocorrelation and heteroskedasticity (Newey-West standard errors), we applied the sequential break point analysis of Bai and Peron (2003) with a significance level of 5 percent to four exchange rates and the years with convertibility. The lira was left out as it lacks sufficient continuous observations with convertibility. This exercise provides some interesting insights. First, the French franc is undervalued (mean $= -7.3$ bps, t-statistic $= -1.76$) for the period 1852–70/1878–83. This pattern is reversed for the years 1884–1914 (21.5 bps, $t = 5.74$). The mark shows no statistically significant deviation from parity and no break is indicated (14.2 bps, $t = 1.58$). For the guilder and the pound we find identical patterns: For the period 1852–65 we have a very strong overvaluation (154 bps, $t = 8.86$; 83 bps, $t = 3.56$, respectively), which is strongly reduced for the second subsample 1866–1914 (29.3 bps, $t = 5.08$; 12.5 bps, $t = 2.60$, respectively).

Finally, we applied a threshold error correction model to our exchange rate data for the period 1866–1914 for the guilder and the pound, as well as a reduced sample for the French franc (1878–1914). For the mark, this model provides no sensible results.[4] In this framework we take into account non-linear adjustment,[5] as the exchange rate may adjust differently depending on whether we have a "small" or a "large" past deviation from parity for the exchange rate y:

$$\Delta y_t = \lambda_1 \left(y_{t-1} - yp_t - a_1 \right) + \varepsilon_t, \text{ if } abs\left(y_{t-1} - xp_t \right) < \tau$$
$$\Delta y_t = \lambda_2 \left(y_{t-1} - yp_t - a_2 \right) + \varepsilon_t, \text{ if } abs\left(y_{t-1} - xp_t \right) \geq \tau$$
$$\lambda_1, \lambda_2 \leq 0;$$

This model is usually motivated by transaction costs: If the deviation from parity is too small to recover transaction costs of arbitrage, we have no or only a minor adjustment of the exchange rate ($\lambda_1 \sim 0$). For large deviations we have full or nearly full adjustment to parity, as arbitrage is profitable ($\lambda_2 \sim -1$). Moreover, we allow for a systematic overvaluation ($a < 0$) or undervaluation ($a > 0$) of the Swiss franc exchange rate, which may differ across the two regimes. The threshold τ is not known and is therefore estimated using a grid search minimizing the sum of squared residuals.

---

[4] There is no significant regime change for this currency. The linear model shows a surprisingly slow adjustment estimate ($\lambda = -0.328$, t-value $= -2.74$) and no significant deviation from parity ($\hat{a} = 0.00087$, t-value $= 0.84$).

[5] This approach is employed in Bernholz and Kugler (2011) and Kugler (2011) for the dynamic adjustment of exchange rates in different local markets.

Table 11.3: *Estimation results threshold autoregressive model log, Swiss franc to French franc, guilder, and pound exchange rate, 1866–1914, France 1878–1914*

$$\Delta y_t = \lambda_1 \left(y_{t-1} - yp_t - a_1 \right) + \varepsilon_t, \, if \, abs\left(y_{t-1} - xp_t \right) < \tau$$
$$\Delta y_t = \lambda_2 \left(y_{t-1} - yp_t - a_2 \right) + \varepsilon_t, \, if \, abs\left(y_{t-1} - xp_t \right) \geq \tau$$
$$\lambda_1, \lambda_2 \leq 0;$$
$$Var(\varepsilon_t) = \sigma^2 / n_t$$

Heteroskedasticity caused by varying number of monthly observations (n_t) in some years is taken into account in estimation by transforming the observations (multiplication by $1/n_t^{1/2}$).

	a_1	λ1	a_2	λ2	τ	R^2	DW
French franc	0.00159 (0.00036)	−0.496 (0.192)	−0.00926 (0.0036)	−1.977 (0.727)	0.0038	0.312	2.54
Dutch guilder	0.00220 (0.00060)	−1.071 (0.159)	−0.0055 (0.00213)	−1.081 (0.346)	0.0038	0.550	2.31
British pound	−0.0050 (0.0120)	0.109 (0.238)	−0.00108 (0.00094)	−0.671 (0.0629)	0.0026	0.338	2.08

Note: Standard errors in parentheses.

The results of this analysis are presented in Table 11.3. First, we note that the estimated threshold τ is very low and in the range between 0.26 and 0.38 percent. This is consistent with results for the guilder/pound exchange rate provided by Kugler (2014), which show a strong reduction of the threshold estimate for adjustment of the exchange rate during the nineteenth century. For the French franc we report a relatively weak adjustment within the τ-band and a high adjustment coefficient in absolute value outside the band, which is however not statistically different from −1. According to the arbitrage model, under transaction costs we would expect no adjustment within the band. However, this adjustment may be triggered by non-arbitrage payments caused by export and imports of goods, services, and capital. It is interesting to note that the a-coefficients estimates, which are statistically highly significant, have different signs: Within the band we obtain a positive estimate, indicating a long-run undervaluation of the Swiss franc of approximately 16 bps, whereas for the case of large deviations from parity we find a negative intercept term, indicating a long-run overvaluation of the Swiss franc of 9 bps. The same pattern holds true for the Dutch guilder, with a 22 bps undervaluation within the band and a 55 bps overvaluation outside the band. Interestingly, the intercept estimate differs between regimes, whereas the adjustment parameter is very close to -1 in both regimes. For the pound we find a random walk behavior of the exchange rate within the τ-band in line with the arbitrage model and we therefore cannot estimate a_1 in a reliable way, as λ_1 is not statistically different from zero. However, the a_2 is negative too, but not statistically significant. These findings indicate that in "normal" times there is a tendency to undervaluation of the Swiss franc, whereas in "extreme" times we have a tendency to overvaluation of it. Thus it appears that some properties of the "strong" Swiss franc since World War I were present already in the "long" nineteenth century.

PURCHASING POWER PARITY AND TRENDS IN THE REAL EXCHANGE RATE FOR THE SWISS FRANC 1914–2010

In this section we will consider the development of the Swiss franc since 1914. Recall from Part II of this book that this period witnessed the transition to an international paper standard which was completed with the adoption of flexible exchange rates for major currencies in 1973. During this period we had very different monetary standards for the Swiss franc. After the breakdown of the classical gold standard in 1914, Switzerland experienced roughly ten years of inconvertibility of banknotes and flexible exchange rates. The exchange rate against the dollar was de facto fixed again in late 1924 at the prewar parity, and gold convertibility was resumed in 1929. The revived gold standard was short-lived, however, soon falling victim to the Great Depression. Switzerland, as a member of the gold block, maintained gold parity longer than most other countries, but finally reduced the gold content of the franc by about 30 percent and suspended gold convertibility in fall 1936. Subsequently, the country moved to a paper standard and operated with exchange controls and (after 1941) a split dollar market for trade and financial transactions. Switzerland did not join the Bretton Woods institutions after World War II, but de facto fixed the exchange rate according to the rules of the Bretton Woods system. In this framework the international payment system was liberalized, and in 1958 all major currencies adopted convertibility for current transactions. The inconsistency of US monetary and fiscal policy with a fixed gold price of \$35/oz during the 1960s then led, after attempts to save the system through exchange rate adjustments, to the breakdown of the Bretton Woods agreement over the period 1971–3. Since then we have lived in a world with inconvertible paper monies and correspondingly fully flexible exchange rates.

This short account of the development of the Swiss franc and the international monetary system makes clear that for this period, deviations from metallic parity are no longer a useful yardstick for assessing the strength of a currency. Instead we use the relative purchasing power parity model, including the possibility of a deterministic trend in the real exchange rate, mainly caused by different relative productivity and terms of trade developments in two countries under consideration. Therefore, we may differentiate between two sources of nominal strength of a currency: first, a "PPP component" stemming from relatively low trend inflation and a more stability-oriented monetary policy, and second, a "real component" resulting from relative productivity gains.

This analysis is carried out for the pound and dollar exchange rate of the Swiss franc using annual data from 1914 to 2010 and the CPI of the three countries involved. The data source for the exchange rates and the Swiss CPI is the SNB's "Monthly Statistical Bulletin"; British and US inflation data are taken from Officer and Williamson (2013). The annual series used are averages of monthly data. First of all we have to check whether the PPP model is meaningful with this data. Therefore we run some static regression cointegration tests, reported in Table 11.4. We selected this approach instead of a multivariate method, such as Johansen's test based on an error

Table 11.4: *Regression residual deterministic cointegration tests SFr/£ and SFr/$,*
1914–2010

$$y_t = b_0 + b_1 x_t + b_2 t + \varepsilon_t$$

y: log exchange rate, *x*: log relative CPI

Exchange rate	Method	b_1	b_2	R^2	DW	Engle-Granger t	Hansen test
SFr/£	OLS	0.9235*** (0.0616)	−0.00996*** (0.00145)	0.9807	0.4095	−4.636**	
	FMOLS	0.9167*** (0.0860)	−0.00986*** (0.00213)	0.9805	0.4270		0.3736
SFr/$	OLS	1.123*** (0.2329)	−0.00887*** (0.00187)	0.8850	0.2771	−3.602*	
	FMOLS	1.242*** (0.2578)	−0.00727*** (0.00248)	0.8830	0.2863		0.35649

Notes: Newey-West standard errors in parentheses; *, **, *** indicates significance at the 10, 5, and 1 percent levels, respectively.

correction system, simply because the switches in the exchange rate regime lead to changes in the adjustment dynamics and a constant EC model over the entire sample is clearly mis-specified.

The results presented clearly point to deterministic cointegration between the two exchange rates and the relative price level with unit elasticity as implied by PPP. First, the Engle-Granger test rejects the null hypothesis of no cointegration; second, the Hansen (1992) parameter instability test (null hypothesis of cointegration) does not reject it. Moreover, both OLS and FMOLS estimates indicate that the slope coefficient is statistically clearly different from zero, but not from one.[6] The deterministic trend is highly statistically significantly different from zero. These estimates indicate that we have an annual real trend appreciation of the Swiss franc amounting to 1 percent and 0.9 percent for the pound and the dollar, respectively. These results are confirmed by unit root tests for the real exchange rate including a deterministic trend: The ADF-test statistic for the null hypothesis of a unit root is -4.498^{***} (£) and -3.472^{**} ($),respectively.

Figure 11.2 visualizes the PPP relationship using restricted estimates with unit elasticity. The trend coefficient is slightly changed, to -0.0084 (£) and -0.0097 ($), respectively.

We see from Figure 11.2 that the pound exchange rate is less volatile than that of the dollar: The residual from the log PPP regression (left-hand scale) has a standard deviation of 0.13, approximately 13 percent, whereas this value is very close to 20 percent for the dollar. The fixed exchange rate periods, in particular the Bretton Woods years, are neatly visible and we clearly see the accumulated appreciation pressure of the Swiss franc against the dollar during this period. Interestingly, the pound exchange rate appears to be in long-run equilibrium in 2010, whereas the dollar is *c.* 7 percent below the equilibrium value.

Figure 11.2 does not allow for differentiating between the two sources of the nominal appreciation of the Swiss franc. It gives no information on how many of the long-run exchange rate developments are due to a pronounced price stability/low inflation policy on the part of the SNB and to the real appreciation of the Swiss franc, respectively. Figure 11.3 provides some information on this issue. It shows the hypothetical development of the exchange rate without any real appreciation and the fitted

---

[6] OLS as well as FMOLS estimates are super-consistent. However, FMOLS corrects for possible endogenous regressors which invalidate statistical tests based on autocorrelation corrected covariance matrix of OLS estimates (Hamilton, 1994, pp. 571–629).

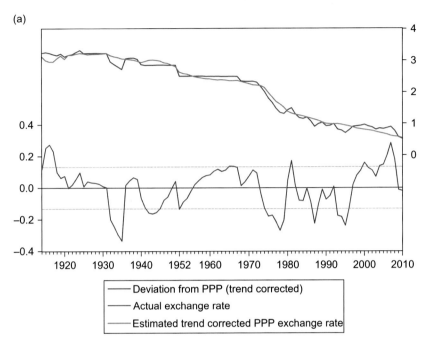

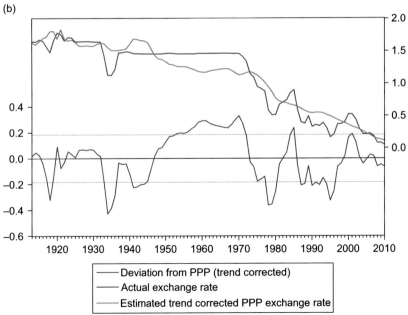

Figure 11.2: Fitted values and residuals from trend-corrected PPP model, Swiss franc, (a) (Sfr/£, log) and (b) (Sfr/US$, log) 1914–2010

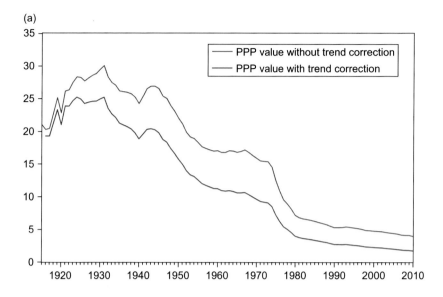

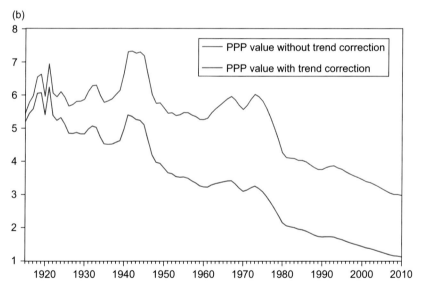

Figure 11.3: Fitted PPP values with and without real trend correction, Swiss franc, (a) (Sfr/£, log) and (b) (Sfr/US$, log) 1914–2010

values presented before including the deterministic trend in the exchange rate. The "pure" PPP component of the Swiss franc's appreciation against the pound is impressive. It implies that the value of the pound fell from the gold standard parity of 25.20 Fr. in 1925 to approximately 4 Fr. in 2010.

The further reduction through real appreciation to 1.7 Fr. appears relatively small compared to the decline of the pound caused by an over-expansive monetary policy during the past nearly one hundred years. For the dollar, this picture is different: We note a fall from the gold standard parity of 5.18 Fr. to a PPP value of approximately 3 Fr. The real appreciation reduced this equilibrium value to 1.1 Fr., nearly one third of the "pure" PPP component.

These results lead to the question: What is behind the trend of the Swiss franc's real appreciation against two currencies of highly developed countries with a similar real per capita income level? In our view, the most convincing explanation is the so-called Balassa-Samuelson effect. In contrast to the United States and UK, Switzerland is characterized by a highly productive exports sector, while the productivity of the domestic sector producing non-tradable or protected goods is relatively low. Under these circumstances, competition in the labor market leads to excessive (compared to productivity) wages, and correspondingly high prices in the domestic sector. This leads then to an appreciation of the real exchange rate calculated with a general price index like the CPI. However, we should mention that the importance of the Balassa effect is controversially discussed in the literature and some authors argue that changes in the terms of trade are the real origin of real Swiss franc appreciation.[7]

Table 11.5 contains some results on the dynamic adjustment of exchange rates and relative price levels. To this end an error correction model was estimated for three sub-periods, namely 1916–45, 1946–71, and 1973–2010. The selection of these periods is motivated by international monetary regimes. The first time span is characterized by flexible exchange rates, interrupted by a short gold standard interlude from 1925 to 1931 (pound) and 1933 (dollar). The second period is of course motivated by the fixed rate system of Bretton Woods, and in the last period we have a flexible exchange rate regime for the currencies considered. Besides the error correction coefficients γ_1 and γ_2, we report the R^2 and the residual standard error of the two EC equations. For World War I, World War II, and the interwar period, we find a highly significant adjustment of the exchange rate to PPP disequilibria and no statistically significant response

---

[7] The Balassa-Samuelson effect is supported by the econometric analysis of real exchange rates and labor productivity in OECD countries for the period 1970–92 provided by McDonald and Ricci (2007). The use of total factor productivity data from 1984 to 2008 leads Gubler and Sax (2014) to the contrary conclusion and confirmation of the robust effect of the terms of trade on the real exchange rate, as stressed by Sax and Weder (2009).

Table 11.5: *EC model estimates SFr/£ and SFr/$ for sub-periods, 1914–2010*
y: log exchange rate, x: log relative CPI

$$\Delta y_t = \gamma_1 \left(y_{t-1} - b_0 - x_{t-1} - b_2 t \right) + a_{11} \Delta y_{t-1} + a_{12} \Delta x_{t-1} + \varepsilon_{1t}$$

$$\Delta x_t = \gamma_2 \left(y_{t-1} - b_0 - x_{t-1} - b_2 t \right) + a_{21} \Delta y_{t-1} + a_{22} \Delta x_{t-1} + \varepsilon_{2t}$$

	γ_1	γ_2	R^2 Δy	R^2 Δx	se Δy	se Δx
SFR/£ 1916–1945	−0.344 (0.169)	0.09992 (0.0871)	0.139	0.0601	0.0942	0.0486
SFR/£ 1946–1971	−0.0166 (0.146)	0.699 (0.263)	0.151	0.534	0.0308	0.129
SFR/£ 1973–2010	−0.481 (0.113)	0.0229 (0.0384)	0.418	0.620	0.0774	0.0263
SFR/$ 1916–1945	−0.408 (0.120	0.0834 (0.0824)	0.394	0.109	0.0804	0.0554
SFR/$ 1946–1971	−0.0228 (0.0291)	0.264 (0.0440)	0.0448	0.777	0.0101	0.0152
SFR/$ 1973–2010	−0.377 (0.124)	−0.0007 (0.0163)	0.283	0.678	0.0971	0.0129

Note: Standard errors in parentheses.

of the relative price levels. The adjustment of the dollar rate is marginally faster than that of the pound rate: 41 and 34 percent of a deviation from PPP is corrected within one year. Moreover, standard error and R^2 estimates indicate that the dollar rate is less volatile and more predictable than the pound rate. Thus the dominance of flexible exchange rates is mirrored in the estimated exchange rate dynamics. For the Bretton Woods period we get, as expected, a reversed adjustment dynamic: The relative price level adjusts to deviations from PPP and there is no statistical evidence in favor of an adjustment of the exchange rate. This process is particularly fast for the pound, where we find an adjustment of 70 percent within one year (dollar: 26 percent). This is probably caused by the highly open Swiss and British economies, with strong effects of the exchange rate on the CPI in both countries, whereas the US CPI hardly reacts to the exchange rate given the high degree of closedness of the US economy in the early postwar period. The post-1973 period is characterized by exchange rate adjustment and no significant CPI reactions to deviations from PPP in all three countries. This adjustment is marginally faster than in the period 1916–45 and the predictability of exchange rate fluctuations of the pound appears higher in the post-1973 period than in the earlier period, whereas this is not true for the dollar.

PURCHASING POWER PARITY AND TRENDS IN THE REAL SWISS FRANC/EURO EXCHANGE RATE 1978–2014

Figure 11.4 displays the quarterly development of the real effective exchange rate index (log) of the Swiss franc against the countries of the current eurozone. Before turning to the econometric analysis of these data we have to mention two differences to our analysis of dollar and pound. First, we now consider an effective exchange rate index defined in the usual way, with an increase denoting an appreciation of the Swiss franc. Second, the data on the euro exchange rate are to some extent synthetic data, as they include the exchange rates of the national currencies before the creation of EMU. In this sense the data are likely to be less reliable than the data for currencies such as the dollar and the pound, which existed over the entire sample.

Figure 11.4 clearly shows the real appreciation trend of the Swiss franc against the currencies of the eurozone and against the euro after 1999. The crucial question is whether this trend is a random walk with drift or a

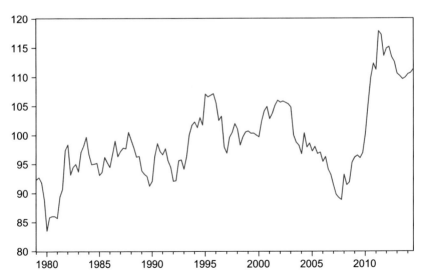

Figure 11.4: Real effective SFr/Euro (zone) exchange rate, log, Jan. 1999 = 100, 1978–2014

Data source: Table G1a, www.snb.ch/de/iabout/stat/statrep/statpubdis/id/statpub_statmon_arch_xls.de

deterministic linear trend, as was shown to be the case for the dollar and the pound using annual data since 1910. In the former case we have no long-run anchor for the real exchange rate, whereas in the latter we have reversion to a linear deterministic trend. Figure 7.1 suggests that appreciation was particularly strong during the first couple of years of the flexible exchange rate period. This is plausibly caused by a "repressed" appreciation during the late Bretton Woods years and the transition to flexible rates. Moreover, the process of European monetary integration effectively started in the late 1970s with the creation of the European Monetary System (EMS). Therefore, we used a slightly reduced sample from 1978 to 2014 for our econometric analysis of the Swiss franc/euro real exchange rate.

Application of the ADF unit root test and the KPSS stationarity test points to a deterministic trend of the real exchange rate. The unit root hypothesis can be rejected with a marginal significance level of 6.4 percent (ADF = −3.343) whereas the stationarity hypothesis for the deviation from a deterministic trend cannot be rejected at any reasonable significance level (KPSS = 0.074). The slope of the trend function is slightly larger than 0.1 percent, amounting to an annual trend real appreciation of approximately 0.45 percent. We may note in passing that this result supports the Balassa explanation of the trend appreciation of the Swiss franc. It is approximately half the size of the estimate for the United States and UK. It is plausible that the core EMU countries share, to some extent, the Swiss characteristics of productivity differences between the export and domestic sector.

Figure 11.5 shows the implication of this trend behavior of the real exchange rate for the nominal effective exchange rate. This figure tells us that in late 2014 the nominal exchange rate was about 5 percent above the trend line. This is rather small compared to the estimated 12–15 percent over- and undervaluation of the Swiss franc that was experienced in 2011 and 2008, respectively.

The residual displayed above can be well approximated by an AR(1) process with AR coefficient equal to 0.89. This implies that the average half-life of a shock is approximately six quarters.

In order to explore the dynamics of the exchange rate, we estimated an error correction model with deterministic cointegration. The estimation with a lag length of 4 for the first difference terms is reported in Table 11.6.

The two error correction coefficient estimates have the expected sign. However, only the coefficient in the exchange rate equation is statistically significant and relatively large in absolute value. Thus the relative price level is indicated to be weakly exogenous and the adjustment to long-run

Table 11.6: *EC model estimates SFr/Euro, 1978–2014* y: log exchange rate, x: log relative CPI

$$\Delta y_t = \gamma_1 \left(y_{t-1} - b_0 - x_{t-1} - b_2 t \right) + \sum\nolimits_{i=1,4} \left(a_{11} \Delta y_{t-i} + a_{12} \Delta x_{t-i} \right) + \varepsilon_{1t}$$

$$\Delta x_t = \gamma_2 \left(y_{t-1} - b_0 - x_{t-1} - b_2 t \right) + \sum\nolimits_{i=1,4} \left(a_{21} \Delta y_{t-i} + a_{22} \Delta x_{t-i} \right) + \varepsilon_{2t}$$

	γ_1	γ_2	R^2 Δy	R^2 Δx	se Δy	se Δx
SFR/Euro	−0.111 (0.00376)	0.00422 (0.00835)	0.107	0.239	0.0219	0.0031

Note: Standard errors in parenthesis.

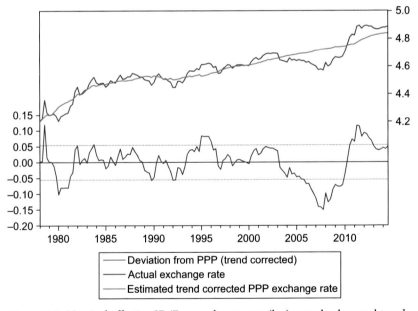

Figure 11.5: Nominal effective SFr/Euro exchange rate, (log): actual values and trend (fitted values), 1978–2014

equilibrium is brought about by exchange rate adjustment. Within a quarter, approximately 11 percent of equilibrium deviations are corrected in this way. Note that this estimate is in line with the annual adjustments of 48 percent and 37 percent estimated for the pound and the dollar, respectively, during the flexible exchange rate period.

CONCLUSIONS

The Swiss franc is usually seen as having been a relatively weak currency in the nineteenth century, up to World War I. Our analysis corrects this assessment to a certain extent. Deviations from metallic parities of the Swiss franc provide interesting insights. While the French franc was somewhat undervalued relative to the Swiss franc (with a mean of -7.3 bps) in the periods from 1852 to 1870 and from 1878 to 1883, this pattern was reversed in the years 1884 to 1914 (+21.5 bps). The mark shows no statistically significant deviations from parity until World War I. For the guilder and the pound we find identical patterns: For the period from 1852 to 1865 we see very strong overvaluation (+154 bps and +83 bps, respectively), which was much reduced during the years 1866 to 1914 (+29.3 bps, +12.5 bps, respectively). Judged against this background, the Swiss franc seems to have been a relatively "normal" currency in the nineteenth century, with periods of strength and weakness alternating.

Comparisons with the Zürich gulden at the time of the introduction of the Swiss franc show equal or lower deviations from parity for the franc than for the gulden. In this sense, the new Swiss franc seems to have been a successful replacement of the older (local) currency for international transactions.

Interestingly, a threshold error correction model indicates a tendency of the nineteenth-century Swiss franc toward undervaluation in "normal" times, while in "extreme" times (with "large" adjustments) a tendency to overvaluation existed. Thus it appears that an element of the "safe haven attribute" developed by the Swiss franc over the twentieth century was already present in the "long" nineteenth century.

In the periods after World War I, the Swiss franc experienced a strong real and nominal trend appreciation against both the pound and the dollar, the only two other major currencies which survived the political and economic disasters of the twentieth century. The real appreciation of the franc followed a stable deterministic trend with an appreciation rate of nearly 1 percent per year, presumably caused by the Balassa effect. Removing the real trend from the nominal exchange rate shows a strong equilibrium appreciation of the Swiss franc caused by inflation differentials, in particular after World War II. As with interest rates, we see an acceleration of this development in the Bretton Woods years and its continuation after the transition to flexible exchange rates. A similar pattern of real and nominal appreciation of the Swiss franc also occurred against the euro and the previous currencies of the eurozone countries, with a trend real appreciation of slightly less than half a percentage point since 1978.

12

Monetary and Macroeconomic Effects of Swiss Banking and Finance 1890–2010

In the nineteenth century, without a central bank, the history of money in Switzerland was a history of specie and of private and public note-issuing banks competing with each other. In Chapters 2 and 3, and then again in Chapter 8, we have reviewed Swiss banks and the development of the Swiss banking sector with respect to their role as issuers of paper money before the creation of the SNB in the period 1905–7. In contrast, in the twentieth century, with the country now having a central bank, the banking system no longer played the same central role for the analysis of money and monetary processes. Under a system of central banking, a currency is "made" by the central bank, not by commercial banks.

Consequently, there is no special need to discuss the development of banking in order to understand the monetary developments under the central bank regime. Neither the internal and external strength of the Swiss franc – with low inflation and real appreciation – nor the very high real income level achieved by the Swiss economy have been mainly caused by the Swiss banking and financial sector. Of course, banks are part of the environment which influences the central bank and the results of its actions, along with many other actors and influences. In this sense, their role needs to be taken into account in order to understand monetary policy and its effects. It is erroneous, however, to see the banking sector and its structure – including banking secrecy – as the primary force shaping macroeconomic variables, such as the price level, exchange rates, or the level of interest rates and their fluctuations. This does not mean, obviously, that a well working and reasonably efficient financial sector is not important for economic development. That is true for every country, and Switzerland is no exception in this respect.

This stands in strong contrast to a widely held view according to which the economic success experienced by Switzerland over the twentieth century is to a large extent based on the country's financial sector, in particular banks. The foreign demand for Swiss financial services, it is said, led to high incomes and returns in the financial sector, as well as to money and capital inflows which allowed Switzerland to attain a high level of capital per capita and correspondingly high real wages. These developments, the argument goes on, were in particular fostered by Swiss banking secrecy legislation introduced in 1934. This allowed foreigners to avoid taxes on bank accounts and securities deposited with Swiss banks, with some of these funds even being of illegal origin. In consequence, foreigners were willing to accept low pre-tax returns in Switzerland, explaining the low real and exchange rate-corrected interest rates experienced by Switzerland since World War I.

However, as we have already pointed out in Chapter 10, Swiss banking secrecy and tax benefits offer no convincing explanation for the low level of Swiss interest rates, as the low interest rates are also documented for Swiss franc assets created outside Switzerland (i.e., euro currency markets) and most fixed interest rate securities deposited in Switzerland by foreign investors are denominated in foreign currencies.

Nevertheless, the development of the Swiss financial sector and its international relations is of interest in itself. We know from the statistics on portfolio holdings of residents and non-residents at Swiss banks that have been published by the SNB since 1999 that large stocks of assets are involved in this business: The franc value increased from approximately 2.8 trillion (6.8 times GDP) at the end of 1998 to 5.1 trillion (9.4 times GDP) at the end of 2013.[1] This is exceptional by any international standard, and wealth management clearly creates a lot of income for Swiss banks. Learning more about the historical development of these activities would be of great interest. Unfortunately we have no direct information on these portfolio stocks deposited with Swiss banks for periods prior to 1998. However, recently, historical series of Swiss GDP disaggregated into the contributions of different sectors were made available for the entire period since 1890. This allows us to analyse an indicator of the importance of the financial sector for Swiss economic development during the past 120 years, besides consideration of the development of bank balance sheets relative to GDP.

A second aspect that we will briefly touch upon in this chapter is the relevance of foreign money and capital inflows for Swiss economic development. Today Switzerland is known as a large exporter of capital, with net foreign assets of nearly 800 billion francs (1.3 times GDP) and with large

---

[1] Data source: Monthly Statistical Bulletin of SNB, Table D51, www.snb.ch/de/iabout/stat/ statrep/statpubdis/id/statpub_statmon_arch_xls_de.

current account surpluses.[2] These data are only available in their present form for the period since 2000. However, we have some estimates for the trade balance in goods and services going back to 1890, and current account data for some sub-periods (including factor incomes and unilateral transfers). These data allow us to make an informed guess as to the date when Switzerland turned into a net capital exporter and no longer had to depend on foreign capital for economic development. Moreover, in this chapter we consider the development of Switzerland's foreign assets and liabilities, and their implications, since 1999.

THE CONTRIBUTION OF THE FINANCIAL SECTOR TO GDP, BANKS' BALANCE SHEETS, AND BANK LEVERAGE: DATA AND DESCRIPTION

Figure 12.1 shows the development of the financial sector's share (banking and insurance) in nominal Swiss GDP from 1890 to 2010. No data are available for earlier periods. In the late nineteenth century, the sector contributed less than 2 percent to Swiss GDP. This share then increased to about 5 percent in 1930, after a short decline during World War I. World War II and the first twenty-five postwar years show a decline of the GDP contribution to 3 percent, the same level as 1913/14. From 1970 onwards we note a very strong and volatile expansion of the financial sector, reaching a peak of 12 percent before declining again to 10 percent during the recent financial crisis.

Figure 12.2 displays the ratio of the total balance sheet of the banking sector relative to GDP since 1890. Up to 1975 this ratio moved in a relatively narrow range between approximately 1.3 and 2.2. We note a strong contraction of the balance sheet during the two World Wars. In the past forty years we see a tremendous increase in the banks' balance sheet, which was mainly driven by an expansion of foreign activities and a concentration process of large banks (a reduction from five such banks to two). The two large banks' balance sheet share reached a peak of about 70 percent in 2007. Note that the two indicators (share in GDP/balance sheet to GDP ratio) are highly correlated.

These two figures show that the financial sector's great importance in Switzerland is a historically quite recent phenomenon, starting long after political, economic, and monetary stability were firmly established. Moreover, it is questionable whether the rapid expansion of the financial sector

---

[2] Data source: Monthly Statistical Bulletin of SNB, Table R, www.snb.ch/de/iabout/stat/ statrep/statpubdis/id/statpub_statmon_arch_xls_de.

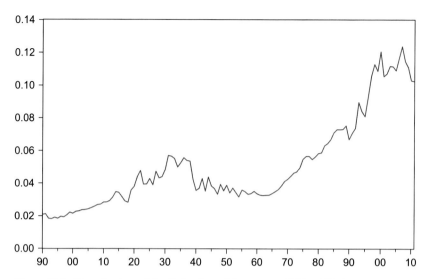

Figure 12.1: Contribution of the Swiss financial sector to GDP, 1890–2010
Data source: Swiss economic and social history database, Table Q17a, Q18a, Q18b,
www.fsw.uzh.ch/hstat/nls_rev/overview.php

over the past few decades has really been beneficial for the country. At least two aspects raise doubts about the blessings of the financial and banking boom since 1975.

First, the size of the Swiss banking sector relative to GDP has grown to reach extraordinary dimensions in international comparison. Along with this, an exceptional degree of concentration – with only two large banks, both of which are "too big to fail" – has been reached. This creates high economic, legal, and political risks, particularly under present circumstances of international pressure to stamp out tax evasion.

Second, this expansion was driven by a tremendous increase in leverage, which made the banks very vulnerable to losses on their assets. This increase in leverage was a very dangerous development, without visible advantage for the Swiss economy. The figures below, borrowed from Junge and Kugler (2013), show series of the leverage (total balance sheet relative to equity) of the Swiss banking sector, Swiss real GDP growth, and the interest spread between mortgages and savings deposits or medium-term bank bonds since 1881, the year of the federal banking act. It is striking to note that, from 1881 to 1945, banks operated with considerably more capital than is the case today. Leverage was well below 10, particularly before World War I. We saw a doubling of leverage after World War II, to

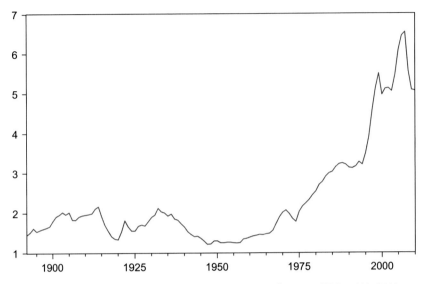

Figure 12.2: Balance sheet of the Swiss banking sector relative to GDP, 1890–2010
Data definitions and sources: balance sheet of discount banks, land credit banks, cantonal banks, and
large banks before 1906, all banks except private banks and foreign banks from 1906 (Swiss
economic and social history online database, www.fsw.uzh.ch/hstat/nls/ls_files.php?chapter_var=./o;
SNB historical statistics www.snb.ch/de/iabout/stat/statrep/statpubdis/id/statpub_histz_arch#t3; and
monthly bulletin www.snb.ch/de/iabout/stat/statpub/statmon/stats/statmon/statmon_D1_1)

17 during the Bretton Woods period; subsequently, leverage reached a
peak of 24 in 2000 and 2007, but it recently declined again, back to the
level of the 1970s.[3] The highly volatile development of the past twenty
years is mainly attributable to the leveraging and deleveraging process at
the large banks during the period of euphoria, the crisis during the Swiss
real estate boom in the 1990s, and then the build-up of the subprime
bubble after 2004. During the entire period, long-term Swiss economic
growth remained close to 2.5 percent per year, and there is no indication
that growth was fostered by this increase in bank leverage (see Figure 12.3).
On the contrary, if there was any change at all, we would identify a slight
decline in average growth over the past thirty-five years. Thus there is no

---

[3] The increase in leverage between 1945 and 2010 might have been even more spectacular
if hidden reserves held in the postwar period were included in the measure of leverage. Of
course, there are no reliable statistics on hidden reserves and the extent of this effect is
difficult to quantify.

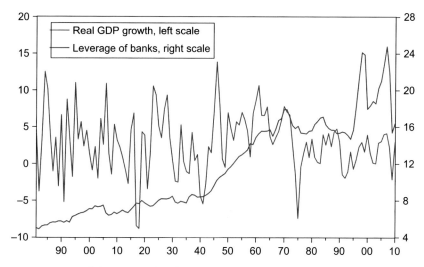

Figure 12.3: Bank leverage and real GDP growth, Switzerland, 1881–2010
Data source: see Junge and Kugler (2013), figure 3

prima facie evidence that the secular rise in banking activity and leverage elicited a corresponding upward trend in economic growth.

Moreover, as shown in Figure 12.4, the trend in interest rate spreads between bank lending and bank borrowing does not suggest any improvement for bank customers during the period of strongly increasing leveraging of banks. We show this for three interest rates that are available for our long historical timeframe, namely mortgages on the one hand and savings and medium-term bank bonds on the other. The latter spread appears clearly stationary despite the trend increase in leverage. Interestingly, the former spread actually widens with the trend increase in leverage, indicating worsening credit conditions or higher costs of financial intermediation by banks during the past 130 years.

Obviously, these are very general observations across many different banks. They ignore changes in asset quality and maturity profiles, as well as many other potential determinants of economic growth and interest rates besides leverage. Nevertheless, they do not provide any support for claims that the expansion and concentration process was of particular benefit for the Swiss economy. Finally, we may mention that econometric models estimated by Junge and Kugler (2013, section 5) show that the leverage-driven expansion of the Swiss banking sector increased the probability of the occurrence of a financial and banking crisis and a subsequent crisis-

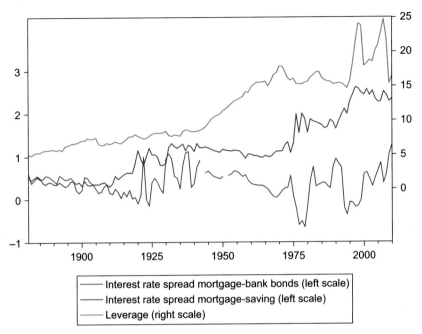

Figure 12.4: Bank leverage and interest rate spreads (%), Switzerland, 1881–2010
Data source: see Junge and Kugler (2013), figure 4

related permanent reduction of the level of real GDP – approximately 17 percent on average, if judged by the experience of the severe crises of 1911, 1931, 1991, and 2007.

THE CONTRIBUTION OF THE FINANCIAL SECTOR TO GDP, BANKS' BALANCE SHEETS, AND BANK LEVERAGE: SOME ECONOMETRIC RESULTS

This section provides some econometric results on the dynamic interrelationship between the financial and banking sector and the rest of the economy. This serves as a supplement to the results presented in the preceding section and provides additional information on the argument that beyond its direct contribution to GDP, the financial and banking sector is an important driver of growth in the other sectors of the economy. To this end we present a VAR analysis of the growth rates displayed in Figures 12.5 and 12.6, namely those of the real GDP contribution of the financial and non-financial sector, overall nominal GDP, and banks' balance sheet, respectively.

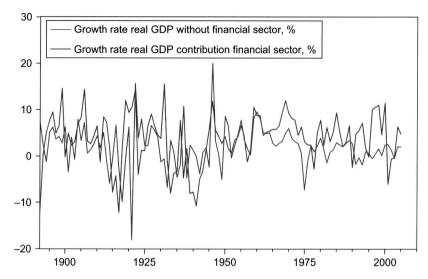

Figure 12.5: Real GDP growth contribution of the financial and non-financial sectors, %, Switzerland, 1881–2010
Data source: see Figure 12.1

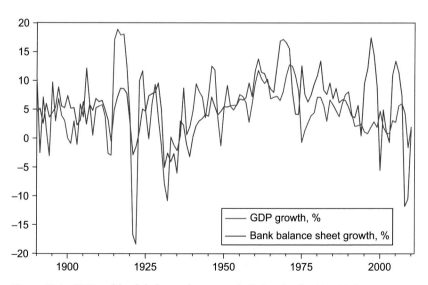

Figure 12.6: GDP and bank balance sheet growth, Switzerland, 1881–2010
Data source: see Figure 12.4

Table 12.1: *VAR results real growth of financial (x) and non-financial sectors (y),*
Switzerland, 1890–2010

	1893–1945	1946–1973	1974–2005
Granger causality x to y	4.91*	8.18**	0.287
$X^2(2)$	(0.086)	(0.017)	(0.866)
Granger causality y to x	4.06	8.73**	1.19
$X^2(2)$	(0.131)	(0.013)	(0.551)
Correlation of VAR residuals	0.024	0.435**	0.091

Marginal significance in parentheses, *, **, *** indicates statistical significance at the 10, 5, and
1 percent levels, respectively.

Figures 12.5 and 12.6 suggest a time-varying correlation between the
growth rates of the GDP contribution of the financial and non-financial
sectors, as well as GDP growth and bank balance sheet growth. Therefore
we tested for the stability over time of the two equations of a VAR model
with lag length 2. Indeed, the application of the Bai-Perron multiple break
test procedure indicates that the growth rates displayed in Figure 12.5 and
12.6 have two break points, namely 1946 and 1974. Interestingly, these
mark the beginning and end of the Bretton Woods system.

Table 12.1 reports the most important estimation results relevant to our
question for the three sub-periods. Besides the Granger causality test
(significance of lagged values of the other variable in the VAR model),
we report the contemporaneous correlation of the VAR residuals. We note
that in the first sub-period up to 1945, there is no or only a very weak
relationship between the two series. The Granger causality test is insignificant at the 5 percent level and the residual correlation is practically zero.
This pattern changes for the Bretton Woods period (1946–73): We find a
highly statistically significant feedback relationship and a high residual
correlation. For the most recent floating exchange rate period, with its
strong expansion of the banking sector, we find no statistically significant
relationship between the growth rates of the financial and non-financial
sectors, which show independent growth patterns. Thus, the years from
1946 to 1973 are exceptional in an overall perspective, with a strong lagged
and contemporaneous feedback relationship of growth rates. One explanation for this could be that the Bretton Woods system's strong restrictions
on international capital flows linked banks more to domestic development,
whereas this was not the case under the liberalized regimes of international
capital flows characterizing the recent and the gold standard eras.

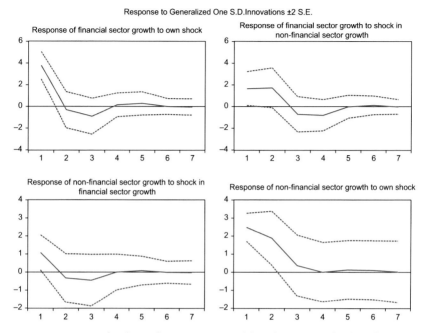

Figure 12.7: Generalized impulse response, VAR(2) real GDP growth of the financial and non-financial sectors, Switzerland, 1946–1973

Figure 12.7 shows the generalized impulse response of the VAR model for the period 1946–73. This approach, introduced by Pesaran and Shin (1998), treats both variables symmetrically, and not asymmetrically like the standard Choleski decomposition with its recursive representation of residual correlation. This is important in our context, with a high residual correlation. This exercise shows a somewhat stronger and longer-lasting response of the financial to the non-financial sector than can be seen the other way around: A 4 percent shock in the financial sector leads to a 1 percent one-year response of the non-financial sector, whereas a 2.5 percent non-financial shock results in a 2 percent response of the financial sector over two years.

Table 12.2 reports the most important estimation results for the VAR model for nominal GDP and bank balance sheet growth. As data for aggregate nominal GDP is available for the period since 1851, we use an extended sample. The Bai-Perron approach indicates one structural break in 1916 and we report results for two sub-periods. We note that in the first sub-period up to 1915 there is no relationship between the two series

Table 12.2: *VAR results balance sheet (x) and GDP non-financial sector (y) growth, Switzerland, 1852–2010*

	1852–1915	1916–2010
Granger causality x to y	1.40	11.89***
$X^2(2)$	(0.497)	(0.003)
Granger causality y to x	0.142	1.65
$X^2(2)$	(0.932)	(0.438)
Correlation of VAR residuals	0.121	0.174*

Marginal significance in parentheses, *, **, *** indicates statistical significance at the 10, 5, and 1 percent levels, respectively.

indicated. The Granger causality test is insignificant at any reasonable significance level and the residual correlation is statistically not different from zero. This pattern changes for the 1916–2010 period: We find a highly statistically significant lagged influence of balance sheet on GDP growth and a moderately positive correlation of the VAR residuals. This suggests a strong effect of bank balance sheet expansion on GDP growth. This conclusion is, however, premature: The high statistical significance of the Granger causality test is brought about by lag one and two coefficients with opposite sign. This leads to a mainly transitory influence of balance sheet growth on GDP growth, as illustrated by the generalized impulse response of the 1916–2010 VAR model estimates displayed in Figure 12.8.

In summary, based on all the empirical results provided in this chapter, we conclude that there is no convincing empirical evidence that Switzerland's monetary and economic success has been predominately created by its financial sector. A more justified conclusion would be, rather, that the financial sector (among others) has profited from the exceptional political and economic stability of the country.

SWISS TRADE AND CURRENT ACCOUNT BALANCE 1890–2010

Unfortunately, a data series for the entire period 1890–2010 exists only for the trade balance in goods and services. For the current account (including factor incomes and unilateral transactions), estimates are available only for the interwar period (1921–39) and from 1948 to 1991. An elaborate balance of payments statistic has been provided by the SNB since 2000. We display both international balances in Figure 12.9, measured as a share of GDP. We note first that the two series move together for the periods

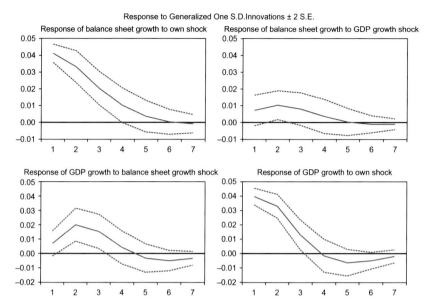

Figure 12.8: Generalized impulse response, VAR(2) GDP and bank balance sheet growth, Switzerland, 1916–2010

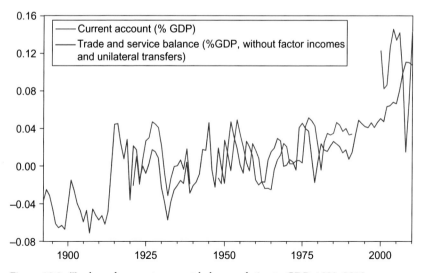

Figure 12.9: Trade and current account balance relative to GDP, 1890–2010
Data source: Swiss economic and social history data base, Table Q17a, Q18a, Q18b), www.fsw.uzh.ch/hstat/nls_rev/overview.php; Monthly Statistical Bulletin of SNB, Table Q1, www.snb.ch/de/iabout/stat/statrep/statpubdis/id/statpub_statmon_arch_xls_de

where both are available, and that the current account balance is mostly positive and tends to exceed the trade balance. This suggests that Switzerland has been a net international creditor since the interwar period. Moreover, for the 1948–91 period, there seems to exist a two-year lag between the trade balance and the current balance. For the most recent years, we observe very high volatility of the current account, which is caused by highly volatile capital returns during the 2001 and 2008 financial crises.

The Swiss trade balance shows three different characteristics. Before World War I, Switzerland had a persistent trade deficit of approximately 4 percent of GDP. From 1915 onwards, the country moved to a trade surplus with a mean of around 2 percent. After the breakdown of the Bretton Woods system we note an upward trend of the trade balance, peaking at a level of approximately 10 percent of GDP in 2010. The pattern displayed in Figure 12.9 suggests that World War I represented a major break in the development of Swiss foreign balances. It marks the beginning of a transition from a trade deficit to a trade surplus in goods and services, which then resulted in a current account surplus from 1925 onwards and a net international creditor position for Switzerland. Thus Swiss economic development's dependence on foreign money and capital was only a characteristic of the "long" nineteenth century, and has clearly not been relevant for the past 100 years.

SWITZERLAND'S FOREIGN ASSETS AND LIABILITIES 1999–2014

This section provides some information on the development of Swiss foreign assets and liabilities since 1999, when detailed quarterly data became available. This exercise is motivated by Switzerland's sustained large current account surplus over the past twenty years and the resulting huge net foreign asset position, as mentioned before. Usually, net capital exports or imports are seen as a passive consequence of consumption and investment decisions reflected by the current account. However, this view may not be appropriate in a world with highly integrated financial markets (Borio, Shin, and James, 2014). Under such circumstances, gross "excess financial elasticity" of capital movements may itself be an important driver of macroeconomic development. This aspect, which appears to have been important in the most recent financial crisis as well as in the crises of the early 1930s, may be of particular relevance for Switzerland, with its internationally important financial sector and its multinational firms, resulting in very large gross foreign assets and liabilities.

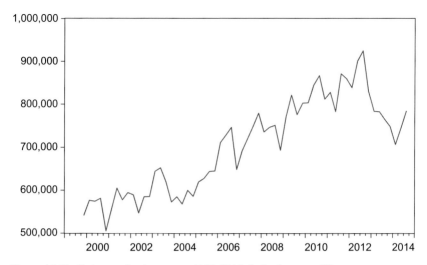

Figure 12.10: Swiss net foreign assets, 1999–2014, Swiss francs, millions
Data source: Monthly Statistical Bulletin of SNB, Table_R4, www.snb.ch/de/iabout/stat/statrep/
statpubdis/id/statpub_statmon_arch_xls_de

Figure 12.10 displays the quarterly development of Swiss net foreign
assets since the end of 1999. We observe an increase of approximately
80 percent in net foreign assets from 1999 to 2012, followed by a 20 percent
decline over the subsequent two years. The latter development is surprising
given the fact that Switzerland maintained a large current account surplus,
in the range of 60 to 80 billion francs, in 2012–14. Note, however, that this
hardly discussed fact relegates the SNB's heavily disputed book losses on its
international reserves – in a small two-digit billion franc range – to an issue
of minor importance relative to the overall book losses of the Swiss
economy on its net foreign asset position.

To understand this divergent development of the current account and
net foreign assets, we have to consider gross foreign assets and liabilities
and their currency structure. Figure 12.11 shows the development of Swiss
foreign assets (SNB and non-SNB owned) and liabilities. We observe
tremendous growth of assets, leading to a level that was twice as large in
2014 in comparison to 1999, and nearly seven times GDP. Until 2009, this
growth was mainly driven by the private sector's accumulation of foreign
assets. However, after that non-SNB foreign assets grew relatively weakly
and the growth in foreign assets was dominated by a tremendous accumulation of central bank international reserves, which reached a level of
approximately 500 billion francs in 2014. Therefore, the private sector

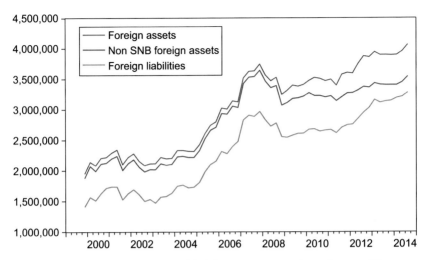

Figure 12.11: Swiss foreign assets and liabilities, 1999–2014, Swiss francs, millions
Source: Monthly Statistical Bulletin of SNB, Table_R4, www.snb.ch/de/iabout/stat/statrep/
statpubdis/id/statpub_statmon_arch_xls_de

substituted foreign assets with domestic (Swiss franc) assets created by the central bank. Foreign liabilities grew at nearly the same pace and recently reached a level that is more than five times GDP. The strong growth of these gross figures is caused by the tremendous expansion of the financial sector which we documented earlier in this chapter, and conforms with the "excess financial elasticity" hypothesis of Borio, Shin, and James (2014).

Most interesting is the currency composition of Swiss foreign assets and liabilities. Figure 12.12 displays the shares of Swiss franc-denominated assets and liabilities. The share of Swiss franc-denominated assets increased slightly from around 16 percent in 1999 to around 18 percent in 2008. Since then we note a decrease, to slightly more than 12 percent in 2014. Interestingly, we see that the franc's share in foreign liabilities was always substantially larger. It remained close to 55 percent until 2008; from then onwards we see a tremendous increase of this share, reaching 65 percent in 2014. This development is probably caused by the increasing attractiveness of the Swiss franc as a safe haven currency in the recent crises. In addition, at the zero lower bound of short-term interest rates, the Swiss franc's trend appreciation makes it internationally interesting from a rate of return perspective, in contrast to the periods of substantially lower Swiss interest rates in the past, as discussed in Chapter 10. These conditions mean that we have a currency mismatch between foreign assets and

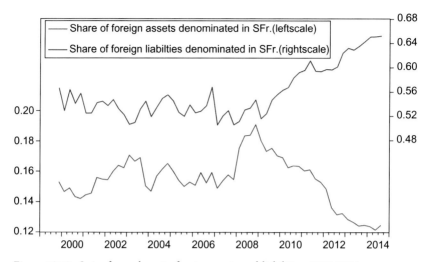

Figure 12.12: Swiss franc share in foreign assets and liabilities, 1999–2014
Source: Monthly Statistical Bulletin of SNB, Table_R3, www.snb.ch/de/iabout/stat/statrep/statpubdis/id/statpub_statmon_arch_xls_de

liabilities, which increased strongly in recent years. This implies that the Swiss economy bears a large and increasing exchange rate risk. For instance, a 10 percent appreciation of the Swiss franc in 2014 leads to a 8.8 percent loss on foreign assets, whereas foreign liabilities are only reduced by 3.5 percent, given the foreign currency shares of 88 percent and 65 percent, respectively. Therefore, we see that the notable decrease in Swiss net foreign assets in recent years is mainly driven by a strong franc appreciation and an increased currency mismatch.

CONCLUSIONS

Our analysis in this chapter of the role of the Swiss financial system and its contribution to Swiss GDP shows that the perception of banks' and the financial sector's paramount importance for the economic success of Switzerland is false. First of all, recall that Switzerland's per capita income was already high in international comparison in the nineteenth century (see Chapter 1), when Swiss banking was still rather unimportant. In the late nineteenth century, the financial sector's contribution to Swiss GDP was still less than 2 percent. This share then increased to about 5 percent in 1930, but it declined again to 3 percent in1960, the level seen in 1914.

Finally, from 1970 onwards, the Swiss financial sector embarked on a very strong and volatile path of expansion, reaching a peak of 12 percent in the 2000s, before declining again to 10 percent during the recent financial crisis. Banks' balance sheet data in relation to GDP followed a similar course.

This shows that the great importance of the financial sector in Switzerland is a historically quite recent phenomenon, starting long after the country's political, economic, and monetary stability was already firmly established. Beyond this, the rapid expansion of the financial sector over the past forty years, which went along with a huge increase in bank leverage, undoubtedly generated large returns but also created high risks for the country – risks which became clearly visible in the financial crisis of 2008. The empirical results we provide in this chapter allow us to conclude that there is no convincing evidence that Switzerland's monetary and economic success has been predominately created by its financial sector. A more justified conclusion would be that the financial sector has profited from the country's exceptional political and economic stability.

Swiss trade and current account balance data show that World War I represented a major break in the development of Swiss foreign balances. It marked the beginning of a transition from a trade deficit to a trade surplus in goods and services, which then resulted in a current account surplus from 1925 onwards and a net international creditor position of Switzerland. Thus Swiss economic development's dependence on foreign money and capital, while being characteristic of the "long" nineteenth century, has clearly not been relevant in the past hundred years.

The development of Switzerland's foreign asset and liability positions, marked by strong growth in both since 1999, reveals an expanding currency mismatch between assets and liabilities over recent years, creating a large and increasing exchange rate risk for the Swiss economy.

Conclusion

In innumerable ways, the present reflects the past. Decisions by our parents, grandparents, and their ancestors – along with the events of their own times, which they could not influence themselves – have shaped the world in which we live today. In this way, the present and the past are inseparably linked; the former cannot really be understood without knowing the latter. Seen from this perspective, the study of history asks for no further motivation.

Yet, above and beyond this, it is legitimate and reasonable to ask what we can learn from history. Obviously, the world is in continuous motion and the problems of the present always differ in one way or another from those of the past. Nevertheless, many relations and patterns remain more or less unchanged over long periods of time, and many questions recur in slightly altered forms in later periods. In this sense, the study of history can provide useful insights and lessons valuable for today.

This applies, among many other fields, to the history of money and currency. Monetary and financial arrangements are among the central institutions shaping our economies and societies. This book has tried to show that Swiss monetary history offers a wide range of experiences relating to many questions which, not least in view of the current turbulence in worldwide money and financial markets, continue to be, or have become once again, of great relevance. The following stand out.

THE VITAL IMPORTANCE OF POLITICAL AND FINANCIAL STABILITY FOR THE RISE OF A CURRENCY

At its inception, the Swiss franc was not exactly predestined to become one of the world's most stable and successful currencies. Created through the Federal Coinage Act of 1850, two years after the foundation of the modern federal state of Switzerland, the new Swiss franc was essentially a satellite currency of the French franc. This continued to be the case for the first fifty years of its life, until the establishment of the Swiss National Bank in the period 1905–7. During this period, the Swiss franc was far from being the strong currency that we know today. As we have seen, it was just an "average" currency, with alternating phases of weakness and strength relative to other currencies used at the time. In the decades before World War I, the Swiss franc was characterized by an interest rate "malus" with respect to the French franc, rather than the interest rate bonus we are familiar with today.

Since the outbreak of World War I, the Swiss franc's value has increased hugely against all other currencies. In 1914, the US dollar was worth 5.18 Francs; in 2015, by contrast, it could be purchased for less than 1 Franc. The relative loss of value was even greater in the case of all other currencies. In 1914, the pound sterling was worth just over 25 francs; at the time of writing it stands at about 1.3 francs. The relative loss of value is particularly pronounced in the case of the former partner currencies in the Latin Monetary Union – the French franc and, even more extreme, the Italian lira, whose values in Swiss francs at the time of the euro's introduction in 1999 had to be measured in terms of thousandths.[1] As for the German mark, created after German unification in the 1870s, it lost its value completely during the German hyperinflation of the early 1920s.

The Swiss franc's advance from a satellite of the French franc to an independent and strong currency of international importance went hand in hand with Switzerland's political and social consolidation and its increasing economic success. The country's firm determination to remain independent and to maintain financial and monetary stability – traits which have always been particularly characteristic of Switzerland when compared to other countries – played a key role in this respect. In a social and political environment characterized by instability, tension, and strife, it is extremely difficult to establish and maintain a stable monetary order. The fact that Switzerland has been spared wartime turbulence for a century and a half, due to both political prudence and fortuitous circumstances, has naturally also helped in creating the stability and trust from which the Swiss franc benefits today.

---

[1]   At the end of 1998, the old French franc and the Italian lira were valued at 0.0024 and 0.00084 Swiss francs, respectively. See also Kugler (2012).

MONETARY, FINANCIAL, AND ECONOMIC STABILITY ARE INTERDEPENDENT

While the Swiss currency's stability has benefited from Switzerland's growing political and economic success, it is also true that the country's focus on monetary and financial stability has made an important contribution to political and economic consolidation. The two go hand in hand. Steady money and well-functioning, efficient financial structures are among the most important achievements of an economic and social system. A stable currency, in particular, is one of our most valuable public goods, comparable to an efficient system of law, of public security, or of public finance and taxation. Without it, a liberal economic and social order cannot effectively develop.

Economic history is full of examples that show how problematic or, indeed, failing currencies can harm the efficiency of an economic system and, in extreme situations, lead to economic and political collapse. In the course of the nineteenth and twentieth centuries, Switzerland succeeded – to some extent through slow and painful experience – in creating institutions and systems that proved robust and resistant to this danger. An acute public awareness of the importance of monetary stability and reliability has been instrumental for this development.

Contrary to a widely expressed view, it is not true, however, that the stability and success of the Swiss economy over the past hundred years is to a large extent due to the international role of Swiss banking and finance, in particular Swiss banking secrecy. Our analysis of the role of the Swiss financial system and its contribution to Swiss GDP shows that this perception is without foundation. Switzerland was already a high-income country in international comparison in the nineteenth century, and the great importance of the financial sector in the Swiss economy is a historically quite recent phenomenon. Furthermore, the huge increase in bank leverage which went along with the rapid expansion of banking and finance since 1970 created not only high returns, but also high risks for the country – risks which became evident in the financial crisis of 2008. Thus we do not arrive at the conclusion that Switzerland's monetary and economic success has been predominately created by its financial sector. Rather, the financial sector has profited from the exceptional political and economic stability of the country.

METAL-BASED VERSUS PAPER-BASED CURRENCIES

Together with many other countries, Switzerland made the transition from a metal-based currency to a purely paper-based fiat money regime during the course of the twentieth century. The clearest and most definitive break in this process was the worldwide transition to flexible exchange rates after the breakdown of the Bretton Woods standard at the beginning of the 1970s. The demise of the traditional metal-based currency systems actually dates back to the early years of the century, when the international gold standard broke down following the start of World War I. However, currency arrangements in the years between the two World Wars and during the Bretton Woods era in the postwar period remained strongly influenced by the ideas of gold standard orthodoxy, and maintained important elements of a metal-based currency and a linkage to gold.

The transition from fixed to flexible exchange rates at the beginning of the 1970s represented an enormous increase in central banks' power, while at the same time vastly extending their accountability to the public. Not until they were freed from the responsibility to maintain a fixed gold parity – and the implied subordination of monetary policy to the restrictions of balance of payments equilibration – were central banks fully able to conduct an autonomous monetary policy directed primarily at domestic objectives. By removing all linkages between money in circulation and the amount of a currency metal available, this step gave central banks much more freedom and flexibility in their monetary policy. Needless to say, however, this also created great temptations and risks. Not for nothing can the twentieth century be described as the century of inflation. The experiences of the most recent financial and debt crises, in particular, have again raised doubts among many observers about the current paper-based money system.

Nevertheless, proponents of metal-based currency systems would do well to remember that even these systems can lose their stability anchors – and have often done so in the past. History books are full of cases where the value of coin deteriorated, or where supposedly fixed metal-based parities were abolished or changed for reasons of political expediency. Consequently, we should avoid a naïve, idealizing view of metal-based currencies. These currencies were based on a self-imposed commitment on the part of monetary authorities to maintain a fixed metal content of the currency unit "for all eternity." Self-imposed commitments are valuable and useful. They establish barriers that provide protection from overly opportunistic changes. But ultimately they are only as good as the political determination to comply with them on which they are dependent.

Moreover, even metal-based currencies played strictly by the rules do not provide an unlimited guarantee of price level stability. Only when the real structures of an economy remain constant over time is this strictly the case. If there are shifts in the productivity of metal mining, however, or if there is a growth-based increase in periodic supplementary demand for currency metal, there may be permanent alterations in the price level, even under a metal-based standard.[2] What is more, one need only examine the history of the Swiss currency during the nineteenth century to find manifold illustrations of the fact that metal-based currency systems can be marred by serious inefficiencies.

COMPETITION AND MONOPOLY IN MONEY AND CURRENCIES

The choice between competition or monopoly in the area of coinage and money has occupied the minds of economists across the ages. Should governments be granted a monopoly over currency, banknotes, and bank regulation, or is it preferable that free competition exists between the issuers of currencies and money? The question of competition and monopoly arises at various levels. At the most basic level, it concerns the definition of the currency unit and the minting of coins. Next, it relates to the issue of paper money in the form of banknotes, and finally, it involves the creation of money in the form of bank deposits. The monetary history of Switzerland in the nineteenth century provides a wealth of experience concerning these questions.

Historically, the view became clearly established that money, being characterized by strong network effects, displays aspects of a public good and hence naturally tends toward centralization and monopoly. Today's scholarly assessment predominantly confirms this position. Swiss monetary history is consistent with this point of view. After its introduction in 1850, the new Swiss franc rapidly and without difficulty established itself as the national currency. Clearly, the transition from the previous chaos of multiple coinage and monies to a uniform national currency met a real need and made a decisive contribution to the efficiency of the Swiss monetary and payment system and the strength of the Swiss economy overall.

In the preceding period, from 1820 to 1850, Switzerland had provided a rare example of true currency competition, with free choice between currency denominations comparable to Hayek's proposal of 1978. The lack of any national currency unit gave independent note-issuing banks complete

---

[2]   The best known historical example of this is the "price revolution" in Europe in the early modern period, triggered by the fact that production costs of silver in the Latin American colonies of Spain collapsed permanently.

freedom in the choice of the currency basis for the banknotes they issued. This competition was successful insofar as the purchasing power of the issued banknotes remained stable and no bank failures and crises resulted from it. However, the banknotes created by issuing banks were not much in demand – an indication of their lack of attractiveness and efficiency in practice.

This phase came to an end with the introduction of the new Swiss franc in 1850. From 1850 to 1881, the Swiss monetary system – which now featured one common, dominant currency, the new Swiss franc – was characterized by competition between independent note-issuing banks, both public (cantonal) and private. Until the banknote act of 1881, however, the banking system remained largely unregulated. Judged by the criteria of financial and monetary stability, this competition between issuing banks was reasonably successful. However, it was plagued by a lack of general acceptance and mutual recognition of the banknotes in circulation. In terms of efficiency, this system thus was no success, creating in turn a tendency toward the introduction of common quality requirements through regulation.

From 1881, statutory federal regulation placed severe restrictions on banks' reserve, liquidity, encashment, and issuance policies. Until 1905, a system of limited banking freedom prevailed, characterized by heavy regulation of the banknote business, yet no state banknote monopoly. The "homogenization" of banknotes achieved through this regulation was successful in promoting their acceptance and the efficiency of the payment system. However, competition between issuing banks no longer worked effectively under these new conditions: Over-issue of banknotes resulted, leading to currency weakness and, finally, the establishment of the Swiss National Bank. The quest for efficiency thus ultimately led to the centralization of banknote issuance – consistent with the idea of money as a natural monopoly. Although the system based on competition worked, it was marred by shortcomings in terms of efficiency. These shortcomings gave rise to regulatory interventions, which in turn destroyed the foundation for the disciplinary effect of competition and, ultimately, led to centralization.

THE IMPORTANCE OF MONETARY STABILITY AS THE MAIN OBJECTIVE OF CENTRAL BANK POLICY IN A PAPER MONEY SYSTEM

The transition to a purely paper-based currency lacking a firm link to gold or any other currency metal has fundamentally changed the role and position of the central bank and its policies. This applies to Switzerland just as it does to other countries. Previously, the rules of the metal-based currency, which tied money in circulation to the available supply of a currency metal, automatically ensured the long-term stability of the value of money (price stability). Once that link disappeared, this was no longer the case. Ensuring the stability of the value of money became the overriding, central task of central banks.[3]

In a purely paper-based money system, the central bank's capacity for creating money is, in principle, unlimited. Monopolies can give rise to misuse, in the case of state currency monopolies as well as in other cases. Monetary history provides ample illustration of this fact. How can we ensure that the central bank will meet its responsibility and withstand the temptation to abuse its power and over-issue its money? From today's vantage point, this can best be achieved through clear constitutional and statutory standards which commit the central bank to a precise mandate, combined with strict accountability requirements vis-à-vis the general public and its elected representatives.

In the past, central banks have often been asked to pursue a variety of different objectives, including price stability, full employment, growth, a stable exchange rate, and equilibrium in the balance of payments. However, over time, recognition has grown that the simultaneous pursuit of a multitude of – often irreconcilable – targets puts too much of a burden on central banks and monetary policy. As a result, none of the named objectives may really be met. The task assigned to central banks becomes ill-defined and arbitrary, as no clear restrictions on their actions are established.

It is obvious and logical to specify long-term price stability as the prior objective of monetary policy. Only the central bank, no other policy institution, can perform this task. In a paper-based money system, maintaining price stability must be the primary concern of the central bank's monetary policy. Financial stability and cyclical stabilization of the real economy can be added to this as subsidiary tasks. Note, however, that avoiding inflationary and deflationary cycles and the rise of associated expectations creates a framework that allows monetary policy the greatest possible scope for fulfilling these additional tasks. The SNB's monetary policies in the era of flexible exchange rates since 1973, which have strongly reflected these insights and been very successful in international comparison, bear witness to the wisdom of such a view.

---

[3] Naturally, the former tasks of central banks – lending of last resort, promoting the efficiency of the payments system, ensuring an appropriate elasticity of money supply – which had led to their establishment in the nineteenth and early twentieth centuries have not lost their legitimacy through this.

FIXED VERSUS FLEXIBLE EXCHANGE RATES

Over the past century and a half, Switzerland has had extensive experience with both fixed and flexible exchange rates. There are considerable advantages to a system of fixed exchange rates, as long as it works smoothly. This was the case during the era of the classical gold standard, but also for the early years of the Bretton Woods system. However, a fixed exchange rate system presupposes that the members of this system are prepared to conduct mutually consistent monetary policies. They must be committed to a common view regarding the possibilities, objectives, and procedures of monetary policy, in order for the system to be viable and functional.

Ultimately, a system of this kind calls for agreement not just in the monetary field, but also on the basic principles governing policies in certain other areas, particularly fiscal stability and flexibility of goods and factor markets. In the long run, insufficient willingness to respect these requirements leads to the build-up of unsustainable international imbalances and to efforts to stabilize the system by means of administrative interventions and measures, such as trade impediments and restrictions on capital movements, or the establishment of international transfer mechanisms. Inevitably, this renders the system frail and unstable.

In such cases, a system of fixed exchange rates can create a considerable potential for tension and turbulence. Switzerland has experienced this on several occasions in its past, to its great pain: in certain phases of the Latin Monetary Union in the nineteenth century, very intensely during the Great Depression of the 1930s, and then again during the final years of the Bretton Woods standard. It learned that, under such conditions, life with fluctuating exchange rates may be the lesser of two evils, and a regime of flexible exchange rates can be the more attractive alternative. Absent internationally well-anchored, reliable common commitments to monetary and fiscal stability, it becomes preferable to live with the occasional disturbances and turmoil associated with a system of flexible exchange rates, as compared to the dangers and distortions of a deceptive, non-credible system based on wishful coordination without credibility.

SMALL COUNTRY, INDEPENDENT CURRENCY: THE VALUE OF MONETARY SOVEREIGNTY

Under such circumstances, maintaining monetary sovereignty becomes a valuable good, an option not to be relinquished lightly and thoughtlessly. Such sovereignty allows for a return to an autonomous, self-determined monetary policy, even if fixed exchange rate commitments should have been entered into at one time or another. The dangers and risks linked with premature surrender of monetary sovereignty to a higher "community" level, without prior, credible establishment of common policy values, are painfully demonstrated by the current confusion in the eurozone and its economic policies. A comparison of today's Economic and Monetary Union in Europe with the Latin Monetary Union of the nineteenth century is instructive in this regard. The latter implied no surrender of monetary sovereignty to a union-level authority. The definition and the statutory basis of the participant-nation currencies remained national. The Latin Monetary Union was no more than an international agreement for the joint adoption of a given (metal) currency standard. Exit, and a return to a different monetary standard, was possible at any time – very unlike the situation in the European Monetary Union of today.

But is it at all feasible and realistic that a small country like Switzerland can uphold monetary sovereignty and independence in a world of growing global integration? When the European Monetary Union was created in 1999, and even before, predictions were common that the sheer size of the eurozone would imply Switzerland losing its ability to pursue an autonomous monetary policy and maintain the franc as an independent currency. The newly created common European money would establish itself as a parallel currency in Switzerland before long and eventually displace the Swiss franc altogether, it was argued. Developments since then have shown these claims to be false.

Over the first ten years of its existence, the euro did in fact establish itself as a reliable and stable currency, due to the responsible and stability-oriented policies of the newly created European Central Bank (ECB). The euro as an investment and reserve currency gained much in importance. Nevertheless, no notable disadvantages for Swiss monetary policy resulted from these developments. The opposite was the case: If anything, a stable euro, and in particular the disappearance of highly unstable former partner currencies such as the Italian lira, made the SNB's task less difficult. Experience showed once again that an established currency is not easily displaced as a domestic means of payment unless it suffers from extreme weakness itself, and that "small" currencies can well survive next to much "bigger" ones without being subject to automatic erosion.

The much greater challenge to Swiss monetary policy results from the opposite problem, related to the increasing weakness and tension that have plagued the eurozone and the euro in recent times. Doubts about the stability and long-run success of the eurozone have created strong upward pressure on the Swiss franc vis-à-vis the euro, forcing the SNB to temporarily assign the exchange rate a much greater role in monetary policy than it would have preferred in normal times. However, Swiss monetary policy has been faced with this dilemma many times before in the course of its history. The appropriate response has never been to give up monetary independence and autonomy as a consequence of such pressures. Indeed, to sacrifice policy autonomy and a strong currency in order to be able to join a weaker and less stable one, for other than political reasons, would probably be without precedent.

Bibliography

Aliber, R. Z. (1967). Gresham's Law, asset preferences, and the demand for international reserves. *Quarterly Journal of Economics*, **81**(4), 628–38.

Allgöwer, E. (2003). Gold standard and gold standard mentality in Switzerland. Habilitation thesis, University of St. Gallen.

Bai, J. and Perron, Pierre (2003). Critical values for multiple structural change tests. *Econometrics Journal*, **6**(1), 72–8.

Baltensperger, E. (1985). Disinflation – the Swiss experience 1973–1983. *Zeitschrift für Wirtschafts- und Sozialwissenschaften*, **105**(2/3), 271–93.

(2007). The National Bank's monetary policy: evolution of policy framework and policy performance. In SNB, ed., *The Swiss National Bank 1907–2007*. Zürich: NZZ Libro, pp. 569–97.

(2012). *Der Schweizer Franken – eine Erfolgsgeschichte. Die Währung der Schweiz im 19. und 20. Jahrhundert*. Zürich: NZZ Libro.

Baltensperger, E. and Böhm, P. (1984). *Geldmengenpolitik und Inflationskontrolle. Möglichkeiten, Kosten, flankierende Massnahmen*. Diessenhofen: Rüegger.

Baltensperger, E., Fischer, A. M. and Jordan, T. J. (1999). Soll die Schweizerische Nationalbank den Franken an den Euro binden? *Aussenwirtschaft*, **54**(1), 25–48.

Baltensperger, E., Hildebrand, P. M. and Jordan, T. J. (2007). The Swiss National Bank's monetary policy concept – an example of a "principles-based" policy framework. *Swiss National Bank Economic Studies*, **3**, pp. 1–28.

Baltensperger, E. and Kugler, P. (2016). The historical origins of the safe haven status of the Swiss franc. *Aussenwirtschaft*, **67**(2), 1–27.

Baumann, J. (2004). *Bundesinterventionen in der Bankenkrise 1931–1937*. Doctoral dissertation, University of Zürich.

Bazot, G., Bordo, M. and Monnet, E. (2014). The price of stability: the balance sheet policy of the Banque de France and the gold standard (1880–1914). *NBER Working Paper* No. 20554.

Bernanke, B. S. (1983). Nonmonetary effects of the financial crisis in the propagation of the Great Depression. *American Economic Review*, **73**(2), 257–76.

(1995). The macroeconomics of the Great Depression: a comparative approach. *Journal of Money, Credit, and Banking*, **27**(1), 1–28.

(2000). *Essays on the Great Depression*. Princeton: Princeton University Press.

Bernholz, P. (2003). *Monetary Regimes and Inflation: History, Economic and Political Relationships*. Cheltenham: Edward Elgar.

(2007). From 1945 to 1982: the transition from inward exchange controls to money supply management under floating exchange rates. In SNB, ed., *The Swiss National Bank 1907–2007*. Zürich: NZZ Libro, pp. 109–99.

Bernholz, P. and Kugler, P. (2011). Financial market integration in early modern Spain: results from a threshold error correction model. *Economics Letters*, **110**(2), 93–6.

Blaum, K. (1908). *Das Geldwesen der Schweiz seit 1798*. Strassburg: Karl J. Truebner.

Bleuler, W. (1913). *Die Bank in Zürich 1836–1906*. Doctoral dissertation, University of Zürich.

Bodenhorn, H. and Haupert, M. (1996). The note issue paradox in the free banking era. *Journal of Economic History*, **56**(3), 687–93.

Böhler, E. and Keller, P. (1935). *Krisenbekämpfung: Ergebnisse der Krisenpolitik des Auslandes. Grundlagen eines positiven Programms für die Schweiz*. Zürich: Rüegg.

Bolt, J. and van Zanden, J. L. (2013). The first update of the Maddison Project: re-estimating growth before 1820. *Maddison Project Working Paper 4*.

Bordo, M. (1993). The gold standard, Bretton Woods and other monetary regimes: a historical appraisal. *Federal Reserve Bank of St Louis Review*, **75**(2), 123–91.

Bordo, M. and Eichengreen, B., eds. (1993). *A Retrospective on the Bretton Woods System: Lessons for International Monetary Reform*. Chicago and London: University of Chicago Press.

Bordo, M. and James, H. (2007). From 1907 to 1946: a happy childhood or a troubled adolescence? In SNB, ed., *The Swiss National Bank 1907–2007*. Zürich: NZZ Libro, pp. 28–107.

Bordo, M. and Kydland, F. (1995). The gold standard as a rule: an essay in exploration. *Explorations in Economic History*, **32**(4), 423–64.

Bordo, M. and Redish, A. (2016). Putting the "system" in the international monetary system. In D. Fox and W. Ernst, eds., *Money in the Western Legal Tradition*. Oxford: Oxford University Press, pp. 595–610.

Borio, C., James, H. and Shin, H. S. (2014). The international monetary and financial system: a capital account historical perspective. *BIS Working Paper* No. 457.

Bosshardt, A. (1961). Schweizerische Währungspolitik vor 25 Jahren. *Aussenwirtschaft*, **16**(2), 117–54.

Büttler, H.-J., Gorgerat, J.-F., Schiltknecht, H. and Schiltknecht, K. (1979). A multiplier model for controlling the money stock. *Journal of Monetary Economics*, **5**(3), 327–41.

Burckhardt-Bischoff, A. (1865). *Die Zeddelbanken in der Schweiz und das Bedürfnis einer einheitlichen Noten-Circulation*. Basel: Balmer u. Riehm.

Cameron, R. (1967). *Banking in the Early Stages of Industrialization*. New York/London/Toronto: Oxford University Press.

Capie, F., Goodhart, C. and Schnadt, N. (1994). The development of central banking. In F. Capie, S. Fischer, C. Goodhart and N. Schnadt, eds., *The Future of Central Banking: The Tercentenary Symposium of the Bank of England*. Cambridge: Cambridge University Press, pp. 1–261.

Cassis, Y. (1991). L'histoire des banques suisses aux XIXe et XXe siècles. *Schweizerische Zeitschrift für Geschichte*, **41**, 512–20.

Coombs, C. A. (1976). *The Arena of International Finance*. New York: John Wiley & Sons.

Cramer-Frey, C. (1880). *Die Regulierung des Banknotenwesens in der Schweiz.* Zürich: Schweizer-Zeitfragen.

Crettol, V. and Halbeisen, P. (1999). *Die währungspolitischen Hintergründe der Goldtransaktionen der Schweizerischen Nationalbank im Zweiten Weltkrieg.* Zürich: SNB.

Degen, B. (2014). Arbeiterbewegung. Available from *Historisches Lexikon der Schweiz,* www.hls-dhs-dss.ch/textes/d/D16479.php.

Denzel, M. A. (2010). *Handbook of World Exchange Rates, 1590–1914.* Burlington: Ashgate.

Durrer, M. (1984). *Die schweizerisch-amerikanischen Finanzbeziehungen im Zweiten Weltkrieg: Von der Blockierung der schweizerischen Guthaben in den USA über die "Safehaven-Politik" zum Washingtoner Abkommen (1941–1946).* Bern: Haupt.

Eichengreen, B. (1992). *Golden Fetters: The Gold Standard and the Great Depression, 1919–1939.* New York and Oxford: Oxford University Press.

(1996). *Globalizing Capital: A History of the International Monetary System.* Princeton: Princeton University Press.

Eichengreen, B. and Flandreau, M. (1996). The geography of the gold standard. In J. Braga de Macedo, B. Eichengreen and J. Reis, eds., *Currency Convertibility: The Gold Standard and Beyond.* London: Routledge, pp. 113–43.

(1997). *The Gold Standard in Theory and History,* 2nd edn. London: Routledge.

Einaudi, L. (2001). *Money and Politics: European Monetary Unification and the International Gold Standard (1865–1873).* Oxford: Oxford University Press.

Ettlin, F. and S. Gaillard (2001). Die 90er Jahre in der Schweiz – Eine wettbewerbsfähige Wirtschaft braucht eine stabilisierende Geldpolitik. In J. Furrer and B. Gehrig, eds., *Aspekte der schweizerischen Wirtschaftspolitik.* Chur/Zürich: Rüegger, pp. 267–93.

Fior, M. (1997). *Die Schweiz und das Gold der Reichsbank. Was wusste die Schweizerische Nationalbank?* Zürich: Chronos.

Fisher, I. (1934). *Stable Money: A History of the Movement.* New York: Adelphi.

Fischer, S. (1986). Friedman versus Hayek on private money. *Journal of Monetary Economics,* **17**(3), 433–9.

Flandreau, M. (2000). The economics and politics of monetary unions: a reassessment of the Latin Monetary Union, 1865–1871. *Financial History Review,* 7, 25–44.

Friedman, M. (1960). *A Program for Monetary Stability.* New York: Fordham University Press.

Friedman, M. and Schwartz, A. J. (1963). *A Monetary History of the United States, 1867–1960.* Princeton: Princeton University Press.

Furrer, N. (1995). *Das Münzgeld der Alten Schweiz.* Zürich: Chronos.

Gesell, S. (1916). *Die Natürliche Wirtschaftsordnung durch Freiland und Freigeld.* Les Hauts Geneveys.

Grossen, J. M. (2001). Transactions germano-suisses sur l'or pendant la Seconde Guerre mondiale. In UEK, ed., *La Suisse, le national-socialisme et le droit.* Publications de la Commission Independante d'Experts Suisse – Seconde Guerre Mondiale, 18. Zürich: Chronos, pp. 127–215.

Gubler, M. and Sax, C. (2014). *The Balassa-Samuelson Effect Reversed: New Evidence from OECD Countries.* Mimeo, Swiss National Bank and University of Basel.

Guex, S. (1993). *La politique monétaire et financière de la Conféderation Suisse, 1900–1920.* Lausanne: Payot.

Gygax, P. (1901). *Kritische Betrachtungen über das Schweizerische Notenbankwesen mit Beziehung auf den Pariser Wechselkurs.* Zürich: Müller.

Halbeisen, P. (1998). Bankenkrise und Bankengesetzgebung. In S. Guex, ed., *Krisen und Stabilisierung: Die Schweiz in der Zwischenkriegszeit.* Zürich: Chronos, pp. 61–79.

(2005). Goldstandard oder "Manipulierte Währung"? Partikularinteressen und Währungspolitik in den 1930er-Jahren, *Traverse*, **1**, 168–76.

(2006). Cool lover? Switzerland and the road to European monetary union. In P. Clement and J. C. Martinez Oliva, eds., *European Central Banks and Monetary Cooperation after 1945.* Frankfurt: European Association for Banking and Financial History, pp. 97–117.

Halbeisen, P. and Müller, M. (1998). Die schrittweise Nationalisierung des Geldes: Von der Einführung der Schweizer Währung (Münzreform) zur nationalen Kontrolle über das Geldwesen (Gründung der Nationalbank 1907). In A. Mosser, ed., *Österreichs Weg zum Euro: Aspekte – Perspektiven – Handlungsräume.* Veröffentlichung der Österreichischen Gesellschaft für Unternehmensgeschichte, 20. Wien: Manzsche Verlagsbuchhandlung, pp. 63–86.

Halbeisen, P., Müller, M. and Veyrassat, B., eds. (2012). *Wirtschaftsgeschichte der Schweiz im 20. Jahrhundert.* Basel: Schwabe.

Halbeisen, P. and Straumann, T. (2012). Die Wirtschaftspolitik im internationalen Kontext. In P. Halbeisen, M. Müller and B. Veyrassat, eds., *Wirtschaftsgeschichte der Schweiz im 20. Jahrhundert.* Basel: Schwabe, pp. 983–1075.

Hamilton, James D. (1994). *Time Series Analysis.* Princeton University Press.

Hansen, Bruce E. (1992). Tests for parameter instability in regressions with I(1) processes. *Journal of Business and Economic Statistics*, **10**(3), 321–35.

Hayek, F. (1978). *Denationalisation of Money – The Argument Refined.* London: The Institute of Economic Affairs.

Homer, Sidney and Sylla, Richard (2005). *A History of Interest Rates.* Hoboken, NJ: John Wiley & Sons.

Hoffmann, H. (1982). *75 Jahre Schweizerische Nationalbank. Der "heilige Krieg" im Kampf für goldfeste Wechselkurse gegen den "heiligen Krieg" für indexfestes Preisniveau.* Bern: Liberalsozialistische Partei des Kantons Bern.

Iklé, M. (1970). *Die Schweiz als internationaler Bank- und Finanzplatz.* Zürich: Orell Füssli.

Jöhr, A. (1915). *Die Schweizerischen Notenbanken, 1826–1913.* Zürich: Orell Füssli.

Junge, G. and Kugler, P. (2013). Quantifying the impact of higher capital requirements on the Swiss economy. *Swiss Journal of Economics and Statistics*, **149**(3), 313–56.

Katzenstein, P. J. (1985). *Small States in World Markets: Industrial Policy in Europe.* Ithaca, NY and London: Cornell University Press.

(2003). Small states and small states revisited. *New Political Economy*, **8**(1), 9–30.

Kalkmann, P. (1900). *Untersuchungen über das Geldwesen der Schweiz und die Ursachen des hohen Standes der auswärtigen Wechselkurse.* St. Gallen: Zollikofer.

Kaplan, J. J. and Schleiminger, G. (1989). *The European Payments Union: Financial Diplomacy in the 1950s.* Oxford: Clarendon Press.

Kehoe, T. J. and Ruhl, K. J. (2007). Are shocks to the terms-of-trade shocks to productivity? *NBER Working Paper* 13111.

Keller, C. (1871). Die Crisis des Jahres 1870. In Schweizerischer Handels- und Industrieverein, ed., *Drei Gutachten über das Schweizerische Banknotenwesen.* Bern: Schweizerischer Handels- und Industrieverein.

Keynes, J. M. (1919). *The Economic Consequences of the Peace.* London: Macmillan.
   (1923). *A Tract on Monetary Reform.* London: Macmillan.
   (1936). *The General Theory of Employment, Interest and Money.* London: Macmillan.
Klauser, P. (2007). The National Bank and its role in the Second World War. In SNB, ed., *The Swiss National Bank 1907–2007.* Zürich: NZZ Libro, pp. 550–66.
Kohli, U. (2004). Real GDP, real domestic income, and terms-of-trade changes. *Journal of International Economics,* **62**, 83–106.
   (2010). Concluding comments: the SNB's monetary policy framework ten years on. *Swiss Journal of Economics and Statistics,* **146**(1), 425–30.
Körner, M. (1991). Vom Geldwesen in der alten Schweiz. In Schweizerischer Bankverein, ed., *700 Jahre Schweizer Münzen.* Basel: Schweizerischer Bankverein.
   (1993). Schweiz. In Hans Pohl, ed., *Europäische Bankengeschichte.* Frankfurt am Main: Fritz Knapp.
Kueng, L. (2007). *The Revival of the Note Issue Paradox: Free Banking in Switzerland between 1872 and 1881,* https://ssrn.com/abstract=2746487
Kugler, P. (2011). Financial market integration in late medieval Europe: results from a threshold error correction model for the Rhinegulden and Basle pound, 1365–1429. *Swiss Journal of Economics and Statistics,* **147**(3), 337–57.
   (2012). Grosse Währung eines kleinen Landes: Fluch oder Segen? *Die Volkswirtschaft,* **1/2**, 27–30.
   (2014). *The Changing Regime of the Pound/Guilder Exchange Rate 1600–1912.* Mimeo, University of Basel, January 2014.
   (2016). The Bretton Woods system: design and operation. In D. Fox and W. Ernst, eds., *Money in the Western Legal Tradition.* Oxford: Oxford University Press, pp. 611–20.
Kugler, P. and Rich, G. (2002). Monetary policy under low interest rates: the experience of Switzerland in the late 1970s. *Swiss Journal of Economics and Statistics,* **138**(3), 241–69.
Kugler, P. and Weder di Mauro, B. (2002). The puzzle of the Swiss interest island: stylized facts and a new interpretation. *Aussenwirtschaft,* **57**(1), 49–63.
   (2004). International portfolio holdings and Swiss franc returns. *Swiss Journal of Economics and Statistics,* **140**(3), 301–25.
   (2005). Why are returns on Swiss franc assets so low? *Applied Economics Quarterly,* **51**(3), 351–72.
Kundert, H. (1907). Was bringt uns die Nationalbank? *Wirtschaftliche Publikationen der Zürcher Handelskammer,* 5, April.
Lambelet, J.-C. (1999). *Le mobbing d'un petit pays – onze thèses sur la Suisse pendant la Deuxième Guerre mondiale.* Lausanne: Editions l'Âge d'Homme.
Landmann, J. (1905). *Das Schweizerische Bankgesetz.* Zürich: Schulthess.
Lescaze, B., et al. (1997). *Une monnaie pour la Suisse.* Genève: Editions Suzanne Hurter.
Linder, W. (1994). *Swiss Democracy: Possible Solutions to Conflict in Multicultural Societies.* New York: St. Martin's Press.
   (2012). *Schweizerische Demokratie. Institutionen, Prozesse, Perspektiven,* 3rd edition. Bern/Stuttgart/Wien: Haupt.
Longfield, S. M. (1840). Banking and currency. *Dublin University Magazine.*
Mangold, F. (1909). *Die Bank in Basel, 1844–1907 und die Entwicklung des Konkordats der schweizerischen Emissionsbanken.* Basel: Bank in Basel.

MacDonald, R. and Ricci, L. (2007). Real exchange rates, imperfect substitutability, and imperfect information. *Journal of Macroeconomics*, **29**(4), 639–64.

McCallum, B. T. and Nelson, E. (2010). Monetary policy for an open economy: an alternative framework with optimizing agents and sticky prices. *NBER Working Paper Series*, 8175.

McCulloch, J. R. (1831). *Historical Sketch of the Bank of England.* London: Longman, Rees, Orme, Brown & Green.

Meltzer, A. H. (2004). *A History of the Federal Reserve, vol. 1: 1913–1951.* Chicago: University of Chicago Press.

Menghetti, P. (1993). *Banktheoretische Überlegungen: Eine Empirische Untersuchung der Schweizerischen Emissionsbanken von 1883–1906.* Winterthur: Schellenberg.

Mishkin, F. S. (2007). Die Inflationsdynamik hängt von den Erwartungen der Menschen ab. *Neue Zürcher Zeitung*, April 28/29.

Morys, M. (2013). Discount rate policy under the classical gold standard: core versus periphery (1870–1914). *Explorations in Economic History*, **50**(2), 205–26.

Müller, P. (2003). La bataille pour le franc. La Suisse entre déflation et dévaluation (1931–1936). In P. Müller, I. Paccaud and J. M. Schaufelbuehl, eds., *Franc suisse, finance et commerce. Politique monétaire hélvetique 1931–1936. Les relations de la Suisse avec l'Angleterre (1940–1944) et la France (1944–1949).* Lausanne: Editions Antipodes, pp. 7–145.

Müller, M. and Woitek, U. (2012). Wohlstand, Wachstum und Konjunktur. In P. Halbeisen, M. Müller and B. Veyrassat, eds., *Wirtschaftsgeschichte der Schweiz im 20. Jahrhundert.* Basel: Schwabe, pp. 191–222.

Neldner, M. (1996). Bankenfreiheit und Noten-Überemission. Der Schweizer Franken und die "Small Note Mania" in Schottland. *Swiss Journal of Economics and Statistics*, **132**(2), 177–95.

(2003). Competition necessarily tends to produce excess: the experience of free banking in Switzerland. *German Economic Review*, **4**(3), 389–408.

Neumann, L. (1991). Das Schweizer Münzwesen von 1648 bis heute. In Schweizerischer Bankverein, ed., *700 Jahre Schweizer Münzen.* Basel: Schweizerischer Bankverein.

Niehans, J. (1978). *The Theory of Money.* Baltimore: Johns Hopkins University Press.

Nurske, R. (1944). *International Currency Experience: Lessons of the Inter-War Period.* Geneva: League of Nations.

Officer, L. H. and Williamson, S. H. (2013a). The price of gold, 1257–present. *MeasuringWorth*, www.measuringworth.com/gold/.

(2013b). Annual inflation rates in the United States, 1775–2013, and United Kingdom, 1265–2013. *MeasuringWorth*, www.measuringworth.com/inflation/

Perrenoud, M., Lopez, R., Adank, F., Baumann, J., Cortat, A. and Peters, S. (2002). *La place financière et les banques suisses à l'époque du national-socialisme: les relations des grandes banques avec l'Allemagne (1931–1946).* Publications de la Commission Indepandante d'Experts Suisse – Seconde Guerre Mondiale, 13. Lausanne: Chronos/Payot.

Pesaran, M. H. and Shin, Y. (1998). Impulse response analysis in linear multivariate models. *Economics Letters*, **58**(1), 17–29.

Pestalozzi, L. (1839). *Die Münzwirren der westlichen Schweiz nebst dem Versuche ihrer Lösung.* Zürich: Orell Füssli.

(1849). *Der Schweizerfranken als Eidgenössische Münzeinheit, Gutachten laut Auftrag der Zürcherischen Handelskammer.* Zürich: Orell Füssli.

Peytrignet, M. (1996). Stabilité économétrique des agrégats monétaires suisses. *Geld, Währung und Konjunktur*, **14**(3), 251–79.

Peytrignet, M. and Stahel, C. (1998). Stability of money demand in Switzerland. *Empirical Economics*, **23**(3), 437–54.

Redish, A. (1994). The Latin Monetary Union and the emergence of the international gold standard. In M. Bordo and F. Capie, eds., *Monetary Regimes in Transition*. New York: Cambridge University Press, pp. 68–85.

Rich, G. (2000). Monetary policy without Central Bank money: a Swiss perspective. *International Finance*, **3**(November), 439–69.

(2007). Swiss monetary targeting 1974–1996: the role of internal policy analysis. *Swiss Journal of Economics and Statistics*, **143**(3), 283–329.

Ritzmann, F. (1973). *Die Schweizer Banken. Geschichte – Theorie – Statistik*. Bern: Haupt.

(1996). Schweizerische Notenbanken im 19. Jahrhundert und Free Banking – Diskussionsbeitrag zu M. Neldner, Bankenfreiheit und Noten-Überemission. *Swiss Journal of Economics and Statistics*, **132**(2), 197–201.

Romer, C. D. (1992). What ended the Great Depression? *The Journal of Economic History*, **52**(4), 757–84.

Roth, J.-P. (2007). 70 Jahre nach dem endgültigen Zusammenbruch des Goldstandards der Zwischenkriegszeit im September 1936. *Quarterly Bulletin SNB*, **2007**(1), 42–8.

Ruoss, E. (1992). *Die Geldpolitik der Schweizerischen Nationalbank 1907–1929. Grundlagen, Ziele und Instrumente*. Doctoral dissertation, University of Zürich.

Rüttimann, I. (1865). *Spezialbericht betreffend das Banknotenwesen an die von dem Schweizerischen Ständerathe niedergesetzte Kommission für die Revision der Bundesverfassung*. Zürich.

Rutz, W. (1970). *Die Schweizerische Volkswirtschaft zwischen Währungs- und Beschäftigungspolitik in der Weltwirtschaftskrise – WirtschaftspolitischeAnalyse der Bewältigung eines Zielkonflikts*. Zürich/St. Gallen: Polygraphischer Verlag.

Salin, E. (1964). Devisen-Bann-Wirtschaft? *Kyklos*, **17**(2), 149–64.

Sax, C. and Weder, R. (2009). How to explain the high prices in Switzerland. *Swiss Journal of Economics and Statistics*, **145**(4), 463–83.

Schärrer, M. (1983). Geld- und Bodenreform als Brücke zum sozialen Staat: Die Geschichte der Freiwirtschaftsbewegung in der Schweiz 1915–1952. Doctoral dissertation, University of Zürich.

Schiltknecht, K. (1970). *Beurteilung der Gentlemen's Agreements und Konjunkturbeschlüsse der Jahre 1954–1966*. Zürich: Polygraphischer Verlag.

(1994). Geldmengenpolitik und Wechselkurs: der schweizerische Weg. In F. von Albertini, ed., *Schweizerische Geldpolitik im Dilemma: Geldmenge oder Wechselkurs?* Chur: Rüegger, pp. 57–68.

Schlesinger, W. (1936). *Das Geldproblem in der öffentlichen Meinung der Schweiz, 1803 –1850*. Zürich: Fehr'sche Buchhandlung.

Schmid, W. (1948/1969). *Die Geschichte des Schweizer Frankens*. Bern: Haupt.

Schweizerische Gesellschaft für Volkswirtschaft und Statistik/Swiss Society of Economics and Statistics, eds. (2010). SNB conference on "The SNB's New Monetary Policy Framework Ten Years On." *Swiss Journal of Economics and Statistics*, **146** (1), 9–430.

Schweizerische Nationalbank (1932). *Die Schweizerische Nationalbank 1907–1932.* Zürich: SNB.

(1957). *Die Schweizerische Nationalbank 1907–1957.* Zürich: SNB.

(1982). *75 Jahre Schweizerische Nationalbank: Die Zeit von 1957 bis 1982.* Zürich: SNB.

(2007). *The Swiss National Bank 1907–2007.* Zürich: NZZ Libro.

Schwerdtel, G. (1992). *The Swiss Participation in the European Payments Union 1950–1958.* Bern: Lang.

Selgin, G. A. (1988). *The Theory of Free Banking. Money Supply under Competitive Note Issue.* Totowa, NJ: Rowman and Littlefield.

(1994). Free banking and monetary control. *Economic Journal,* **104**(November), 1449–59.

Selgin, G. A. and White, L. H. (1994). How would the invisible hand handle money? *Journal of Economic Literature,* **32**(4), 1718–49.

Siegenthaler, H. (1985). Die Schweiz 1850–1914. In Fischer, W. et al. (eds), *Handbuch der Europäischen Wirtschafts- und Sozialgeschichte,* vol. 5. Stuttgart: Klett-Cotta, pp. 443–73.

Smith, A. (1776). *An Inquiry into the Nature and Causes of the Wealth of Nations.* London: Strahan & Cadell.

Solomon, R. (1977). *The International Monetary System, 1945–1976: An Insider's View.* New York: Harper and Row.

Spahni, W. (1977). *Der Ausbruch der Schweiz aus der Isolation nach dem Zweiten Weltkrieg: Untersucht anhand ihrer Aussenhandelspolitik 1944–1947.* Frauenfeld: Huber.

Speiser, J. J. (1849). *Noch ein Wort über die Münzfrage, als Erwiderung auf das Gutachten des Herrn Leonhard Pestalozzi.* Bern: Buchdruckerei der Berner Zeitung.

Straumann, T. (2006). Der kleine Gigant: Der Aufstieg Zürichs zu einem Internationalen Finanzplatz. In Institut für Bankhistorische Forschung, ed., *Europäische Finanzplätze im Wettbewerb.* Stuttgart: Franz Steiner Verlag, pp. 139–70.

(2010). *Fixed Ideas of Money: Small States and Exchange Rate Regimes in Twentieth-Century Europe.* Cambridge: Cambridge University Press.

Tanner, J. (2000). Goldparität im Gotthardstaat: Nationale Mythen und die Stabilität des Schweizer Frankens in den 1930er und 1940er Jahren. *Studien und Quellen des Schweizerischen Bundesarchivs,* **26**, 45–82.

Temin, P. (1978). *Did Monetary Forces Cause the Great Depression?* New York: W.W. Norton.

Thornton, H. (1802). *An Enquiry into the Nature and Effects of the Paper Credit of Great Britain.* Ed. F. A. von Hayek (1939). London: Allen & Unwin.

Toniolo, G. (2005). *Central Bank Cooperation at the Bank for International Settlements: 1930–1973* (with the assistance of P. Clement). Cambridge: Cambridge University Press.

Toniolo, G. and White, E. N. (2015). The evolution of the Financial Stability Mandate: from its origins to the present day. *NBER Working Paper* No. 2084.

UEK (1998). *Unabhängige Expertenkommission Schweiz – Zweiter Weltkrieg. Die Schweiz und die Goldtransaktionen im Zweiten Weltkrieg.* Bern: EDMZ.

Weber, E. J. (1988). Currency competition in Switzerland, 1826–1850. *Kyklos*, **41**(3), 459–78.

(1992). Free banking in Switzerland after the liberal revolution in the 19th Century. In K. Dowd, ed., *The Experience of Free Banking*. London: Routledge, pp. 187–205.

Weisskopf, E. (1948). *Das Schweizerische Münzwesen von seinen Anfängen bis zur Gegenwart*. Doctoral dissertation, University of Bern.

White, L. H. (1999). *The Theory of Monetary Institutions*. Oxford: Basil Blackwell.

Zimmermann, R. (1987). *Volksbank oder Aktienbank? Parlamentsdebatten, Referendum und zunehmende Verbandsmacht beim Streit um die Nationalbankgründung 1891–1905*. Zürich: Chronos.

Zurlinden, M. (2003). Goldstandard, Deflation und Depression: Die Schweizerische Volkswirtschaft in der Weltwirtschaftskrise. *Schweizerische Nationalbank, Quarterly Bulletin*, 2, 86–116.

Index

Other books in the series (*continued from p.iii*)

Michael D. Bordo and William Roberds, Editors, *The Origins, History, and Future of the Federal Reserve: A Return to Jekyll Island* (2013)

Michael D. Bordo and Ronald MacDonald, Editors, *Credibility and the International Monetary Regime: A Historical Perspective* (2012)

Robert L. Hetzel, *The Great Recession: Market Failure or Policy Failure?* (2012)

Tobias Straumann, *Fixed Ideas of Money: Small States and Exchange Rate Regimes in Twentieth-Century Europe* (2010)

Forrest Capie, *The Bank of England: 1950s to 1979* (2010)

Aldo Musacchio, *Experiments in Financial Democracy: Corporate Governance and Financial Development in Brazil, 1882–1950* (2009)

Claudio Borio, Gianni Toniolo, and Piet Clement, Editors, *The Past and Future of Central Bank Cooperation* (2008)

Robert L. Hetzel, *The Monetary Policy of the Federal Reserve: A History* (2008)

Caroline Fohlin, *Finance Capitalism and Germany's Rise to Industrial Power* (2007)

John H. Wood, *A History of Central Banking in Great Britain and the United States* (2005)

Gianni Toniolo (with the assistance of Piet Clement), *Central Bank Cooperation at the Bank for International Settlements, 1930–1973* (2005)

Richard Burdekin and Pierre Siklos, Editors, *Deflation: Current and Historical Perspectives* (2004)

Pierre Siklos, *The Changing Face of Central Banking: Evolutionary Trends since World War II* (2002)

Michael D. Bordo and Roberto Cortés-Conde, Editors, *Transferring Wealth and Power from the Old to the New World: Monetary and Fiscal Institutions in the 17th through the 19th Centuries* (2001)

Howard Bodenhorn, *A History of Banking in Antebellum America: Financial Markets and Economic Development in an Era of Nation-Building* (2000)

Mark Harrison, Editor, *The Economics of World War II: Six Great Powers in International Comparison* (2000)

Angela Redish, *Bimetallism: An Economic and Historical Analysis* (2000)

Elmus Wicker, *Banking Panics of the Gilded Age* (2000)

Michael D. Bordo, *The Gold Standard and Related Regimes: Collected Essays* (1999)

Michele Fratianni and Franco Spinelli, *A Monetary History of Italy* (1997)

Mark Toma, *Competition and Monopoly in the Federal Reserve System, 1914–1951,* (1997)

Barry Eichengreen, Editor, *Europe's Postwar Recovery,* 1996

Lawrence H. Officer, *Between the Dollar-Sterling Gold Points: Exchange Rates, Parity and Market Behavior* (1996)

Elmus Wicker, *Banking Panics of the Great Depression* (1996)

Norio Tamaki, *Japanese Banking: A History, 1859–1959* (1995)

Barry Eichengreen, *Elusive Stability: Essays in the History of International Finance, 1919–1939* (1993)

Michael D. Bordo and Forrest Capie, Editors, *Monetary Regimes in Transition* (1993)

Larry Neal, *The Rise of Financial Capitalism: International Capital Markets in the Age of Reason* (1993)

S. N. Broadberry and N. F. R. Crafts, Editors, *Britain in the International Economy, 1870–1939* (1992)

Aurel Schubert, *The Credit-Anstalt Crisis of 1931* (1992)

Trevor J. O. Dick and John E. Floyd, *Canada and the Gold Standard: Balance of Payments Adjustment under Fixed Exchange Rates, 1871–1913* (1992)

Kenneth Mouré, *Managing the Franc Poincaré: Economic Understanding and Political Constraint in French Monetary Policy, 1928–1936* (1991)

David C. Wheelock, *The Strategy and Consistency of Federal Reserve Monetary Policy, 1924–1933* (1991)